Racelines

Racelines

Observations on Horse Racing's Glorious History

PHILIP VON BORRIES

MASTERS PRESS

NTC/Contemporary Publishing Group

Library of Congress Cataloging-in-Publication Data

Von Borries, Philip, 1947–
        Racelines : observations on horse racing's glorious history /
    Philip Von Borries.
            p.   cm.
        Includes index.
        ISBN 1-57028-234-X
        1. Horse racing—United States.   I. Title.
    SF335.5.V65   1999
    798.4—dc21   98-41998
                                                                          CIP

Cover design by Nick Panos
Front cover photograph by Lambert/Archive Photos
Back cover photograph by American Stock/Archive Photos
Interior design by Rohani Design

Published by Masters Press
A division of NTC/Contemporary Publishing Group, Inc.
4255 West Touhy Avenue, Lincolnwood (Chicago), Illinois 60712-1975 U.S.A.
Copyright © 1999 by Philip Von Borries
Printed in the United States of America
International Standard Book Number: 1-57028-234-X
99 00 01 02 03 04 VL 19 18 17 16 15 14 13 12 11 10 9 8 7 6 5 4 3 2 1

Dedication

TO THE BREEDERS' CUP, the greatest racing show on the face of God's earth; to the greatest city in America—Chicago; to Keeneland Racecourse and the Red Mile, my home tracks; and to my father and mother—Frank B. Borries Jr. and Betty Earle Borries, who returned Isaac Murphy to the living world.

To my older sister, Betsy, and her husband, David Crean; to my younger sister, Elise; to my cousin Jean Parry, her late husband, David, and their daughter, Meagan; to my older niece, Marla Harris, her husband, Lynn, and their children—Krista and Collin; and to my younger niece, Melony Allison, and her children—Tabitha, Dustin, and Kirsten.

To Tommy Trotter, H. A. "Jimmy" Jones, Tom Rivera, Joe Joyce, Ken Dunn, General J. B. Faulconer, Walter Blum, Johnny Longden, Jim Gluckson, Bernie Hettel, Jack Middleton, W. H. P. Robertson, Dean Hoffman, Bill Doolittle, Kurt Becker ("The Voice"), Caton Metzler Bredar, Mike Cartee, R. James Williams, Gene McLean, Kathy Parker, Kathy Heitz, Joan Colby, Carl Larsen, Rab Hagin, Bruce Jakubek, Maryjean Wall, Jennie Rees, Jane Goldstein, Charlotte Quinn, Jim Peden, Dan Farley, Chris Lincoln, Dave Johnson, Edgar Allen, Tom Hammond, Howard Battle, Mike Battaglia, Dave Hooper, Dale Owens, Toby Callett, Mike Cronin, Doug Donn, Joe Tanenbaum, Jennifer Pierce, Mike Tanner, Al Cadeux, William H. King, John Asher, Keene Daingerfield, Mike

Mercer, Bill Mooney, Louis Hodges Sr., Louis Hodges Jr., and Damon Thayer—all top racing people.

To Bill Kaplan, Marty and Karla Wolfson, Luis Olivares, Jimmy Croll, and Walter Paisley, for time and generosity both inside their barns and racing lives; to Man o' War, Native Dancer, Bret Hanover, Tim Tam, Graustark, Ruffian, Manila, and Niatross—my favorite horses; to Doug, Christine, and Andrew Evans, three of Florida's best; to Greg, Paula, Joanna, Allison and Natalie Sexton—five "good ones" from Louisville; and to Janet Ray, who handled the mail work for this book flawlessly.

To the late Jim Bolus, who had absolutely no equal as a turfwriter, editor, friend, and human being. Also, to his longtime running mate, William F. "Billy" Reed of *Sports Illustrated*, both for his strong friendship and for his generous—and long-standing—support of my late father's groundbreaking work on the legendary Isaac Murphy; to Michele Blanco, who gave me both the signature piece ("Cool Man Caltech") and the signature section ("Hip-Hop") of this book; to Kathy Hamperian, senior manager, desktop support, University of Kentucky Computer Center, for her extraordinary generosity and professional help; to Amy Pettit of the Keeneland publicity department for additional photographic research; to Cathy Cooper Schenck of Keeneland Library for her invaluable help; to Jan Ciochetti, Janice Siska Hjelmgren, Jeanne Frederick, Jennie Ornsteen, and Sally Jessee, five points of brilliant light in my heart; to Fritzi Rose James, Christopher Blanco, and David Schenk, who remind us all daily that the future is indeed bright and rich; to the late Eddie Arcaro, a king of a rider and a prince of a man; to Arlington International Racecourse, whose light will shine again; to Tom Gravitt, whose singular courage is a glittering example for all of us; and to trainer Ray Lawrence Jr. and Rossi Gold, who gave a rookie turfwriter "the big break" he needed.

To five of my Kappa Sigma fraternity brothers—the Reverend Michael Milliken, Gayle House, Tommy Kron (of Rupp's Runts fame— "In our hearts, you'll always be number one"), Hal Dennis and Ron Kissling. Thanks for the good times.

And, to Julianne and Delilah, the two best "radio jocks" in America, who helped me finish this book with their great sounds (WGKS/KISS 96.9 FM/Lexington and Paris, Kentucky); to Phil Copeland, whose music is the best; to David Nemec, who made this book possible; to Stan "the Man" Starks, the perfect friend in thought, word, and deed; and to Ken Samelson, my editor and good "Big Mac" friend, who knows exactly why.

Contents

Introduction

THIS BOOK IS THE product of a basic literary law: If you write on any subject long enough, you're going to want to do a book on it sooner or later. My first racing book (also my first book) came out in 1986. I think that *Racelines* is long overdue.

And please make no mistake about *Racelines*.

It does not espouse a philosophy, nor does it provide answers to the critical questions facing the cosmos in which we live. Nor does it deal with racing's myriad of economic, social, political, or logistical problems. And it doesn't pretend to.

As a consequence, you will not find the jaded, cynical, deadbeat, antihero type—that demigod of twentieth-century American journalism—anywhere in *Racelines*.

Rather, this is a simple anthology of solid Thoroughbred and Standardbred racing stories. All of them share one belief in common: that horse racing (along with baseball) is one of the two greatest sports in the universe, and its participants are a reflection of that.

Two editorial points are of considerable importance.

First, the articles in *Racelines*, which cover a 20-year time span (1979 to 1998), appear here in their original form. They *have not been updated* to protect the integrity of the original article.

Thus, it is paramount that the reader duly note the date of each article. These are listed in the Contents (by year) and also on the lead page of each piece (full date and publication source). They refer either to the article's first publication date, or, if unpublished, its final draft date.

Point two. Articles carrying the "American Racetrack Series" designation indicate pieces done by the author specifically for this book. Because it is far easier and quicker to sell an article than a book, some of those articles appeared in various publications prior to the publication of this book. They are, however, the exclusive property of the author, as is the designation "American Racetrack Series."

It's a varied mix of articles, to be sure. Read and enjoy. And remember: If we both do our job well enough, there may be a sequel.

I

HUMOR

.

Wonder Boy

I love you madly.
(Anonymous jazzman's salutation)

YOU KNOW THE ONE, true great beauty of the horse?
We've landed on the moon, performed heart transplants, built genius-like computers. For our recreation, we've got things like VCRS, television, cassette tapes, radio, laser discs, and MTV *ad infinitum.* We've got cars, trains, and planes that go by horses like they were tied to a pole.

But, for all of that, nothing—and I mean NOTHING—will attract more attention quicker, nor make people goofier, than to put them in the presence of a horse.

It's the great equalizer, the one sure thing that can instantly link (read *bond*) the rich and famous to the downtrodden for life as if they were blood family.

Lots of people say they hate horses.

Yeah, right.

Give these gunslinging hard-asses an apple, let them feed it to a horse, and you'll have a mindless, drooling idiot on your hands quicker than you can say, "I believe in love."

The horse is a humbling experience (we want a paint when we grow up).

For all our conceits, our achievements, our vanities, and our luxuries, we can't live without this creature. You don't have to be rich or esoteric to enjoy them. They've been on this earth so long, it's impossible to imagine a world without them (trust me when I say that man will go extinct long before horses do). They're like milk in a way. You never outgrow your need for them, no matter how old you get.

One basic reason why is their inherent morality and that of their ancillary persona, the greatest hero in all of American history—the cowboy. Horses make more than just a few people pale in their presence, because they are the exact opposite of a goodly portion of the human race.

They don't lie, cheat, steal, sell out their best friends, run up your credit cards, use you, come home liquored up, abuse you, try to snake your best girl, and the like. You get the idea.

They're blood loyal to you, except in cases where you abuse them. And in that case, you're a punk, and you deserve whatever the hell happens to you.

Horses don't talk back to you, they don't drop the dime on you (tell on you), and they've got an innocence and faith in humanity (some of it sadly misplaced) that is utterly beguiling.

In short, a horse can be trusted to the wall, which is a lot more than can be said for some human beings.

All they ask for is routine maintenance: healthy love and attention; quality food and drink; and a clean place to sleep and reside, that abode including a good-sized exercise area.

In addition, horses are functional (they used to carry the mail, and there's another great American hero for you—the Pony Express rider); they're practical (they don't break down like cars); they're interesting historical artifacts (this was our transportation before the car); and they've always been valuable (horse stealing used to be a hanging offense).

And, in the romance department, they simply cannot be beat.

Trying to impress your *femme fatale* (that's French for drop-dead, good-looking woman with the laser stare who won't pay attention to you) with flowers, candy, wine, or violin music?

Try a classic-looking racehorse, pal, and get some real results.

She'll swoon all over the big, gray lug, saying something like:

Ohhh, he's so handsome. Yes, heee is. OHH, YESS heee is. I just LOVE a man in gray. And, just look at allll the white on him. He's got four white feet, and a BIGG, BEAUTFULLL white blaze. Yess, he doess. It looks like Mama's big boy fell in a paint bucket. Oh, yes, it does. And, he's so

bigggg and friendly. I just LOVE him. I wish I had something to feed him.
He looks sooo hungry.

The Lord will never give you a better opening than this.

By the time she finds out the true nature of the beast (you, not the horse), namely that you lied about breeding, owning, training, shoeing, vetting, transporting, and riding him (when those horrible old stewards would let you), you should be at dinner.

She won't want to make a scene in public, and with that much breathing room, you'll be able to explain the situation in full.

If that doesn't work, forget about what we said before, call in your markers for the violinist, the flowers, the candy, the wine, and whatever else you can think of, and tie on tight.

You're going to need it. All of it, because you've got a real hard case on your hands.

Author's Note: This chapter is dedicated to Christina Kearns, my goddaughter, who is one of the great treasures in my life; to Bobby Caldwell, this country's finest singer, bar none; to Clint Eastwood, for two American masterpieces, "Bird" and "Unforgiven"; and to Charlie Bauer, a man of great style—both at the tournament bridge table and away from it.

One-Liners

O N THE RACETRACK, THEY call 'em "cowboyisms": short, quick rejoinders that are all muscle and no fat. What follows is a sampling of some Thoroughbred racing one-liners, which in some cases, as a few purists will note, are longer than one line.

1. "He can run on a concrete highway or over a plowed field."

2. "A lot of horses have class, but no ability. Others have ability, but no class. This one has both . . . in spades."

3. "If I tell you it's Easter in August, you can start painting the damn eggs!" Version #2: "If I tell you an elephant is going to lay eggs, grease the skillet!" (In both cases, a trainer was asked if his horse was a lock for a particular race.)

4. "Her heart is bigger than her stall."

5. "Does this horse have speed? He has more speed than a street junkie. And he'll land up just like one, too. Out of it. Way out of it!"

6. "If you didn't make any mistakes, they wouldn't let you in the track."

7. "Put a bow in his neck, jock, down the backside." (A trainer's instructions to a rider.)

8. "Racing is really an up-and-down game. A trainer friend of mine last year had six horses who won thirty races. This year, he's got thirty horses who've won six races."

9. "You're only as good as your horses. You got to go where they take you. Try it the other way, and you'll never make it as a trainer."

10. "How old am I? Man, I don't even buy green bananas anymore."

11. "You can measure weight, you can measure distance, you can measure the other horses in a race. But you can't measure heart, and that's why my horse won today."

12. "Four-one (4-1) for the poor one!" (An exacta combination that according to superstition will break a losing streak.)

13. "I know a man who came to the races in a $20,000 car and left in a $100,000 bus."

14. "They're a thousand pounds of crystal. One bad step, and you could land up with a lot of broken glass. I wanted something better than that for my family. They deserve some kind of security, and now we've got that." (A trainer's response when asked why he had sold the best runner in his stable.)

15. "That jock is scootin' and bootin'." (An old-time saying about a jockey who breaks quickly from the gate, then opens up a big lead.)

Out of Luck in the Infield

L AST YEAR, ON THE Sunday before the epic Derby battle between Affirmed and Alydar, a close friend invited me to an early morning workout at Churchill Downs.

There, for the first time, I saw visages I had often dreamed about but had never personally enjoyed: the backstretch area, the winner's circle, the grandstand, the clubhouse, the famed Millionaire's Row, and finally, the top of the mountain—the esteemed press box of Churchill Downs.

Now this may not sound significant as racetrack tours go, but please bear with this writer. I had been imprisoned in the Derby infield for seven years, and finally after all that time, I was free to wander anyplace I pleased.

The tour proved to be a terrible ordeal for my host, what with his guest mumbling incoherently . . . and frequently.

Often, he had to lead me by the hand, softly talking to me so as not to excite me, all the while assuring me that no National Guardsmen, armed with those Wiffle-ball bats they called "riot-control batons," would suddenly appear and eject me.

And, by the time the tour was over, my face was scarlet red from the repeated "reality" slaps I had given it every time I reached for my wallet. (This was a free tour, after all, and not the Derby infield, where you paid for everything. Clearly, old habits die hard.)

A typical Kentucky Derby Day infield crowd (Churchill Downs Incorporated)

As we sat eating breakfast in the press box, high above the far and madding crowd (present and future), I poured out my Kentucky Derby story to my host.

In seven years (1970–76), I told him, I estimated I had drunk more than 100 mint juleps; had amassed a total of 87 Kentucky Derby programs that I was sure would someday be collector's items (that famed sporting-memorabilia phrase); had placed 49 losing bets; bootlegged more whiskey than a mountaineer; took and subsequently lost three dates; waited in line for a total of 20 hours to use the men's room (which generally required an ability to swim after the fourth race of Derby Day); and forked out more than $200 in parking and entry fees to attend a horse race that I did not see (to put that total into perspective, my inaugural Derby cost me only $5 parking and $3 admission to the infield).

Early on, I continued, it became apparent to me that some people would do anything—ANYTHING, you hear—to get into the Kentucky Derby infield free of charge.

Consider, I said, the case of the guy who parachuted onto the track in 1970 (my first Kentucky Derby) fifteen minutes before Derby posttime.

The following three years (1971–73) remain encased in a cloak of anonymity. Not so the 1974 running.

That's when the magic of the infield began to disappear, at the 100th running in 1974.

At this point, my host interrupted and offered the opinion that perhaps I felt that way because I had failed to place a winning ticket on the victor, Cannonade, and for eternity, I would just be another loser in the centennial Derby.

El wrongamente, I told him. There was more to it than that. A lot more.

The Derby was hot that year, damn hot, and the infield was packed like a blanket finish with more than 100,000 people (a conservative estimate, I believe) who wanted to be a vital part of some great racing history.

At the entrance to the infield tunnel (infield side) sat a redneck who had placed his picnic blanket square in the middle of all the fans who were going back and forth between the infield and the Central Avenue side of the track.

Shortly after the placement of his blanket, he started taking on people who stepped on his blanket, and I could see that it was going to be a long day.

I stepped back, took a deep breath, and guessed the number eight. Actually, the authorities made it there in about four minutes, and in the blink of an eye removed him, his blanket, his picnic goods—everything—from the site as if he had never existed.

That "epically historic" 100th running also witnessed a streaker bare his buttocks, atop the infield flagpole, to our esteemed royal visitors from England—Princess Margaret and the Earl of Snowden.

Historical purists may claim that the activities stemmed from hostilities dating back to previous wars between our countries.

Actually, as I told my host, it was more basic than that. The royalists—who had better seats, much better seats—were there. Just like the streaker . . . and the flagpole. Kind of like Mount Everest. Something had to be done, in the eyes of those great infield intellects, and was.

The next year, 1975, my body was assaulted as my mind had been the year before. Some moose wearing a Michigan State shirt, with muscles protruding from his neck and his arms hanging—naturally—at a 45-degree angle from his body, began shaking the infield fence furiously.

Quickly, others joined him, until at last he peeled the fence like a banana. Underneath that fence was you-know-who, literally curled up with Andy Beyer's *Picking Winners*, an excellent journal on how to survive at the racetrack. Unfortunately, it provided no information on how to extricate fencing from your face.

Then that moose proceeded to walk through the open fence, along with several hundred other people, with guess-who still pinned underneath.

Briefly, but only briefly, did a cop attempt to stop him. Naively, he asked him, "Where do you think you're going?"

"Out to my damn $10 seat," the Michigan State musclebounder replied. "Got any OBJECTIONS!?"

The cop quickly demurred, and Mr. Michigan State—along with friends—watched the race from near the rail.

I survived one more year, coming up to see Bold Forbes steal the Derby away from odds-on favorite Honest Pleasure in 1976. But that was it. By then, things had really begun to close in on me.

The Missing Persons Bureau was repeatedly interrogating me about the disappearance of my three dates in the early 1970s. The IRS was getting suspicious about my inability to win money at the Derby in all the times I had gone to THE RACE. Even my insurance company got into the act, repeatedly warning me not to go to the Kentucky Derby. (They passionately claimed that the Derby infield was an act of madness, not God, and under no circumstances would they ever pay off the double-indemnity clause contained in my policy.)

But, my friend/host implored, surely you've had some great times at the Derby.

Oh, I have, I replied.

For the last two years (1977 and 1978), I've watched the Kentucky Derby in privacy, away from the roar of the crowd, a mad one at that.

I'm a much happier person now. A better person for it all.

I have a front-row armchair seat, plenty of food and drink, and occasionally I win the Kentucky Derby pool at our party. I don't have to stand in long lines. I'm treated like royalty, like a real person.

All my friends and family say I seem to be at peace with myself. But then, who wouldn't be? The MPB, the IRS, and my insurance company have stopped calling me, and I love it, just absolutely love it.

I finally realized, I told my host as we got up from our breakfast, that the Kentucky Derby and I could never have a meaningful relationship.

Oh, we're still good friends, I added, and I'm happy for the experience, but I'm glad I saw the light before it was too late.

There are a bunch of loose horses out there in the infield. Thank the Lord, I'm not one of them.

II

ARTS
AND LETTERS

The Art of Cigar

A pearl of great value cannot be merely had for the asking.
(Old Arabic saying)

Be aware of wonder.
(Rule 14 of Robert Fulghum's rules of life)

THE STRUGGLE OF AN ARTIST—any artist—is a long and arduous trek to recognized and unqualified success. A host of names from all ages abound.

Michelangelo, one of the first widely successful commercial artists ever, destroyed himself physically painting the Sistine Chapel.

Van Gogh, a tortured genius besieged by mental illness, forfeited first his mind, then part of one ear, and finally his much-lamented life.

Da Vinci, whose works included sketches of flying machines that were the forerunners of helicopters, was ridiculed in his time and long afterward.

Rodin survived controversy and reigns now as one of our greatest sculptors.

Titian, who revolutionized oil painting with his vibrant reds and blues, had the ultimate revenge on his critics, having a brownish-orange color named after him.

And Frederic Remington, Charles Russell, and Charles Schreyvogel pioneered new frontiers on the canvas and in stone with their visceral western art.

There are more examples, but the point has been clearly made.

These artists all endure today because their spectacular work—ageless, timeless, and classic—continues to enrich the world. They have in effect switched positions with their critics. The aforementioned artists, and many more like them (before and since), today enjoy epic reputations while their third-rate detractors languish in anonymity.

And rightfully so.

Internationally acclaimed artist Cindy Wolf didn't start out to become that. It just happened that way, a product of a certain karma in the universe that only insiders fully recognize and understand.

She is proof paramount of the old adage that great artists are neither born nor made, but rather are developed—swept along, up and away, by diverse forces that far exceed genius-like talent.

The Versailles, Kentucky, resident got her first taste of horses at age three and a half riding the family's saddle horse. Further urged by parents who also introduced her to culture and history, Wolf unearthed an overpowering (could it be any other way?) passion for sculpture.

It is a genre she has remained with from her earliest dabblings in wax.

Educated at a women's college in Missouri, where she obtained a B.A. in history and minored in equine sciences, Wolf began her artwork simply as a hobby, mixing it with campaigning her show mare in local competitions.

Remarkably, without formal art training, she now ranks as a highly respected talent in the world of professional sculpture, one that is represented by Frost & Reed, Ltd., the prestigious London gallery that displays her work here and abroad.

The commission by Gulfstream to sculpt Cigar's image in bronze is one of her most monumental equine undertakings. As the signature horse for this decade, one of the greats of this generation, and one of the finest of all time, Cigar—via his achievements—surpasses any horse that Wolf has done to date.

"I am elated to have been selected for Gulfstream's dramatic endeavor," Wolf said in an interview earlier this year. "Cigar has a legion of adoring fans, and I am proud to be one of them."

The life-size statue of "Horse of the World" Cigar will be unveiled today, February 2, at Gulfstream Park in that oval's Garden of Champions. The only one to be immortalized by a statue, he will be the centerpiece of the famed racing palace, which currently features bronze plaques of 75 other champions who have raced at Gulfstream since 1944.

"Cigar has proved his greatness by defeating all opposition during a historic win streak that spanned almost two years," said Douglas Donn,

Doug Donn (Gulfstream Park/Equi-Photo)

Gulfstream President and chief executive officer. "We feel privileged to have received [Cigar's owner] Mr. Paulson's authorization to stand a statue of his champion at Gulfstream."

What are Wolf's feelings about that momentous commemoration?

"It will prompt a range of emotions," she said. "I'll be happy and proud and sad [at the separation from her project]."

Certainly, the gifted artist—who feels that horses represent a substantial part of her destiny and who works on only one project at a time—is more than equal to the task (it takes a giant to know a giant, to paraphrase an old saying).

Nonetheless, the stature of the subject has been a force to be reckoned with, requiring Wolf to corral all of her artistry to capture the magnificence of this wunderkind racer for thousands to see in the days, months, and years to come.

The solitary life of an artist is one that Wolf accepts. Her calling is to capture horse racing's immortals in bronze, her end goal to document the greatness of her subjects long after memories of them have faded.

That is the idealistic, philosophical, and artistic side to her work, which at times has seen Wolf work staggering 18-to-20-hour days (most works of this type require a year; Wolf received the commission from Donn on August 1 of last year). The practical logistics of creating such a work are equally mind-boggling.

To complete a work of bronze, a metal Wolf favors because of its unique qualities, many artists send their scale models to a foundry.

Wolf is among the very few in her meticulous craft who are truly "hands-on" artists from beginning to end, possessing the necessary skills for carrying the work through the entire metal-founding process.

Cindy Wolf's statue of Cigar (Gulfstream Park/Equi-Photo)

The Cigar statue, which Wolf refers to as "he," began its existence in her studio as a one-third life-size scale-model skeletal construction of wood, metal, wire, and foam.

Clay was then applied over the model, whose dimensions were computer-enhanced for accuracy after initial measurements were taken of the stellar racer by Wolf herself.

The personal measurings were, to say the least, an evocative experience.

"The first impression I gained from Cigar as I took those measurements in his stall is the one that has stayed with me throughout the creation of the statue," Wolf recounted. "He drew himself up and let his presence be known to me. It is the feeling he imparted then that has enabled me to instill life and motion into the statue."

With the Utah foundry team of Chuck Quigley and Mike Rubeck—Wolf's associates for more than 11 years—Wolf assisted in the mold making, wax pouring, cleaning, shell building, metal pouring, assembly, welding, and metal chasing.

The statue, in all of its bronze magnificence, left Versailles, Kentucky, for Gulfstream Park on Friday afternoon, January 31. The entire process will be completed at Gulfstream Park with the application of an oxidation procedure to give the bronze its finished color, or patina.

The Cigar statue that is coming to Gulfstream Park is a worthy addition to a select group of horses that literally stand in all their refulgent glory from coast to coast.

Churchill Downs has one of Aristides, the inaugural 1875 Kentucky Derby winner. Belmont is graced by an edifice of 1973 Triple Crown victor and two-time Horse-of-the-Year champion Secretariat. Kentucky Derby triumphant Sea Hero shines over Saratoga.

Arlington International Racecourse features the electrifying photo finish of winner John Henry and runner-up The Bart in the inaugural 1981 Arlington Million.

Classic champion Swaps, the 1956 Horse-of-the-Year whose career scores included the 1955 Kentucky Derby, is part of the racing estate of Hollywood Park. The indestructible handicapper Seabiscuit is similarly honored at Santa Anita.

The 1948 Triple Crown champion Citation (racing's first millionaire and Cigar's copartner on the modern-day win-streak list) has long been a fixture at Hialeah.

And certainly, this list would not be complete without a mention of the legendary Man o' War, a statue of whom resides at the front entrance of the Kentucky Horse Park in Lexington, Kentucky (he was moved there in the mid-1970s from his original resting place in the old Man o' War Park).

So what will one see in Wolf's statue of Cigar? Many things.

First, pieces of his fabulous 16-race win skein (over parts of three racing campaigns) that tied the modern mark set by Citation. That work, incidentally, included four victories here at Gulfstream—the 1995 Gulfstream Park Handicap, the 1995 and 1996 Donn Handicaps, and an allowance race.

Second, the voracious heart ("bigger than his stall" in racing parlance) that earned Cigar two consecutive Horse-of-the-Year titles, enabled him to reel off the big streak, and saw him annex numerous major stakes, all of that done with a bristol-stomping authority that left absolutely no doubt in anybody's mind who "the man" was.

Or what he was all about.

Aristides statue at Churchill Downs (Churchill Downs Incorporated)

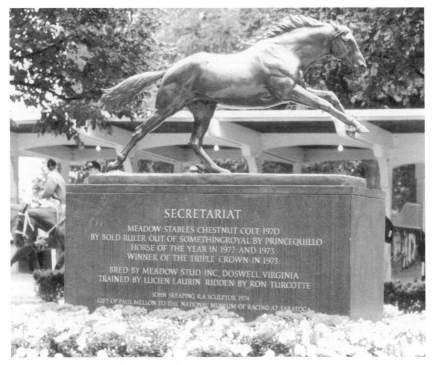

Secretariat statue at Belmont Park (New York Racing Association/Adam Coglianese)

Also, the classic horsemanship of trainer Bill Mott (a consultant on Wolf's project), the regal rides of Jerry Bailey, and the fearless competitiveness of owner Allen Paulson (a highly successful businessman and record-setting flyer with no room in his vocabulary or heart for second place, who audaciously campaigned his charge against all takers nationwide and on one memorable occasion far away from his native land).

And perhaps even several touches of magic.

One piece of that magic is the fact that The Hammer (a moniker Cigar acquired as an unruly youth) was a Christmas gift from Paulson's wife, Madeleine. (It can truly be said that there are a lot of people who would like to get on her Christmas gift list.)

An even larger slice of that mesmerizing magic was the way Cigar single-handedly thrust Thoroughbred racing back on the center stage of newspaper sporting pages, magazines (industry publications, as well as sporting and general-interest periodicals), the old mainstay of radio, and the prince of them all in this electronic age—television.

Sea Hero statue at Saratoga (New York Racing Association/Adam Coglianese)

Here was a megastar in the tradition and mold of the sport's greatest horses, an iron-horse wrecking machine, a dynasty seemingly without weakness or end, an ace who seemed to revel in all the commotion as much as its media sources did.

Wolf's statue will no doubt also mirror the epic foray halfway around the world to Dubai, the land of Arabian (k)nights, where the Seattle Slew grandson prevailed despite a long and arduous journey, a slow start, a deep surface not to his liking, and a physical condition less than 100 percent.

Against All Odds statue at Arlington International Racecourse (Arlington International Racecourse)

Digging deep down inside that seemingly endless reservoir of courage that was his trademark, he prevailed when all the forces of the natural world were set against him.

Indeed, if there was one race that defined Cigar's infinite greatness, it was this race, one that stamped him as a truly "honest" horse—the kind who gave his all every time he went out, and then some.

In an age when inferior services, mediocre workmanship, and second-rate products are the norm, here truly was something that was American-made and seemingly without flaw, as thoroughly reliable and dependable as the sun coming up in the morning. For all intents and purposes, absolutely perfect. The adjectives are endless, but you get the drift.

And, when Cigar retired, he left horse racing as its richest North American competitor ever ($9,999,985), just a few dollars short of being

Statue of Seabiscuit at Santa Anita Park (Santa Anita Park/Benoit Photo)

Thoroughbred racing's first ten-million-dollar horse. Clearly, what you will see in Wolf's sculpture is not a horse just of this time, but of all time.

Look at the all-time win-streak list that follows (each horse's birth year follows in parentheses) and you realize that Cigar's work far transcended just that of Citation, placing him in a company with horses from three different time frames—the eighteenth, nineteenth, and twentieth centuries.

(23) Leviathan (1793)

(21) First Consul (1798)
    Lottery (1803)

Statue of Citation at historic Hialeah Park
(Hialeah Park)

Trainer Bill Mott and rider Jerry Bailey,
both Hall of Famers (Gulfstream Park/
Equi-Photo)

Owner Allen Paulson leads Cigar in after a repeat victory in the 1996 Donn Handicap at
Gulfstream Park. (Gulfstream Park/Equi-Photo)

(20) Fashion (1837)
    Kentucky (1861)

(19) Boston (1833)
    Sweetmeat (1842)

(18) Sally Hope (1822)
    Hindoo (1878)

(17) Beeswing (1830s)
    Alice Hawthorne (1838)
    Boston (1833)
    Hanover (1884)

(16) Luke Blackburn (1877)
    Miss Woodford (1880)
    Citation (1945)
    Cigar (1990)

(15) Rattler (1866)
    Ten Broeck (1872)
    Colin (1905)
    Vander Pool (1928)
    Buckpasser (1963)

(14) Harry Bassett (1868)
    Man o' War (1917)

Soon and forever, this racing demigod we call Cigar will make one more run—into permanent sporting artistic immortality, thanks to the skill of artist Cindy Wolf and the generosity of Gulfstream Park.

What we will see and feel and hear, above all else, will be the eternal song of all life—sporting and otherwise.

It is not enough for our greats to merely win. Rather, they must endure and prevail. In short, they must meet and pass the "ultimate standard"— to be the only one standing at the end of the battle when the bell is rung.

On and off the track, Cigar has more than met that classic standard.

Come February 2, we will witness a mighty and rare moment in both sport and art. We are truly lucky to walk in the light of such geniuses as Wolf and such champions as Cigar.

Hoofprints on Film

THOUGH BASEBALL MAY BE the national pastime, horse racing and horses are in a league by themselves, the sport and athletes most favored by American filmmakers.

The catalogue appended to the end of this article lists some 100 films about horse racing and horses, nearly double the number of baseball films. And, not surprisingly, approximately one-third of that catalogue is devoted to "the king of sports"—Thoroughbred racing.

What follows is a look at what I consider to be the ten best horse-racing (and horse competition) films ever made, followed by a like number of honorable mentions.

All have been gleaned from the master list.

Comprised of eight major categories (Thoroughbred, Standardbred, Quarter Horse, Steeplechase, Rodeo, Polo, Equestrian, and General Interest), the catalogue is clearly rich in its quality, variety, and quantity.

And now, ladies and gentlemen, the envelopes.

THE TOP TEN
Champions (Great Britain, 1983)

If you were to give an Eclipse Award for the best horse-racing film ever made, this movie—along with *Phar Lap*—would share the honor. In addition, they would each get divisional awards as the best modern-era and period-piece horse-racing films, respectively, ever made. Obviously, I think a lot of these two movies.

From its opening, a series of magnificent tracking shots, to its powerful freeze-frame ending, this aptly named film does not disappoint.

Based on the true story of English steeplechase rider Robert Champion, the film vividly recounts his painful victory over cancer and his courageous comeback to take the 1981 Grand National—the world's greatest steeplechase race—with an 11-year-old jumper named Aldaniti, who himself overcame a series of injuries en route to his greatest career triumph.

Scripted from Champion's autobiography (*Champion's Story: A Great Human Triumph*), the film is sterling proof of the old axiom that truth is stranger than fiction.

Ironically, the weakest part of the movie is the section that takes place in the bluegrass country of Kentucky, in and around Lexington, the central-Kentucky area long acknowledged as the horse capital of the world.

This despite the presence of Oscar winner Ben Johnson (*The Last Picture Show*). It makes no difference, though, as this section occupies only a small part of this monumental film.

From start to finish, this film belongs to John Hurt (*The Elephant Man*, *Midnight Express*, etc.), whose physical size and looks give this film a visceral and realistic look rarely seen in horse-racing films. Hurt's performance in the title role of reinsman Robert Champion is dead-on straight, with no false moves: he is a jockey in thought, word, deed, and mannerism.

In lesser hands, *Champions* would have been a simple, formula sports story. In the hands of a classic master like Hurt, however, with his abiding attention to gritty detail and subtle nuance, *Champions* is that rarest of movies—a good, solid film.

One final point about *Champions*.

If the actor playing trainer Josh Gifford—who realized the dream of a lifetime with the Grand National win by Champion and Aldaniti—looks vaguely familiar, well he should.

It's Edward Woodward, star of the pop-TV hit series *The Equalizer*. His powerful presence, including one brutal exchange with Hurt following a minor training mishap, adds further muscle and bone to an already strong film.

Phar Lap (Australia, 1984)

Every good movie has a look, a certain feel, and this film has the best look I've ever seen in any horse-racing film. It has a gristly feel, like hard sand stuck in your teeth. Translated, that means from beginning to end the film has a stark realism rarely seen in horse-racing movies.

Part of that is due to the principal cast, several of whom—notably craggy-faced Martin Vaughan as Henry Telford, the small-time trainer who discovered the champion Australian racehorse Phar Lap (1926–32)—look like they were plucked straight from the racetrack.

Because the movie is also a period piece, it relies heavily on a true re-creation of the times. The movie succeeds magnificently, with not a false prop in sight, its sets and locations totally devoid of any Hollywood phoniness.

All of this is bound together by a hard script that offers a splendid array of moral colors—black, gray, and white—amidst crooked Jockey Club officials; shadowy bookmakers; race fixing of several varieties; physical abuse of a great racehorse; Phar Lap's attempted murder by gangsters; a pragmatically greedy owner (Dave Davis, played to perfection by Ron Liebman) and an equally conniving trainer (Telford); the devoted boy-groom, Tommy Woodcock (Tom Burlinson), who became as big a national hero as the wonder horse he trained for the last win—and start—of his fabled career; and the object of all these bad intentions and good attention, Phar Lap, played by a former show jumper named Towering Inferno.

Like *Champions*, this well-photographed film utilizes several powerful tracking shots and is based on a true story.

To Down Unders (Australians) what Man o' War is to Americans, Phar Lap (who, ironically, had been bred in New Zealand) was a huge gelding (17 hands) who in death became larger than he ever was in life. In short, he was the stuff of which legends are made.

A winner of 37 of 51 lifetime starts, including Australia's most prized classic—the Melbourne Cup—in 1930, Phar Lap's career ended with his sudden death two years later in California, shortly after he had begun his North American campaign.

Translated, his name means "lightning" (it was derived from a West African phrase meaning "wink in the sky").

Sadly, in the wink of an eye it seemed, Phar Lap left, leaving behind several notable effects, including a 14-pound heart (the average is 9 pounds); a folk myth that was even larger; and a bitter, lingering question about his mysterious death.

Australians have claimed for years it was murder at the hands of American gangsters, and because *Phar Lap* is an Australian-made film, the movie subscribes to that popular, nefarious (and always convenient) form of scapegoating: anti-Americanism.

Americans, however, have claimed it was the result of the coppery chestnut (nicknamed the Red Terror) eating contaminated feed, a position held to by numerous turf historians. (A number of them also point out that Americans had absolutely no motive for killing the horse; indeed, the finger points mostly at *Australian* bookmakers and gangsters, whose gambling businesses had been heavily damaged by Phar Lap and were likely to be more so if he returned to Australia.)

While the question of Phar Lap's enigmatic death will probably never be answered definitively, one question was answered with the release of his life story: When was a film going to be made about this great runner, who ran short and long, won under enormous loads of weight, and conceded prolific poundage to his rivals?

It took a little time—52 years—but it was worth the wait.

Bite the Bullet (United States, 1975)

Veteran actor Gene Hackman, perhaps best known for his Oscar-winning performance in *The French Connection*, has fashioned a fine career off sensitive, in-depth portrayals of ordinary men. *The Conversation* (one of Hackman's personal favorites) is another example, and *Bite the Bullet* is yet one more case in point.

Whether you're a fan of Hackman (one of Hollywood's most unlikely-looking stars, who got his big break in *Bonnie and Clyde*), horse racing, or both, you won't be cheated.

An unusual western about the cruel endurance horse races that abounded in the American West between 1880 and 1910, the film is heightened by the richness of its location photography. James Coburn plays Hackman's chief rival and is part of a stellar cast that includes Candice Bergen, Ben Johnson, Jan-Michael Vincent, and Dabney Coleman.

To some, the unusual ending may seem off-balance. Actually, it's a perfect finale to a great horse race and an even greater horse-racing film that sparkles because of Hackman's intuitive understanding of the inherent decency (and quiet heroism) of the common man.

The Reivers (United States, 1969)

The late Steve McQueen reportedly felt uneasy about doing comedy.

That's hard to believe considering his colorful performance in this wild misadventure, based on William Faulkner's Pulitzer Prize–winning novel set in the Deep South around the turn of the century.

McQueen stars as Boon Hogganbeck, a devil-may-care hired hand who "borrows" the new family car for a trip into Memphis. In tow are the owner's grandson (sensitively played by Mitch Vogel) and a black stable hand (Rupert Crosse, who received an Oscar nomination for his hilarious work).

While racing is not the central theme in *The Reivers* (which is southern slang for "the thieves"), it's included in this top-ten list because a horse—and a fabulous horse race—are crucial to the film's resolution.

The race photography in this movie may be the best ever seen on the screen (only *Ben Hur* can compare), complete with "wild sound" audio tracking and lush slow-motion shots. The stellar cast includes Sharon Farrell, Will Geer, and Michael Constantine.

The Appaloosa (United States, 1966)

Marlon Brando movies may be divided into three categories: classics (like *On the Waterfront* and *The Godfather*, both Oscar-winning performances); outright junk (pick any of many); and "sleepers" (like *One-Eyed Jacks*). *The Appaloosa*, a hostile film complemented (like many other selections on this list) by superb location cinematography, belongs in the last category.

Brando plays a down-and-out cowboy whose prized Appaloosa stallion is stolen by a Mexican bandit, deftly portrayed by John Saxon. The resulting violent conflict between the two men works well because of a solid script that avoids stereotyping Saxon's character.

Though the scene where a smoldering Saxon airs his lifelong grievances against American gringos in general and Brando in particular might seem a bit dated today, it was, nonetheless, progressive screenplay writing for its time.

His rage, objectively presented, gives Saxon's character another dimension, one that forces the viewer to acknowledge his position. While we can never agree with his act of theft, and are personally repulsed by his murderous malevolence, we are at least brought to a point where we understand *why* he is like he is.

A hearty, physical movie, *The Appaloosa* concludes with one of the finest examples of marksmanship ever seen on the screen.

Though the horse competition in this film is figurative (Brando's protracted efforts to regain his prized horse), it belongs on this list as much as any other movie.

Historically, the film offers several points worthy of brief mention.

One is the code of the old West, where stealing a man's horse was considered a greater offense than murdering him. As an example, we offer the apocryphal tale of a Texas judge who freed a murderer but sentenced a horse thief to be hanged, telling the latter, "Son, we got lots of men in Texas who need akillin', but we don't have any horses in Texas that need astealin'."

Secondly, the story transports us back to a time when the horse was a way of life, and not just a sporting animal, as it is today.

Finally, *The Appaloosa* is a rich look at this unusual horse itself. Easily identified by its distinctive spotted rump, this breed was developed by the Nez Percé Indians, who once inhabited the region bordering the Palouse River (thus the breed's name) in the Pacific Northwest.

Ben Hur (United States, 1959)

One of Hollywood's most honored films, this spectacle about the conflict between the Jews and the Romans in Jerusalem during the lifetime of Jesus Christ is a dramatic, religious epic that has nothing to do with horse racing. It is included here, though, because of one major scene, the dramatic chariot race between Judah Ben Hur (Charlton Heston) and Messala (Stephen Boyd).

The chariot race is spectacular for two reasons.

Cinematically, the race sequence—one of the most electrifying ever captured on film—features incredible stunt work by Heston's double, Joe Canutt, the son of legendary Hollywood stuntman Yakima Canutt.

Considered to be one of Hollywood's three pioneer stuntmen (along with Richard Talmadge and David Sharpe), Yakima Canutt—a peerless horseman—received an honorary Oscar in 1966, the first one ever awarded to a stuntman.

Historically, this film has rich undertones, though few may realize it. Believe it or not, it is a look at civilization's first horse—the harness horse. That may disturb the "running horse people," but the facts are there. According to the experts, horses—thanks to the wheel—were beasts of draft long before they were beasts of burden, their pony-like size centuries ago precluding men from riding them.

Moreover, chariots dominated the early chapters of warfare. Historians have traced them back to 4000 B.C., a date that precedes the use of cavalry by some 3,000 years. By logical extension, harness horse racing was also the world's first formal equine competition. In the late 1930s in Turkey, archaeologists turned up a circa–1350 B.C. treatise entitled *The Chariot Training Manual.*

Its author was one Kikkulis, a trainer for King Suppiluliumas of Mittani, whose royal trotters are the world's first documented racehorses. (Significantly enough, the kingdom of Mittani was located in the region often called the Cradle of Civilization—Mesopotamia.)

Finally, it should be noted that the Olympics are the world's best-known and oldest formal athletic competition. When the first Olympics were held in 1000 B.C., chariot races were among the events on the program. Not until 800 B.C., say historians, were horse-running races introduced at the games. Enough said.

For the record, the 1959 edition of *Ben Hur* (a remake of a 1926 version, which was a remake of a 1907 version) was a trouble-plagued film that was years in production and cost $4 million to make, twice the going rate at the time.

Nonetheless, the end product proved to be well worth the effort, as this film classic garnered a slew of Oscars, including Best Picture, Best Actor (Heston), Best Supporting Actor (Hugh Griffith), Best Director (William Wyler), Best Cinematography (Robert Surtees), and Best Music (Miklos Rozsa).

The Killing (United States, 1956)

An early classic from director Stanley Kubrick (*2001: A Space Odyssey, Dr. Strangelove, Spartacus, The Shining, A Clockwork Orange*), this is a must-see film for obvious reasons.

Kubrick also wrote the screenplay, and this tense crime drama first brought his work to the attention of critics.

Unusually structured, *The Killing* is an elaborate caper movie about a daring racetrack robbery planned by an ex-convict.

Big Boy (United States, 1930)

The only musical on the top-ten list, and one of the few in the master catalogue, *Big Boy* stars Al Jolson (who made his fame as a blackfaced minstrel singing songs of the Deep South) as a black jockey who wins a big race (the Kentucky Derby) against enormous odds.

Though the script may strain the credibility of many, it is, in fact, one of the *more* historically accurate racing pictures turned out by Tinseltown. During the early years of organized American Thoroughbred racing, black riders dominated the sport.

A prime example was the Kentucky Derby, which black riders worked as if they owned it, taking 15 of the first 28 editions contested between 1875 and 1902.

The most famous of those black riders was Isaac Murphy, a charter member of the National Racing Hall of Fame (which also includes fellow black rider Willie Simms and black trainers Ed Brown and Ansel Williamson). Considered America's first great black athlete and the finest reinsman of the late nineteenth century as well, Murphy was the first rider to win three Kentucky Derbies (in 1884, 1890, and 1891) and also the first to take consecutive renewals of the event.

His prime career triumphs also included four of the first five runnings of the American Derby (once *the* derby in America), run at old Washington Park. Still contested in Chicago, the American Derby is now held at Arlington International Racecourse, where Murphy is notably remembered by a stake race named in his honor.

Big Boy deserves to be remembered for one other reason.

Made shortly after the advent of "talkies," this film may well be the first "sound" horse-racing picture turned out by Hollywood.

The Great American Cowboy (United States, 1974)

The only documentary on the top-ten list, but one of several from the master catalogue, this film won an Academy Award (Best Documentary

Feature) for its voraciously candid look at the hardships and rewards of the American rodeo circuit.

And the opening sky-vaulting footage and resulting free-frame shot alone are worth the price of admission.

This film's centerpiece is the competition between rodeo superstar Larry Mahan and Phil Lyne, a newcomer seeking to dethrone the long-time king of the cowboys.

Fueled by magnificent rawboned and candid photography, *The Great American Cowboy* touches the true heart of this country, and for my money remains the best rodeo picture—feature or documentary—ever made.

That's how damn much I like it.

National Velvet (United States, 1944)

Every list like this has, or should have, at least one good "family" selection, and this one is it (barely nosing out *The Black Stallion*). And, like another selection on the top-ten list (the top-ranked *Champions*), its theme is the Grand National, the world's most prized steeplechase race.

Based on the enormously popular book by Enid Bagnold (the pen name of Lady Jones, wife of Sir Roderick Jones of the famous Reuters Limited News Service of London), this warm and enduring classic centers on a butcher's daughter and a bum kid who train a jumper to win the Grand National.

In the title role of Velvet Brown, Elizabeth Taylor leads a superb cast that includes Mickey Rooney, Donald Crisp, Angela Lansbury, and Anne Revere (who received an Oscar as Best Supporting Actress).

A stunning beauty even at age 12, Taylor delivered a radiant performance in her first major screen role, one that propelled her to stardom and still shines today.

Some critics consider it to be the finest work of her long and productive career. That's a substantial assessment considering that her body of work includes a pair of Oscar-winning efforts (*Butterfield 8* and *Who's Afraid of Virginia Woolf?*).

A decent sequel (British-made) to this film, *International Velvet*, was released in 1978.

HONORABLE MENTIONS

The Black Stallion (United States, 1979)

One of the finest family films ever made, this movie—based on the classic children's book by Walter Farley—features a sparkling performance by Mickey Rooney.

Casey's Shadow (United States, 1979)

The only quarter-horse film in the catalogue, this splendid comedy-drama is a great vehicle for the crusty veteran actor Walter Matthau (*The Bad News Bears*, *The Sunshine Boys*, and an Oscar-winning performance in *The Fortune Cookie*, among others).

This film is based on jockey Randy Romero, who started out riding quarter horses before switching to Thoroughbreds in the mid-1970s. His career work includes piloting undefeated Personal Ensign to a heart-stopping victory over Winning Colors in the 1988 Breeders' Cup Distaff (Personal Ensign's final career start) and a record 181 wins during the 1982 season at old Arlington Park (now Arlington International Racecourse) in Chicago.

A Day at the Races (United States, 1937)

Though a cut below the two best films ever made by the Marx Brothers (*Duck Soup* and *A Night at the Opera*), this film still provides plenty of laughs. Could it be any other way . . . with the Marx Brothers at the races?

Saratoga (United States, 1937)

This vintage film, with America's most fabled (and famous) racetrack and most beautiful racing town as its backdrop, stars Clark Gable, Jean Harlow, and Lionel Barrymore.

Intellectuals may query: What's the plot all about?

Get a life. Who the hell cares? With a location, cast, and subject like that, how can you go wrong?

One tragic note, however. This picture was the last performance by the 26-year-old platinum-blonde Harlow, who died of a kidney disorder shortly before it was completed.

Home in Indiana (United States, 1944)

Brilliantly photographed, this is a harness-racing classic that stars three-time Oscar winner Walter Brennan, Lon McAllister, Jeanne Crain, Ward Bond (who, it seems, was in every great movie ever made), and June Haver.

McAllister, a talented adolescent actor who didn't successfully make the transition to adult roles because of his height, is superb as the young boy who drives a blind filly in the film's climactic race.

Broadway Bill (United States, 1934)

Another oldie but goldie, this fine racetrack drama (a somewhat disturbing work) was directed by the incomparable Frank Capra (*It's a Wonderful Life, It Happened One Night, Mr. Smith Goes to Washington, You Can't Take It with You, Mr. Deeds Goes to Town*). A multiple Oscar-winning director, Capra remade this film in 1950 as *Riding High*.

In particular, note the stylish tracking shots and the brooding close-up of the trainer toward the end of the film.

Junior Bonner (United States, 1972)

Another top work from the late Steve McQueen, this fine rodeo piece is considered by some critics to be the gentlest film ever directed by one of Hollywood's most notorious mavericks, the late Sam Peckinpah (*The Wild Bunch, Ride the High Country, Straw Dogs, The Getaway*).

Charlie Chan at the Racetrack (United States, 1936)

There's nothing deep about this film; it's simply great entertainment starring the original Charlie Chan, the *Swedish-born* Warner Oland.

My Old Man (United States, 1979)

Based on a short story by Ernest Hemingway, this remake of *Under My Skin* (1950) stars Kristy McNichol, Warren Oates, and Eileen Brennan in a well-crafted backstretch tale about a seedy trainer and his protective, horse-loving daughter.

Boots Malone (United States, 1952)

Nicely photographed, this fast-paced racetrack drama stars the late William Holden (*Network, Sunset Boulevard, The Bridge on the River Kwai,* and an Oscar-winning performance in *Stalag 17*) as a shady agent who changes when he helps a young boy to become a jockey.

NOTABLE HORSE AND HORSE-RACING FILM CATALOGUE

Thoroughbred

> *April Love* (remake of *Kentucky*)
>
> *Big Boy*
>
> *Blue Grass of Kentucky*
>
> *Boots Malone*
>
> *The Champ* (1979 remake of the 1931 original and the 1953 version entitled *The Clown*; racing scenes shot at Hialeah)
>
> *Charlie Chan at the Racetrack*
>
> *A Day at the Races*
>
> *Derby Day* (retitled *Four Against Fate*)
>
> *Devil on Horseback*
>
> *The Ex–Mrs. Bradford*
>
> *Fast Company* (the 1953 film, not the 1938 film of the same name)
>
> *The Galloping Major*
>
> *Glory* (story by the late Admiral Gene Markey, husband of Calumet heiress Ms. Lucille Wright Markey)
>
> *The Homestretch*
>
> *Hot to Trot*
>
> *It Ain't Hay*
>
> *Kentucky*
>
> *The Missouri Traveler*
>
> *Money Rider*
>
> *My Old Man* (remake of *Under My Skin*)
>
> *Night Chase* (contains footage shot at Del Mar)

Phar Lap

Pride of the Blue Grass

Racing Blood

The Rainbow Jacket

The Reivers

The Return of October

Salty O'Rourke

Saratoga

Shadow of the Thin Man (part of the famed "Thin Man" series)

Sporting Blood

Stablemates

The Story of Seabiscuit

Thoroughbreds Don't Cry

Three Men on a Horse

Under My Skin (remade as *My Old Man*)

Standardbred

Ben Hur (1959 remake of 1926 version and 1907 original)

The Great Dan Patch

Green Grass of Wyoming

Home in Indiana

Quarter Horse

Casey's Shadow

Steeplechase

Champions

National Velvet

Rodeo

Adventures of Gallant Bess

Arena

Black Rodeo (documentary)

Bronco Buster

The Great American Cowboy (documentary)

Junior Bonner

J. W. Coop

The Lusty Men

Riding Tall

When the Legends Die

Polo

Leave Yesterday Behind

Equestrian

International Velvet (sequel to *National Velvet*)

Sand

Sylvester

General Interest

The Appaloosa

Bite the Bullet

Black Horse Canyon

The Black Stallion

The Black Stallion Returns

Broadway Bill (remade as *Riding High*)

Dime with a Halo

Down Argentine Way (musical)

Easy Come, Easy Go (the 1947 film, not the 1967 movie of the same name)

The Electric Horseman

Equus

An Event

A Girl in Every Port (the 1952 movie, not the 1928 film of the same title)

Gypsy Colt

The Horse in the Gray Flannel Suit

The Horseman

A Horse Named Comanche (original name: "Tonka")

It's a Great Life (part of the "Blondie" series of films)

The Killing

King of the Turf

King of the Wild Horses

King of the Wild Stallions

Little Miss Marker (1934 original remade in 1949 as *Sorrowful Jones*, in 1963 as *Forty Pounds of Trouble*, and in 1980, again as *Little Miss Marker*)

The Littlest Horse Thieves

The Longshot

The Man from Snowy River

Maryland

McHale's Navy

The Misfits

Miss Grant Takes Richmond

Money from Home

My Brother Talks to Horses

My Friend Flicka

The Palomino

Peter Lundy and the Medicine Hat Stallion

The Red Pony (1949 version)

Return to Snowy River: Part II

Ride a Wild Pony

Riding High (remake of *Broadway Bill*)

The Rocking Horse Winner (from a D. H. Lawrence story)

Romance of a Horsethief

The Rounders

Run Wild, Run Free

The Sad Horse

Sing You Sinners

Snowfire

Thunderhead—Son of Flicka

Tip on a Dead Jockey

Top of the Form

Tribute to a Bad Man

Who's Got the Action

Wild Horse Hank

Wild Horses

Wild Stallion

Yankee Doodle Dandy (features a magnificent stage dance sequence—set against a racing background—by James Cagney, who won an Oscar for his performance)

You Can't Buy Luck

Author's Note: This catalogue contains horse-racing films, equine-theme movies, and motion pictures with major racing sequences. Films with a strong gambling theme were put in the General Interest category, as were western-oriented movies (with the specific exception of rodeo films). Movies that could not be specifically classified were also placed in the General Interest category.

Louis N. Hodges Sr., one of the great masters of American racetrack photography (Louis Hodges Jr.)

The Wizard
of Orleans

HE STILL GETS UP every morning between three and five, long before the sun has made an appearance in accordance with the rules of the universe, a habit gained from many years in the sport as a racetrack photographer.

He makes bulletproof coffee that causes his sons, Louis Jr. and Kevin—both excellent racetrack photographers in their own right who now carry on the family business (Arlington Park in the summer and the Fair Grounds in the winter)—to absolutely shudder (no pun intended).

He drinks that potent coffee (so strong that it can bench-press 500 pounds easy, it is said) in the solitude of the den of his Jefferson, Louisiana, home, located just minutes from the nation's third-oldest race-track in downtown New Orleans.

The den is lined with pictures of some of the most famous racehorses in American racing history, a mere sample of what passed through his lens from the late 1940s to the early 1980s.

And, like some of Kentucky's finest horse farms, which house many fine racehorses retired from the great racing wars, the den is filled with great cameras that he "retired" from racing action over the years: five Hasselblads, one Linhof, two Speed Grafics, and one Brooks Variwide.

Now, just months short of his 70th birthday, Louis Nevin Hodges Sr. is engaged to a beautiful lady, has purchased two high-powered and very expensive Leicas, and is talking about hitting the road again as a racetrack photographer.

No senior-citizen discounts for this man, who regards Social Security as something to be endured, not enjoyed. For him, time does not exist, only his photography. At five-foot-six and 165 pounds, Hodges is a cherubic, grandfatherly figure who instantly reminds you of the Wizard of Oz. With a camera.

Mild in manner and eager for all that is good in the world, there is not a trace of macho in him, though he is firm in both opinion and principle.

His strength—which grabs your attention immediately and tells you that here is no ordinary man—is his gentility, a quality seen in the sport about as often as a Triple Crown winner.

That gentility flows forth constantly in his racing stories, which contain not a shred of raw language and are totally devoid of petty jealousies, lingering grudges, and successful acts of revenge. On the rare occasion that he utters a negative word about someone, it translates as constructive criticism, often tinged with regret over a less-than-perfect situation.

Listen to him for even the shortest while and one realizes that as hard as the sport was then, even more so now, Hodges himself never hardened.

And the stories he tells. Oh, the stories.

Hodges came in with Citation and left with Spectacular Bid. His life is a panorama that captivates and mesmerizes you like the facade of sounds and lights the real Wizard hid behind, protecting awesome powers, which if allowed to fall into the wrong hands would have swung the balance unfairly against a much-beleaguered world.

In a fashion, Hodges spent his life "hiding," hiding behind the sounds and lights of numerous cameras, creating the magic of racetrack photographs. Like his cinematic counterpart, Hodges fought the evils of his own world all his life: sloth, apathy, incompetence, and mediocrity. His weapon was an intense, professional pride and skill rarely seen today (a craftsmanship he still retains and passed on to both his sons), as out of time and place as the movie Wizard, who arrived at Oz via a lost balloon.

The naive may view the work of Hodges and other track photographers as nothing more than pictures, an opinion that demonstrates just how unappreciated and misunderstood this type of work is. It is true that

LOUISIANA DERBY – $100,000

J R Straus & I Proler Owners		Run Dusty Run 2nd
H C Pardue Trainer	CLEV ER TELL	A Letter To Harry 3rd
Ray Broussard up	Equals Track Record	1 1/8 Mi 1:48:4
	Fair Grounds New Orleans La 20 March 1977	

A classic "three-way" shot by Louis Hodges Sr. (Louis Hodges Sr.)

the "winner's circle" pictures start out as strictly a commercial endeavour, being sold to owners, trainers, riders, and breeders for their own personal remembrances.

But that is only the beginning.

In time, many of them become art, in some cases a lost art, like the old "five-ways" Hodges used to shoot for stakes races, which included shots of the winner's circle and the trophy presentation; a comeback shot of the winner after the race; a finish-line shot; and a long, horizontal panel at the bottom of the picture displaying the last yards of the stretch run.

The standard today is the three-way, on occasion a two-way, although Hodges's son Louis Jr. is planning to shoot some four-ways this summer at Arlington Park for certain races.

In the end, though, and most importantly, the pictures serve as the most lasting historical record we have of those moments on the turf, preventing some of the greatest races in American history from being just mere race charts and nothing more.

The same cannot, sadly, be said for a craftsman like Hodges, who spent his entire life in that virtual anonymity so typical of his profession (ever hear of pioneers C. C. Cook, J. C. "Skeets" Meadors, or Bert Morgan, or modern-era whizzes Bob Coglianese and Jim Raftery?).

But that does not alter the value of his work, or that of any other racetrack photographer, in the least. And that work includes scores of free publicity and promotional photographs used anonymously by various media and advertising outlets—of barn-area scenes, early-morning workouts, clubhouse celebrities, and paddock gatherings, to name but a few.

As his son Louis Jr. points out, these pictures are the only things that really last from racing. This may seem to some to be a self-serving statement, but you'll find no jury in this quarter to convict him, no matter how much you cry "jury tampering" regarding a February visit that produced the official press book from the famed Swaps-Nashua match race at Washington Park in Chicago in 1955 (credit the senior Hodges); Louis Sr.'s resplendent hospitality; a taste of some of New Orleans' fine beverages, alcoholic and otherwise (credit the junior Louis Hodges); and an introduction to that city's famed rib and beef restaurant Luther's, as well as the procurement of a rare James Dean poster in the French Quarter, plus a tour of the Superdome (credit Kevin Hodges).

Think about it. Horses may die and pass on. Tracks may crumble from age, injury (catastrophic and otherwise), cheap politics, or bad management. Owners may leave the sport. Trainers and riders may retire. Yet, in the end, the pictures endure, much like land does. As Gerald O'Hara told his daughter Scarlett in *Gone with the Wind*, land was the only thing worth having, worth fighting for, worth dying for, because it was the only thing that lasted.

The O'Hara and Hodges families never met, but they are kindred spirits, products of a common background.

Born August 22, 1917, in New Orleans, Louis N. Hodges Sr. was the son of Irish Catholic immigrants Sam and Margaret Hodges, who had come from County Cork.

"It was intended," Louis Hodges Sr. explained during the recent Mardi Gras season, showing traces of a rich New Orleans accent, "that I should go to college. My stepmother, Lydia, a wonderful woman my father married after my real mother died when I was five, was responsible for me becoming a photographer.

"The Depression ended my college hopes. I picked a profession where I could excel and also be in demand. It worked out well since I had, I felt, a flair for the creative and the unusual."

Hodges started out doing studio photography in New Orleans before World War II, for the Wheeling Company. In June of 1941, he joined the U.S. Army Air Force. While in pilot training in Florida, he met and eventually married Dolly Summerlin, who died last year after more than 40 years of marriage that produced two sons and a daughter, Sylvia.

A condition called aereo embolitis, the airman's version of the bends suffered by divers, washed him out as a pilot, but as fate would have it, he eventually landed up with the Far East Air Force photo lab in Manila. Discharged in 1946, Hodges was told by his doctor to get an outside job, and he remembers his entrance into racing like it was yesterday.

"I was standing at the Eastman-Kodak store on Canal Street," he recalled, "and a friend of mine, Joe Sanerans, asked me, 'Hey, Louie. Are you still looking for that special job?' I told him yes and Joe said, 'Well, I've got it for you.'"

Sanerans gave him the name of the local Pinkerton director, and Hodges was shipped out immediately to old Lincoln Downs in Rhode Island. He spent several years doing horse-identification photography there—where he would later pick up his first job as a racetrack photographer—and also in New York.

While Hodges put in time at several tracks, including Lincoln Downs, Blue Bonnets, Sportsman's Park, and Hawthorne, he spent the greatest part of his career working the prime Chicago circuit (first Arlington and Washington Parks, later just Arlington Park) in tandem with the Fair Grounds in New Orleans.

During the span of his five-decade career from the early 1940s to the early 1980s, he also did some harness-racing photography. But it was the runners who provided him the bulk of his livelihood during his long tenure on the racetrack, and for whom, from the start, he always held the strongest affection.

The feelings of love for the sport and its people were ingrained early in his career by a national star who enjoyed much of his success in Chicago and who demonstrated, wildly contrary to popular public opinion, that racing people were an inherently decent lot, equal to if not superior to those found in the outside world.

"A lot of people think that racing is nothing but a thieving sport, a crooked business," Hodges said, "but let me tell you one about W. Hal Bishop [after whom a stake race is named at Arlington Park]. In 1948, I was at the Fair Grounds, and a trainer came up to him and said he needed $5,000 for his payroll. He was short, and had no way to make the payroll.

"Bishop barely moved. He wrote him a check on the spot for $5,000, so a fellow trainer could make his payroll. No interest was ever charged and no paper ever changed hands—in the way of a contract—except that check. A lot of people have criticized racing for being dishonest at all levels, as if that's the norm, but when I saw that, that put a new image in my mind about the sport. I never forgot it."

It was, perhaps, a sign of the times, and how much they've changed over the years. At least that's what Hodges thinks, and he's shot his way through a handful of decades that changed numbers on him five times.

"It's so cutthroat today," he said. "People don't help each other these days the way they did back then. No matter how competitive it got on the racetrack, once the races were over, they were friends—win, lose, or draw.

"Management today is a reflection of that selfish attitude," he went on. "Back then, the sport was run like a well-oiled business, instead of being a self-seeking enterprise, like it is today. If they went back to that old way, racing would be great.

"England is a perfect example of what I'm talking about, where the royal family is as much a part of the sport as the water pails that the horses drink out of."

Hodges left the sport he loved so much in the early 1980s to take care of someone he loved even more, his wife, who was in failing health.

The business, including Hodges Color Service in New Orleans, was turned over to Louis Jr., his oldest son. Though its primary function is lab work for the family tracks and other tracks, it also does racing murals, which are massive enlargements of actual racing photographs.

Trainer Meshach "Mesh" Tenney and owner Rex Ellsworth with 1956 Horse-of-the-Year champion Swaps (Louis Hodges Sr.)

This shot features three American racing classics: a very young Bill Shoemaker with the brilliant Swaps at fabled Washington Park in 1955. Needless to say, racetrack photography doesn't get any better than this. (Louis Hodges Sr.)

Another "Golden Oldie" from the fifties—Lou Hodges Sr.'s famed "flying mane" shot of Nashua (Eddie Arcaro up) at Arlington Park (sister track to Washington Park) in Arlington Heights, Illinois, in 1955 (Louis Hodges Sr.)

Louis Hodges Sr.'s magical and wondrous 1955 picture of the famed Swaps-Nashua match race (Louis Hodges Sr.)

At one time, as Louis Jr. proudly points out, such work had to be sent out of town. No longer is that true, as Hodges Color Service now routinely produces murals. The biggest available size currently is 4 feet by 8 feet, but during the Mardi Gras season they were working on one which when all the separate sections were seamed together would measure 8 feet by 36 feet.

If it sounds big, consider the source.

At the time of his retirement, Louis Hodges Sr. had seen and recorded some of the biggest names in American Thoroughbred racing: Citation, Native Dancer, Dark Star, Swaps, Nashua, Tim Tam, Round Table, Ridan, Secretariat, Alydar, and Spectacular Bid.

Two of his best pictures never involved the winner's circle.

One memorable shot is of Tim Tam, taken shortly after the Calumet star had broken a leg in the stretch run of the 1958 Belmont Stakes, thereby missing a sweep of the Triple Crown.

On business in Kentucky, Hodges stopped off at a Lexington farm and caught a picture of trainer Jimmy Jones flanked by a wailing stable dog on the left and a recuperating Tim Tam on the right. Hodges entitled it *Thoroughbreds Never Cry!!!*, and produced a picture nearly as popular as the horse himself. Another shot, of Ridan, was used in an Absorbine advertisement.

Great horses leave great impressions, but when it comes to pinning Hodges down on the single best horse he ever saw in action, it can't be done. In his mind, it's a dead heat between Citation and Swaps, both with strong Chicago connections, particularly the latter.

Swaps was involved in the grandest racing spectacle Hodges ever saw. That was the famed $100,000 winner-take-all match race in 1955 at old Washington Park between Swaps and Nashua, first and second respectively in that year's Kentucky Derby.

The event, won by Nashua (who later became the first horse syndicated for a million dollars), is considered one of the greatest in American match-racing history, which dates back to 1822, when American Eclipse, a winner of all eight lifetime starts, conquered Sir Charles in the nation's capital.

Sadly, most of the pictures from that Swaps-Nashua match race perished in the fire that leveled Arlington Park in 1985, a month before that year's Arlington Million. However, at least one picture still survives, and it is a curiosity in itself, with both the winners and losers gathered in a circle, all holding trophies.

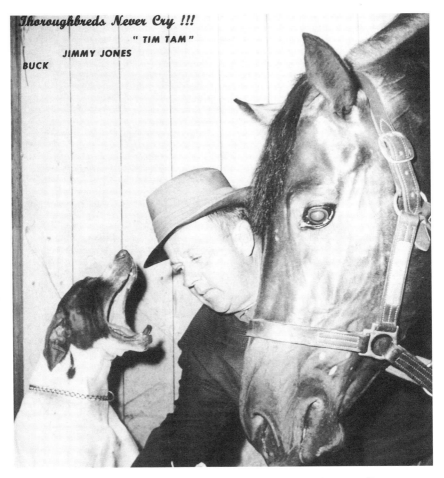

Thoroughbreds Never Cry!!!: Louis Hodges Sr.'s famous "Tim Tam" picture (Louis Hodges Sr.)

Though Hodges, like many others, was surprised at the margin of victory (six lengths), it did not surprise him that the match race had been held in Chicago. This may not sound important, but consider that this was a strong intersectional—actually bicoastal—rivalry that pitted the best of the West (Swaps from California) against the best of the East (Nashua from New York).

So how did the race get held on neutral ground?

The answer is Benjamin Lindheimer, the genius who turned Arlington Park from a cow-town track into a national racing palace. During his reign, the 1930s and particularly the 1940s and the 1950s, Chicago enjoyed its golden years of racing.

At one time, it was said that Man o' War was the standard by which we judged American Thoroughbreds. The same could be said of Hodges's work, which includes this elegant juggernaut of a picture of the great Secretariat. More than a quarter of a century later, its power and beauty remain undiminished by time. Nothing greater can be said about an artist—any artist. (Louis Hodges Sr.)

Back then, in the summer, King Chicago was the place to be and to race. But that was only part of the reason for the site location being in the midwestern hinterlands.

"Lindheimer was an ideas man," Hodges said passionately, his eyes sparkling, his whole being moving with enthusiasm. "He came up with the idea of the match race. At one point, New York tried to take it away from him, but they failed. He was strong, and he got Chicago that big race and some fabulous racing history.

"He exerted more influence on me than any other person I've ever met in racing," Hodges continued. "Someone once said Lindheimer was 21 years old when he was born, and it was the truth. He was generous to a fault, and if you had an idea or suggestion that would help improve the plant, he didn't care who you were, he was willing to listen.

"One thing you had to remember about him, though. If you made a mistake, tell him. He wouldn't tolerate any nonsense. If you tried to cover the mistake up, or, for God's sake, tried to pass the blame off on somebody else, he'd nail you to a cross."

Lindheimer was just one of the many racing greats that Hodges naturally accrued as a friend over the years, that group notably including such trainers as W. H. Bishop; Hall of Famer Marion Van Berg ("he always had time to stop and talk to you"); and the trainer of Swaps, Mesh Tenney ("very businesslike and very easygoing").

Hodges also well remembers the legendary Ben Jones, whose Calumet outfit was a dominant force in Chicago racing during the city's golden era of racing. For all that wealth, though, Jones passed no gold into Hodges's hands.

"I got along with him fine," said Hodges with a laugh, "but he never bought any pictures. He thought I should give him the picture for free, because he trained for Calumet."

And certainly Chicago never lacked for top-notch riders during its golden years.

In the 1950s, it had a jockey colony that included Eddie Arcaro, Bill Shoemaker, and Bill Hartack. Though the first two were his personal favorites, Hartack made a strong impression on Hodges.

"This is not to be construed as a knock," Hodges said, "but Hartack was his own worst enemy because of his incredible competitive spirit. If Hartack had had Shoemaker's low-key disposition, his career would have been altered [and remember that Hartack shares the Kentucky Derby riding record with Arcaro, each having won the event five times]. I really believe that his despondency over losing affected his mental attitude."

As for Hodges, there never really were any losers for him, just winners. Years of them.

"Everything I have and I am, I owe to racing," he said proudly.

Lingo

E ACH AMERICAN SPORT HAS its own special language, but none perhaps is as colorful or more steeped in historical tradition than the vocabulary of the oldest of all the major American spectator sports, Thoroughbred racing.

Here's a sample of its most popular terms.

FURLONG

The basic unit of length of all Thoroughbred races, today as in the past, is the furlong, a distance of one-eighth of a mile (220 yards exactly).

The word comes from a combination of Old English words meaning "furrow long." According to scholars, the phrase was used by English farmers in measuring land to be tilled, usually with a horse attached to a plow.

PURSE

The purse of a race, or its monetary value, can range from a few thousand dollars for a low-level claiming event to millions of dollars for a race like the Breeders' Cup Classic ($4 million).

But today, the winners of a race can no longer claim it the way their ancestors did. In times past, after winning reinsmen had crossed the finish line, they could reach up and pull down an actual purse that hung on a pole. The purse contained the prize money for that event.

BUG BOYS

Bug boys, or apprentice riders, are so named because of the asterisk or "bug" placed next to their name in the racing forms and programs, denoting a specific weight allowance given to beginning jockeys.

CHALK PLAYERS

Chalk players, or "chalkies," bettors who habitually play the favorites in a race, are so named from the days when the odds were recorded on slates with chalk, not on huge tote boards as they are today.

Since favorites required more action with the chalk because they were the most heavily played horses, the bettors who gambled on them were named chalk players in their honor.

SCRATCH

This refers to a horse who is withdrawn from a race.

The term dates back to the old days of racing, when a line was drawn through a horse's name on huge betting boards around the track to let the public know that the horse would not be running in that particular race.

Today, an electronic tote board (and the track announcer) quickly lets the public know when a horse has been scratched.

Still, the manual form of scratching endures on the part of the racing fan, who, when informed of a horse's withdrawal from a race, draws a line through ("scratches through") that horse's name on their racing form or program.

STAKES RACES

The major types of races in the Thoroughbred sport include the stakes race, the richest of all racing categories.

They are special events in which the racetracks add money to various "stakes" put up by owners in the form of nomination, entry, and starting fees. Hence, the names "stakes" and "added money" for these lucrative events.

An example of a stakes race is the Kentucky Derby.

CLAIMING RACES

The most commonly seen race in the Thoroughbred sport is called a claiming race; approximately two-thirds of the sport's contests are claiming events.

In this type of race, any horse can be bought ("claimed") for a specific price, which is listed on the entry sheets, racing forms, and programs.

Less today than in olden days, claiming races were called "platers," a reference to the silver plates that owners of winning claimers once received.

STEEPLECHASE RACES

Although you rarely see steeplechase (jumping) events on Thoroughbred racing cards today because so few bettors care to take that big of a gamble, these type of races have a long and colorful history.

They are descendants of "steeplechasers," an old style of riding in which opponents chased each other across the countryside, using the steeples of country churches as their landmarks.

HANDICAPS

"Stakes" races and handicaps comprise the two richest types of races in the sport. However, the conditions of a handicap are slightly different than those of a stakes race.

In handicap races, more weight is assigned to better horses, less to inferior horses, in an effort to equalize the chances of all entered in the race.

The weights, based upon past performances of the competitors involved, are assigned by the racing secretary in a hypothetical effort to bring all the horses in a handicap race to the finish line at the same time.

The term *handicap* comes from the phrase "hand-in-cap," an old French game of chance in which all contestants had an equal chance of winning or losing.

An example of a well-known handicap race is the Santa Anita Handicap.

The 1958 edition of the Kentucky Derby, America's most beloved "stake" race, was won by Tim Tam (#3). Second place (or "place") went to Lincoln Road (on the rail), while third place (or "show") went to Noureddin (to the left of Tim Tam and Lincoln Road). In the background is the "pari-mutuel" (tote) board. The finish line represents the end to a 1¼-mile race (ten "furlongs"). (Keeneland Library/J. C. "Skeets" Meadors)

SILKS

In the old days of racing, the material of a jockey's jacket and cap was silk. Hence, the term *silks* to describe that garb.

The term endures to this day. However, the material of a modern-day rider's cap and jacket is nylon, which is more durable, easier to clean, and much less expensive than silk.

WIN, PLACE, AND SHOW

Win is self-explanatory: your horse finishes first. The origins of *place* and *show*, however, are a little vague.

Many historians and scholars say that the term *place* (meaning to finish second in a race) goes back to the times when the runner-up's number was "placed" on the finish board beneath the winner's number.

Show (meaning to finish third in a race), according to the same sources, refers to the old-time act of "showing" the number (of the third-place horse) to the crowd before putting it up on the finish board.

PARI-MUTUEL

The wagering system most used around the world today, including in the United States, is the pari-mutuel system, in which each person bets against all the other bettors in a particular race, with the racetrack acting as the intermediary who holds the money and then distributes it.

Pari-mutuel is an Americanized version of the French phrase *Paris Mutuels*, which refers to betting machines invented in France during the 1870s to thwart crooked bookmakers who then roamed the grounds.

Though the name has been slightly changed, the system has not.

The word *mutuel* is French for "among ourselves" (freely translated, it means "betting among ourselves"), and the only time today that a race-track actually forks out its own money is when a minus pool occurs. This happens when a track cannot make its legally required minimum payoff and so must use its own money to pay off the tickets.

BOOKIE

The term *bookie*, rapidly shortened from *bookmaker*, originated years ago in England, where these men worked the track grounds, taking and recording bets offered to them in a little book.

For the record, England is one of the few countries in the world where bookies are still legal.

RINGER

A *ringer* is a horse running under the name of another horse that it looks like, a scheme usually instigated by a party or parties desiring to pull off a big betting coup.

Most historians agree that the word *ringer* probably came from the game of horseshoes, frequently played around the racetracks, in which a "ringer" described any shoe encircling the bar at which it was thrown. Since the shoe closest to the bar received the highest point award, only a close inspection could separate multiple ringers, or identical look-alikes.

Lingo II
Charley Horse *and* Shutout

L ONG HAILED AS the King of Sports, the sport of Thoroughbred racing, interestingly enough, has provided baseball—our other great national sport—with several terms for the diamond game's vocabulary.

One of them is *charley horse.*

That term, which describes a muscle strain or pull, may have the most fascinating historical background of any word or phrase in baseball's lexicon.

Most historians and etymologists attribute the phrase to a mid-seventeenth-century British king, Charles I, who habitually palmed off his aging guard horses, or "Charleys," onto the London police force.

In time, broken-down horses picked up the tag of "old Charleys." The moniker was later taken over by baseball, whose ballparks utilized the services of the old horses. If a ballplayer was seen limping around, he was likened to the old horses and said to have a "charley horse."

Some historians, however, say the phrase came into popular usage courtesy of Billy Sunday, a late-nineteenth-century ballplayer (for the Chicago White Stockings, forerunners of the Chicago Cubs) who later became a nationally known evangelist.

Sunday supposedly coined the phrase in 1886 following a trip to the local racetrack, where he and his band of teammates had bet on a horse named Charley, who went lame during the race and finished last.

The next day, teammate George Gore was denied an easy inside-the-park home run after pulling a muscle rounding second base. As Gore limped into third base, Sunday—so the story goes—exclaimed, "Look! Here comes that 'Charley' horse!"

Other sources, however, credit the popularization of this enigmatic term not to Sunday, but to another Chicago White Stockings player of that same time, Joe Quest.

An apprentice in a machine shop (co-owned by his father) prior to entering professional baseball, Quest—as did his teammates—occasionally suffered a tightness of the legs. Because no one had a name for it, Quest called it a "charley horse" after his father's horse, Charley, who had strained his legs from constantly pulling heavy loads in the machine shop.

The other notable term that Thoroughbred racing has given baseball is the word *shutout.*

When a pitcher "shuts out" a team, a phrase dating back to the 1870s, the pitcher prevents them from scoring a run.

This is much like the race fan who fails to pick even one winner during the day at the racetrack, or who just misses getting a bet down ("placed") at the last minute.

III

HIP-HOP

Calder Race Course, home to one of the best two-year-old programs in the country (Calder Race Course/Jean Raftery Photos)

The Force of Life

Get busy living, or get busy dying.
(Morgan Freeman in *The Shawshank Redemption*)

R IDER MIKE MORGAN'S APPEARANCE in today's In Reality aboard Ernie Retamoza's Irish Gates is vivid proof that the greatest theater in the world is not live theater, the kind you see on Broadway (or at a movie theater), but rather the theater of Thoroughbred racing.

No Hollywood scriptwriter of any decent reputation could possibly have dreamed up this scenario. If they had, they would have been summarily fired and blacklisted.

It is a story that far exceeds the parameters of the twilight zone of credibility.

And yet there it stands, well and alive, proof paramount of the old saying that truth, indeed, is stranger than fiction. And a hell of a lot more fun, too.

So here it is, Mr. Morgan's and Mr. Retamoza's story in all its grandeur.

A veteran rider, successful for years on the Midwest circuit, Mike Morgan was operated on for throat cancer earlier this year, just days after the May 6 Kentucky Derby. That was the last riding action he saw until he piloted Irish Gates on Friday, September 22, at Turfway Park.

No big deal, except that the doctors didn't feel he'd be back until later—much later, maybe like Churchill in November, or Turfway in December. Get the picture? You're outta here, pal. Don't call us. WE'LL call you. When we're good and ready.

"I could have told those doctors he was going to be back sooner," Retamoza said earlier this week, as a broad smile slowly engulfed his matinee-idol-look-alike face.

"They operated on him the Thursday after the Derby [May 11]. Know what he was doing three days before, on that Monday? Working horses! He was in surgery something like 12 hours. I saw him shortly after the surgery, and he was walking down the hall. God, tough as nails, I tell you that. I think the reason he's back so soon is because he's so fit and he's so damn tough."

Well, this story isn't just about courage; it's also about loyalty, another attribute that's as valuable and beautiful these days as a collection of "Liberty standing" quarters, the most exquisite American coin ever made.

Let's be real specific here.

When it comes to Mr. Retamoza, his handsome picture ought to be underneath the word *loyalty* in the dictionary. He continues to ride Morgan, supports him both as a trainer and longtime friend, believes in him ("I love having him on my horses because he's smart and he's got all that experience").

The standings don't matter to Retamoza. Morgan's back and that's all that counts. He'll be riding. No agents need apply to attempt to sway Mr. Retamoza's mind. It's a done deal, and a good one at that.

And there's yet another side to this, one that the preeminent short-story teller of this country—O. Henry—would fully appreciate. It also proves how arduous this trip to the Florida Stallion Stakes has been for everyone concerned.

Retamoza wanted to send a hot little runner named Coach Gate to the In Reality. Coach Gate was a son of Gate Dancer, and he was a horse that Morgan considered to be the best he'd ever ridden in some two decades of service in the irons.

But it wasn't to be, because the forces of life intervened. Healthy one day, Coach Gate was gone almost as quickly because of a staph infection of the hock. But the Lord does provide. There was a backup, another Gate Dancer son named Irish Gates, and the world of the Festival of the Sun will see him in action today.

Mike Morgan and Irish Gates before the running of the 1995 In Reality Stakes (Calder Race Course/Jean Raftery Photos)

How does Morgan feel about all this: his first national ("ship-in") mount since his surgery, his first stake mount since returning to the races, his riding in general?

"It feels great to be riding again," he said. "There is nothing—I mean nothing—like riding. That's why I worked some horses three days before the surgery [in the rain]. I told Janice [his wife] that I had to. I love it. I can't explain it except to say it's what I do for a living . . . and I love it."

What chance does this trio have in the In Reality?

Considering their past track record (Retamoza, by the way, has entered three maidens in stakes races in his career, and won with all of them), is it really wise to discount them? (There's karma to these here guys.)

But that's not really the point.

In the face of large odds, they are here, ready to run. And there are two basic lessons in life to be learned from them. First, it's not whether you win or lose that counts, but whether you survive. Despite enormous, grievous losses in both their respective quarters, Retamoza and Morgan will answer the bell today.

And secondly, heroes and heroines—people of gigantic courage and character—still walk the grounds of the earth. As that "giant" character of classic literature, the beloved and courageous Tiny Tim, once said long ago, "God bless us, one and all."

Indeed, sir, indeed.

Down to the Sea(cliff)

Hope can set you free. So can a damn fast, undefeated racehorse.
(Old racetrack saying)

Down to the sea in mighty ships we shall go.
(Variation on lines from *The Book of Common Prayer*)

MR. JAMES BROWN, THE hardest-working man in show business and primo soul artist of a golden era now just a memory, meet trainer Bill Kaplan, who—like you in previous years—has a great hit on his hands and is seemingly headed for the stars with no end in sight.

"I feel good," Kaplan said earlier this week at his office in Barn 50. "Really good." (Pause.) "More important, the horse feels good. He's training well, eating up, and looks great. He's really something."

"All I want is for Seacliff to remain undefeated one more race," added Kaplan, as a slow smile began to curve around his face.

The object of his gargantuan affection, not to mention the current pride and joy of Calder, is the much-vaunted Seacliff. Undefeated in four career starts, Seacliff recently became the third racer in history to sweep a division of the Florida Stallion Stakes when he took the September 30 In Reality Stakes.

That completed a sweep of the open division of the Florida-bred two-year-old series, which began with the August 5 Dr. Fager and the September 9 Affirmed. Seacliff's work duplicated a feat previously turned out by Smile in 1984 and Naked Greed in 1991 (to date, the filly division of the Florida Stallion Stakes—the Desert Vixen–Susan's Girl–My Dear Girl triad—has never been swept).

Seacliff (Calder Race Course/Jean Raftery Photos)

And now, the bay Valid Appeal son—who took his career debut by 4½ lengths on July 15 at Calder—is headed for the mecca of it all: the Grade 1, $1 million, 1¹⁄₁₆-mile Breeders' Cup Juvenile at Belmont on Saturday, October 28. For the record, Seacliff isn't the only Calder racer slated to run in the Breeders' Cup; Marty Wolfson is sending Chaposa Springs and The Vid to New York, too.

"We'll work him once before he leaves for New York," Kaplan said of the Herb and Ione Elkins–owned racer, "probably five-eighths or three-quarters of a mile. Then once more up there in New York, probably three-quarters."

"Besides Seacliff," Kaplan allowed, "I'm sending Goldarama [a graded stakes-placed mare owned by Mr. and Mrs. Elkins and partners] up to New York on Friday. She could race on the Thursday or Friday preceding the Breeders' Cup championship day, or in an undercard race on Breeders'

Seacliff sweeps the 1995 open division of the Florida Stallion Stakes with a win in the grand finale—the September 30 In Reality. (Calder Race Course/Jean Raftery Photos)

Cup Day." Both horses will be set out shortly, because Kaplan wants them to have plenty of time—roughly two weeks—to acclimatize to their surroundings and the racetrack.

"I bought twenty tickets for my friends and family," Kaplan continued, displaying a trait indigenous to great press-publicity trainers like Jimmy Croll of Holy Bull fame (that is, a simple salutation and one question are about all one needs for a complete interview; trainers like Croll and Kaplan will do the rest). "I'm really looking forward to it.

"It's a true homecoming for two reasons. One, because I was born there [in Brooklyn], and secondly, because there are a lot of ex–Calder people up there at Belmont. People like Kenny Noe, Terry Meyocks, and Don Combs."

A former pilot (who used to own Air South) and CPA, Kaplan now finds himself in the position of training probably one of the five best two-year-old males in the country, that quintet also including Maria's Mon, Hennessy, Honour and Glory, and Diligence.

Unlike them, yea, any of the name two-year-olds in the country who will be coming in for the race, the magnetic Seacliff is undefeated. Let's put that in all caps: SEACLIFF IS THE ONLY MAJOR COMPETITOR FOR THAT RACE WHO IS UNDEFEATED.

Trainer Bill Kaplan (Calder Race
Course/Jean Raftery Photos)

"We're going in with a lot of hope and also the realization that we'll be running against the best in the country," Kaplan said during one Sunday morning interview.

"It was a great experience last year [with My Dear Girl victress Fortune Pending in the Breeders' Cup Juvenile Fillies], and I think that serves us well for this year."

All this begs a question. Does one of Florida's finest have a "star personality"?

"He's good, very professional," Kaplan replied. "The only problem we have is when we're walking him around the shed row. He thinks *he's the boss.*"

A warm smile appears on Kaplan's amused countenance like a ray of sunshine as he delivers the punchline: "We're *still* negotiating that one."

"He's just an average-sized horse," Kaplan adds, "but his heart is bigger than his stall. I love him."

The last part of the response cries out for a timeless question favored by cynics, the jaded, and the low of heart: Mr. Kaplan, do you love horses more than people?

The streetwise Kaplan explodes into laughter, then delivers a get-real one-liner: "No, but they're better at going a mile and a sixteenth."

Touché. And roll on, Calder knight, roll on.

Author's Note: Unplaced in the 1995 Breeders' Cup Juvenile, Seacliff was retired in late December 1996. The bay colt (Valid Appeal–Eloquack, by Elocutionist) left the racetrack with five wins and one second from eleven starts, and career earnings of $456,300. His lifetime work included a victory in the 1996 Spectacular Bid Stakes (G3) and a second in the 1996 Jersey Shore Breeders' Cup (G3).

In the Land of Mantle

NEW YORK HAS to hold some grand memories for one Martin Daryl Wolfson.

As a youngster, his father—racing giant Louis Wolfson of Affirmed and Roman Brother renown—managed the unparalleled act of getting Marty Wolfson into the hallowed Yankee Stadium dugout, where he was the subject of a group of pictures with such Yankee greats as Mickey Mantle, Roger Maris, and Whitey Ford.

A young Marty Wolfson flanked by Yankee greats Mickey Mantle (left) and Roger Maris (Photograph courtesy of Marty and Karla Wolfson)

The treasure of them all is Wolfson sitting on the Yankee bench flanked by the M&M boys of emerald summers gone by—the late Mickey Mantle and the late Roger Maris.

Unless you're an intellectual or running on batteries, this is what Wolfson's picture does to you:

73

It brings back the richness of an innocent era long gone by, to days when wealth—for a young boy—was defined by a Trapeze glove (well broken in), a Schwinn bicycle, several good pairs of jeans (which always carried at least three packets of Kool-Aid, which could be eaten or drunk), a pair of well-worn Converse sneakers, a Hillerich & Bradsby Louisville Slugger bat (a sacred and cherished one was the Rocky Colavito model), a steady allowance (whose sole purpose was to feed your constantly growing baseball-card collection), and a sister (or sisters) who posed absolutely no problems.

You ate anything you wanted (your ultimate meal was a cheeseburger run through the garden, an ice-cold cherry Coke, and hot French fries lathered in ketchup), and as often as you wanted, because you could.

You were lean and flat-bellied from all that baseball, not a trace of fat on you (no amount of pinching by anyone ever produced a scintilla of fat on you).

Adults, particularly those on diets, loathed you; your family doctor considered you a medical marvel; your grandparents revered you because you cleaned your plate (and you loved them mightily in return because they fed you anything you wanted).

The best day in your life you were strutting around the diamond, a baseball cap—with at least two or three cards stuck inside to make it stick up like the pros'—tilted in the style of your hero, a wad of gum in your mouth accentuating your youthful arrogance, telling all who would listen to your madness that the home run you had just hit was just like those of the Mick.

You even had the number to prove it, number seven—Mantle's number, *his number and his alone*, which had been sewn, colored, painted, glued, taped, even nailed onto your favorite baseball shirt, a white shirt with colored sleeves.

It didn't get no better.

Those golden mornings, afternoons, and days—which inexorably washed away into inky darkness spiced by little white punctuation marks called stars and a big crystal ball called the moon (the only thing that terminated your baseball)—seemed as infinite as the universe.

You were young, could drive a baseball into east Hell, and time had no meaning. Life was an endless baseball game. Let adults worry. You had the Mick, and all was right with the cosmos.

It was that simple. No Visa bill, no mortgage, no car payments, no women, no nothing except baseball.

Wolfson's picture is a treasure from a mystical past, a remnant from easier times. Its companion, of sorts, hangs in Blinkers here at Calder—a photograph of Mantle wearing a Calder hat and holding up a Calder program.

Years later, Wolfson's Yankee Stadium photograph continues to shine despite its age. It is what they call a classic. It endures because it exudes two rare commodities—youthful innocence and boundless joy.

And it sets one to thinking.

Premise number one: That's Marty Wolfson in those pictures, next to the Mick. Premise number two: I'm a personal friend of Marty. Premise number three (and here's the long reach

Calder Race Course–based trainer Marty Wolfson, one of the best young conditioners in the country (Calder Race Course/Jean Raftery Photos)

by the first baseman): That makes me a friend of Mickey Mantle. (Someone crank down the sugar level in that Kool-Aid. Please.)

Things are different now. Much different.

Postseason play now consists of divisional, pennant-playoff, and World Series action. Long gone is the baseball world of two leagues of eight teams each and a simple World Series between the AL and NL champs.

And the racing world is now topped off by the Breeders' Cup, a $10 million, seven-race series that incorporates this country's richest race—the $3 million Breeders' Cup Classic. (Back in 1960, it was a $287,000-plus Garden State Stakes.)

To that familiar sporting ground, Wolfson is planning to trek—if it all works out—with a solid tandem of The Vid and Chaposa Springs. It is his first Breeders' Cup foray, but odds are it won't be the last for Wolfson, who's in the midst of his fourth straight million-dollar year.

Besides The Vid and Chaposa Springs, his most notable work of recent years includes Forever Whirl, a former claimer Wolfson sent on to win the

Marty Wolfson's filly masterpiece: Grade 1 stakes winner Chaposa Springs (Calder Race Course/Jean Raftery Photos)

Flamingo Stakes and the Ohio Derby, and multiple stakes winners Mr. Angel and Miss Gibson County. And that's just the cream of the crop.

What are his plans for the Breeders' Cup?

"The Vid will go in the [Breeders' Cup] Mile," Wolfson said Monday morning, "and Chaposa Springs will go in the [Breeders' Cup] Sprint. However, I'm looking at an 'undercard' race on Breeders' Cup Day for her [Chaposa Springs]. I'm waiting to see how they weight her."

Why are you sending a filly against the boys in the Sprint?

"It's tough to ask, but Jerry [Bailey, her projected rider, who is also slated to pilot Mr. Vid] says she has enormous talent," Wolfson explained.

The Vid winning the 1994 Tropical Turf Handicap (G3) at Calder (Calder Race Course/Jean Raftery Photos)

"And if you look at the race, fillies have done pretty good—two wins and three seconds in the last six years or so."

For the record, Chaposa Springs is a multiple graded-stakes winner who earlier this year took the Grade 1 Test. The Vid, who Wolfson says likes his races "spaced every six weeks to two months," most recently ran third in the Arlington Million.

As said before, Wolfson's sojourn this year to the Breeders' Cup—the World Series of racing—is no accident, but rather the product of long, hard, well-calculated work that had a very definite beginning.

"Probably my favorite horse is Forever Whirl," he said. "I claimed him and he became a major stakes winner.

"That, in turn," Wolfson continued, "got the business really going. We got a lot of press shipping around the country, and as a result, we started to pick up clients.

Karla Wolfson, the other half of the highly successful Wolfson stable (Calder Race Course/Jean Raftery Photos)

"The other reason for the stable's success in the last few years is Karla [Wolfson's wife]. She's been working here in the stable for the last five years, and it's no accident that we've enjoyed our best years since she started working with me full-time.

"She works hard, very hard, and she keeps me focused. I couldn't have done it without her."

Life is good, and it may be about to get even better in the land of Mantle.

Powder Break
Was No Powder Puff

Size don't mean nothing at all. The good ones
always stand tall and run big. Always.
(Old racetrack saying)

I F POWDER BREAK HAD been created a human being instead of a fabulous racehorse, her name would have given her trouble. It's an optical illusion, precisely the kind of thing that leads Cro-Magnon bullies to mistakenly pick on someone they think is weaker.

Only they're not.

You can almost hear the conversation as she walks down the street. On the opposite side is the village idiot who wants to impress a few of his friends. Loudly, he says, "Ohhhh, Powwwderrr Breakkk. Why don't you go powder your nose, darling?"

Everyone laughs uproariously. They stop as the recipient slowly crosses the street and walks right into the middle of the crowd, which engulfs her because of her minuscule size.

She is face-to-face with her tormentor, who towers over her. Her eyes are one icy, laser stare. There is a nervous silence (and she is the only one who *hasn't* broken into a sweat).

She looks up at her detractor and speaks one line, turns and walks away.

And this is what she says: "Hey, redneck. Make fun of me again and I'll slap your face off your head."

By the time she makes it across the street, the crowd has vanished.

Powder Break (Calder Race Course/Jean Raftery Photos)

Only Powder Break wasn't a human being. She was instead a pony-sized filly—no bigger than a whisper—whose style was to come aflyin' at the end.

Powder Break, in short order, was a grand piece of work.

Speak her name today, and trainer Luis Olivares's face still lights up like a Christmas tree as his hand instinctively reaches for the VCR machine and the tapes in his barn office. It's showtime! The good ones do that to you. They get in your heart and stay there.

"She was one of the three best horses I've ever trained, along with Flying Pidgeon and Groomstick," Olivares said in a recent interview in his office.

"I'm very attached to her," he continued, "because she had lots of problems and still won. She had emphysema at three. We were about two-thirds of the way through the year. I had taken her to Saratoga [in August 1984], and she got sick on me. She was on a two-race win streak, and she was gone for the year. Second start back in 1985 [in February], she wins.

"Later that season [1985], she had just about completely healed up from a broken splint bone [in her right front leg]. She's doing so well that we send her to New York. She wins the New York Handicap (June 2). Unbelievable. But that was her.

"She was a midget. Pony-sized, around 15 hands or so. She didn't have the body to go three-quarters, but she had the stamina to go two miles.

"I didn't need to work her hard. She was aggressive. I don't know where she got that big heart from, but she was a runner. Wasn't afraid of any other horse, no matter how big the horse was.

"Powder Break was something else, really was. She never lost on the grass here at Calder [three stakes, one allowance race in four starts]. She won stakes three of the four seasons she raced [1983–86]. She improved every season she raced [$8,960 as a rookie, then $92,515, followed by $185,436, topped off by nearly $377,480 in her last season]. And she beat the boys."

The victory against the males came in the 1986 Pan American Handicap at Gulfstream Park, in which stablemate and $1.30–to–$1 favorite Flying Pidgeon ran third.

"That was her greatest career race, her greatest win," Olivares said. "No question. They both got stopped [she and Flying Pidgeon], but she picked it back up quicker than he did. She was smaller, and it was easier for her to do that. She paid $18.40 to win. Uptown Swell ran second, and the entry of Palace Panther and Mourjane ran off the board [fourth and sixth respectively at $2.50–to–$1 odds]."

Powder Break was more, much more, than numbers, but no discussion of her would be complete without at least a cursory glance at her record. It confirms everything Olivares says and thinks about her.

A 1981 dark bay daughter of Transworld out of the Boldnesian mare Bold Gee Gee, Powder Break—a multiple graded-stakes winner owned by Florida stockbroker Robert Green—won 11 of 44 career ventures, ran second seven times, and finished third five times for earnings of $664,391.

The bulk of those numbers were posted on the lawn, where Powder Break banked $653,181 off a 30-10-7-3 slate.

Her major career wins included the Pan American Handicap (G1), the Grade 2 New York Handicap, and the Grade 3 La Prevoyante Handicap (here at Calder).

Other stake wins included the Office Queen (also a local stake) and divisions of the Queen Isabella, the My Charmer (at Calder also), and the Key Largo Stakes.

Major placings included seconds in the Grade 2 Orchid and Black Helen handicaps, and a third in the Vineland Handicap (G3).

And when it came to distance, Powder Break—on her preferred surface, the turf—had more range than an all-star shortstop, winning from $1\frac{1}{16}$ miles to $1\frac{1}{2}$ miles.

She got around, too, her stakes action taking her to a host of places, like Belmont, Saratoga, Aqueduct, Laurel, the Fair Grounds, Golden Gate, Garden State, Hollywood Park, Santa Anita, and Louisiana Downs, as well as Calder, Gulfstream, and Hialeah.

Here's the last word on this mighty mite, whose regular riders were Santiago Soto and Jose Santos, and whose list of vanquished foes included males like Flying Pidgeon, Palace Panther, and Uptown Swell, and females like Shocker T., Scorched Panties, and Chetski.

In 1990, Calder held the inaugural Powder Break Handicap. It was won by Sez Fourty . . . trained by Luis Olivares.

"When I won that race, it was incredible," Olivares said. "I really wanted to win that race for her. I felt so good in my heart. It brought back all those great memories of her, all those races she had won for me, and all those great horses she had beaten."

Memories don't fade, and that's why the Powder Break Handicap—a $1\frac{1}{8}$-mile turf affair for three-year-old fillies—will be run here at Calder for the fifth time on Grand Slam Day IV, Saturday, October 21.

Cool Man Caltech

I play it cool
And dig all jive.
That's the reason
I stay alive.
My motto,
As I live and learn,
is:
Dig And Be Dug
In Return.
(The poem "Motto," by Langston Hughes)

THIS IS THE WAY we imagine Caltech.
Angular, sleek, lean, athletic. And, to use an oft-heard phrase, "tall, dark, and handsome." Possessed of classic good looks, which were actually complemented by the wire-rim glasses he wore off the playing field. A comparison that comes to mind instantly is the Superman–Clark Kent tandem.

Only, Caltech was no cartoon character. He was for real.

Here it is. If one could visualize a combination of Vince Gill and Jimmy Stewart (in looks, physique, and demeanor), you'd pretty much have Caltech. Add a burgundy-and silver-leather-sleeved letter jacket, and you'd be all the way home.

He had a ready smile and a kind word for all. He always signed autographs. Always. There wasn't an ounce of pretense in his body. And with good reason.

He had been raised right by good people: they wouldn't have tolerated anything less from their son. He was to be a *gentleman*—now, there's a dinosaur term for you—at all times. No matter how great an athlete he was.

His heart was true. You had to look no further than his "steady," a girl he had known since grade school, for gosh sakes. Their romance was a *fait accompli*, a $500 Latin way of saying that they were destined to get married.

As to be expected, Caltech was well-groomed and well-dressed at all times. In short, he was a smart, decent, good-looking kid with a world of athletic talent that impressed other people more than it did him.

And he had another hallmark of a fine being.

He bettered everyone he came in contact with. Small wonder that men respected him, women adored him, children idolized him, friends worshiped him, coaches wished for more of his kind.

Some people fight all their lives for genuine respect; Caltech, it seemed, had had it since the day he was born, and on him, it fit like the act of breathing fits all living things—naturally and regular-like.

Caltech could have been a star in any of the three major sports. If football, he would have been a Frank Gifford halfback or a Roger Staubach quarterback. If basketball, he would not have been a power or finesse forward. He would have been the rarest type of forward—a Bill Bradley forward (a Rhodes scholar with a great outside shot).

But Caltech best suits baseball, the other great American sport (besides horse racing), and this is what he would have been like:

Caltech would have been a star outfielder. In the mold of Roberto Clemente. Possessed of a howitzer-like throwing arm. You can just hear the third-base coach yelling at a runner who's been thrown out: "What're you!? Stupid!? It's book around the league that nobody, I mean *NOBODY*, runs on Caltech. He's got a damn cannon out there. Get your mind right, kid!"

He also had a catlike bat, which meant he could just as easily crush a homer to right as he could whip—pull—a ball down the left-field line for a double. Mess up your fielding on the latter, and Caltech would be standing on third by the time the dust had cleared, because he had spellbinding speed that would make a cheetah look slow.

And he had a special presence—both as a player and a person. Bowie Kuhn once declared that Roberto Clemente, whom no one called "Bob" for obvious reasons, "had a touch of royalty."

Caltech was a lot like that. Whether at rest, walking, or running, he had a shimmering cool that was magnetic. He was electric, man, right down to the way he wore his cap.

But Caltech wasn't a person.

Just as we imagine him—the incomparable and irreplaceable Caltech (Calder Race Course/Jean Raftery Photos)

He was a racehorse who went young well before his time. No doubt, this is what the hollowed-out losers remember most about Caltech. That's their nature. It's also precisely what separates them from the living.

Here is the story of Caltech as the living and the kind of heart know it.

Trained by Eduardo Azpurua Jr. and owned by the partnership of David Romanik, Bradford Beilly, and Stewart Beilly, the handsome chestnut racer posted a 20-6-1-1/$726,944 ledger during his four-year stay on the racetrack (1988–91).

The majority of that work was accomplished on the lawn—five wins and a third from nine starts for a bankroll of $709,624. His top career win was a wire-to-wire, 1¾-length job under saddle master Rene Douglas in the 1989 Budweiser International Handicap (G1) at Laurel at near 14-to-1 odds over a field that included crackerjack turfsters Yankee Affair, Sunshine Forever, and Citidancer II.

A converted claimer who became a multiple graded-stakes winner, Caltech packed it all into that three-year-old campaign, taking five of thirteen starts and earning $695,340 off scores in the Grade 1 Budweiser International, the Grade 3 Lawrence Realization, and the Manalapan (a 3¼-length win here at Calder).

That magical three-year-old campaign ended with starts in the Breeders' Cup Turf and the Hollywood Turf Handicap, both Grade 1 events, where he faced heavy heads like Prized and Frankly Perfect.

A tendon injury limited his four-year-old season (1990) to one start. Retired and sent to stud, Caltech served the 1991 season at Vintage Acres farm near Ocala. Put back into training in August 1991, he made what turned out to be his final career foray on October 5, 1991. A few days later, he was gone, the victim of a freak training accident.

The shock was enormous for Romanik, a prominent Miami attorney who is also the general counsel for Gulfstream Park. An article in the now-defunct *Racing Times* left little doubt of that, reporting that Romanik felt as if he had lost a member of his family.

Continuing on, it quoted him saying, "We gave him doughnuts, coffee, and peppermints in the morning. He had taken on human qualities."

There are many lessons to be learned from all of this, but here is the greatest one of them all: *The true worth of any quality being is how they lived and how they were loved.*

Saturday's second running of the Caltech Handicap, a 1½-mile grass race for three-year-olds and up that is part of Grand Slam IV Day, is proof that Caltech lived well and is loved mightily.

A Portrait in Paisley

QUICKLY, THE SIMPLE became complex.

The intent was a routine publicity profile for a weekend edition of the Maywood Park program; the subject was Walter Paisley.

I merely sought a cursory glance at his life, a lush racing life. I got more. Much more. I got a profile on life itself. It was as if you were watching *Dragnet* ("just the facts, ma'am, just the facts") and suddenly found yourself watching *The Grapes of Wrath*.

The exterior part of Paisley's life and career has been well chronicled.

Driver Walter Paisley (United States Trotting Association)

He is 47, a divorced father of two sons, has been driving for over three decades, and is a multiple titlist—and fixture—on the Chicago circuit.

One of six Chicago drivers with over 3,000 career wins, at the start of this year the Berwyn, Illinois, native was the top-ranked Chicago pilot on the all-time wins and money lists with 4,477 scores (10th) and $23 million-plus (13th).

Perennially among the nation's leaders, last season he had 287 victories (21st) and a career-best $2.24 million (16th).

The youngest driver ever to compete in the Hambletonian (at age 18 in 1959), over the years Walter Paisley has handled so many good ones (Royce, Rambling Willie, Sir Dalrae, Braidwood, Tricky Dick N., Hi Tech Society, George S., Spotlite Lobell, Iggy Magoo, etc.) that the list makes *Gone with the Wind* read like a short story.

Behind those great numbers, however, is another side of this Chicago king and Illinois Hall of Famer. Few have seen this side, though it is out there on a daily basis, like the program. It is an integral part of Paisley, one he carries with him wherever he goes.

A ruddy-complected man, Paisley brushes his close-cropped hair straight back. It reveals an angular, lined, and weathered face that is ruggedly handsome in the finest Hollywood tradition. One envisions a movie agent saying, "That face of yours has got character, Paisley. It looks lived in. I like that. Come here. I'm gonna make you a star!"

Clear and penetrating eyes dominate the face, part of a presence that is quiet but still commanding. He projects a physicality—with his face, his clothes, and his manner—that breathes the word *driver*. Even his name could only belong to a driver. When God made him, you sense the Lord had just seen *Ben Hur*.

He did not disappoint me once. Indeed, he continually surprised me with his answers to the profile, their intelligence and candor exceeded only by the speed with which he replied.

Like his answer to what his biggest accomplishment was. Not his 4,000-plus career winners as one would assume (a bad habit he quickly broke me of), but his horses earning a million or more dollars the last 15 straight years.

"That's kind of hard to do," he added modestly.

For the uninitiated, Paisley knows the true meaning of the word *hard*, and the real value of money.

In the beginning, he suffered times more lean than his five-foot-eight, 140-pound frame. Thirteen years (note the number) of futility, just 242 wins, and slightly more than $500,000 in purse earnings. Most would have quit. Paisley didn't, proof paramount that you can measure everything on the racetrack but heart, that indefinable tangent that separates a winner from a loser.

Though the struggles to eat well (and regularly) are long over, the scars of that hunger obviously linger on for this man who was anything but an overnight success.

Is it merely coincidence, then, that his racing colors are the colors of money, green and white?

Early on, he showed his class by passing on a question about his biggest disappointment (the only one of some two dozen he did not answer). How easy it would have been to point to 1975, when he lost his only chance for a national title by just two wins (ironically to fellow Chicagoan Daryl Busse).

He crosscut time with his heroes, his childhood ones (old-time driver Red Ross and 1950s heartthrob Ricky Nelson) causing his face to explode into a wide smile. And the present? Who else? Herve Filion, the game's winningest reinsman.

His happiest moment, he was asked.

Again he bypassed the obvious and said Braidwood—a horse he bought for $10,000 who turned out to be a "world beater" in his words—winning the Midwest Pacing Derby. Why? Perhaps because that racer perfectly personified Paisley's life and career.

I invaded his privacy accidentally with a question about his saddest day. He never broke stride.

"The day my dad died," he told me, then adding after a slight pause, "which was also the same day my marriage broke up."

Boom! Down, but not out. Strong man, this guy Paisley.

His work ethic and his sense of equality showed up in a fill-in-the-blank question about what he'd do if he were president. "I'd make taxes the same for everybody. It would be a flat rate, like 20 percent." One could just picture the rich running for cover under President Paisley.

Another fill-in-the-blank question: What do people say behind your back?

"I wish he'd be in a better mood when he loses," he said without smiling. Even off the track, the competitive fires blaze furiously.

We came to the end of the profile, running neck and neck with an upcoming race. Paisley was to drive, but despite repeated calls, he did not budge. He was determined that we make it across our finish line first.

I asked one more fill-in-the-blank question: "Nobody knows I'm . . .," it began.

I had stepped on a raw nerve.

"Always doing my best, and real sensitive," he said so softly that I nearly spilled a cup of coffee leaning forward to hear it all.

For an instant, it was deathly still. Then he broke the tension by smiling. Assured that the profile was completed, he left quickly.

To idolize is to defile, so let us leave Walter Paisley—steadily closing in on his 5,000th career winner—with this: in the 1950s, novelist William Faulkner said in his Nobel Prize acceptance speech that mankind must not only survive and endure, it must prevail.

Paisley's life—filled with gargantuan numbers taken the hard way—says he has prevailed in the fullest sense of Faulkner's words. Loudly. Majestically.

We can all learn from Mr. Walter Paisley.

Author's Note: Walter Paisley retired in 1993 with 5,712 career winners.

IV

BIG STATS

This grand three-way shot captures champion trainer Dale Baird in his greatest moment in the sport—his record 7,000th career winner with Yasuo on May 3, 1996, at Mountaineer Park. (Mountaineer Park/Mountaineer Photo Service)

Illinois Racing News (June 1996)
Also appeared as "Leading Trainers of All Time"
in The Thoroughbred Times (June 29, 1996)

Cruising Past 7,000 and Climbing

The Record Journey of Trainer Dale Baird

ASK ANYONE WHAT PITCHER has won the most major-league baseball games, and many will come up with the answer (Cy Young) right off the bat, many times complete with the total (511, which is a signature figure like Ty Cobb's major-league record .367 lifetime batting average).

Those who don't know it can still find it easily enough by going to the bible of major-league baseball, *The Official Encyclopedia of Baseball*.

First published in 1969, this widely respected and best-selling reference work is reissued every three or four years, an updating that essentially quenches the thirst for every major facet of "the sunshine game," which, not coincidentally, has long been known as the National Pastime.

Now answer this question: Who is Thoroughbred racing's winningest trainer?

And it should be stated in advance that the answer may surprise many, an indication that if ever a sport cried out for a basic reference work like major-league baseball's "Big Mac" (as it is called by many, a reference to its publisher, Macmillan, and its gargantuan size), it is Thoroughbred racing, which was in operation long before America's first major-league circuit, the National League, began play in 1876.

The answer is Martinsville, Illinois, native Dale Baird (born April 17, 1935; began training in 1960), who according to *Daily Racing Form* statistics recorded his 7,000th career winner on Friday, May 3, at Mountaineer Park with Yasuo.

Also the first man to send out 6,000 winners, Baird once again went where no trainer had gone before.

That is a lot of winner's circle pictures for a man who has never been among the national training gentry (D. Wayne Lukas, Shug McGaughey, Bill Mott, Charlie Whittingham,

Record-setting champion trainer Dale Baird (Mountaineer Park/Mountaineer Photo Service)

etc.) with a marquee-name horse, his lone national attention being a record dozen national races-won crowns.

Much of that lack of acclaim is the result of Baird having plied his trade for years in West Virginia at Mountaineer Park and Charles Town, tracks far removed from the national racing centers and the ancillary national racing media.

Nonetheless, his impressive win total is a feat that places him head and shoulders above his colleagues, one that would fail to impress only those running on batteries.

The way to the top, however, has been rather circuitous mathematically for Baird, who just a decade ago was playing second fiddle to that American racing icon Jack Van Berg.

Baird sent out his first winner, New York, on August 18, 1961, at Ellis Park in Kentucky. A grandson of 1935 Triple Crown winner Omaha, New York took the afternoon's first race (a six-furlong contest) under the hands of Robert Wilkerson.

Owned by Baird as well, New York was the favorite in the race, perhaps an early recognition by some of Baird's talents. In any event, New York was a harbinger of things to come.

The Master of Winners—Dale Baird—looking for more winners (Mountaineer Park/Mountaineer Photo Service)

Now fast-forward to the 1984 season, when Baird notched his 4,000th career winner, which he methodically followed up with his 5,000th winner (Stuffed Johnnie) at Mountaineer Park on August 5, 1988.

His 5,000th victor might have attracted more attention if not for the fact that the year before, Jack Van Berg had become the first trainer to saddle 5,000 winners, his groundbreaking triumph coming with Art's Chandelle (which Van Berg also owned) at Arlington International Racecourse near Chicago on July 15, 1987.

Time has a way of evening things out, though, and on August 13, 1992, Baird established a new watershed mark for American trainers, becoming the first conditioner to reach the 6,000-win career mark when Irish Laser captured a 5½-furlong race at Mountaineer Park.

By virtue of his most recent feat, Baird is now further engraving a record that is to this sport and every trainer who has ever saddled a winner what Cy Young's 511 lifetime major-league victories is to baseball and to every pitcher who has won a major-league contest.

For the record, Baird's unprecedented 12 American races-won titles have come in three different decades.

His first was in 1971 (245), which was followed by a short-lived record of 305 in 1973 (the first man to saddle 300 winners in a season, Baird saw that mark broken the following year by Jack Van Berg).

In 1979, Baird commenced a run of four straight championships, registering 316 victories that year, then following up with 306 in 1980, 349 in 1981 (the 1979–81 work made him the first trainer to post three consecutive 300-win seasons), and 276 in 1982.

Next came a nation-leading 249 winners in 1985.

His most recent work has been the national races-won crown the last five straight years: 296 in 1991, 256 in 1992, 269 in 1993, 247 in 1994 (a tie with Mario Beneito), and 286 winners in 1995.

The last-named was his 12th national races-won crown as a trainer, eclipsing the old record of 11 held by Hirsch Jacobs. In addition, Baird has earned 12 races-won titles as an owner, one less than the record 13 turned out by Marion Van Berg. That group includes the last six straight years, 1990 through 1995.

Though he has enjoyed the bulk of his success via claimers, Baird's roster of career winners includes stakes winners Helken Special, French Bow, and Dust Appeal.

Completing the list of the top three race-winningest trainers of all time are Jack Van Berg and King Leatherbury.

Through April 15, 1996, Jack Van Berg (born June 7, 1936, in Columbus, Nebraska) held down the second-place spot on the list of all-time winningest trainers with 6,108 victories.

Leatherbury (born March 26, 1933, in Baltimore, Maryland) occupied the third spot on the list of the sport's all-time winningest trainers with 5,424 victories through the same date.

JACK VAN BERG

A Hall of Famer who is the son of the late Hall of Famer Marion Van Berg (1896–1971), Jack Van Berg is best known for his work with

Jack Van Berg (*The Thoroughbred Times*)

classic winners Gate Dancer (a record-setting Preakness winner) and Alysheba.

The latter, the 1987 Horse-of-the-Year whose career victories included the 1987 Kentucky Derby, the 1987 Preakness, and the 1988 Breeders' Cup Classic, retired as the world's richest race-horse (his career $6,679,242 bankroll was surpassed earlier this year by Cigar with that one's triumph in the inaugural Dubai World Cup).

A multiple national titlist, Van Berg has topped the national trainers list in races won nine times (1968, 1969, 1970, 1972, 1974, 1976, 1983,

1984, and 1986) and in money won once (1976).

In 1976, he became the first trainer in American Thoroughbred racing history to lead the country's trainers in both races won and money won in the same season. His work that year included a record 496 victories.

KING LEATHERBURY

A fixture for years on the Maryland circuit, Leatherbury has sent out such stakes winners as Ameri Valay, Buffels, Catatonic, Heading Home, I Am the Game, Longest Drive,

King Leatherbury (*The Thoroughbred Times*)

Owned By Us, Taking Risks, Thirty Eight Go Go, Thirty Eight Paces, and Wait For the Lady. His first career winner was Mister L. in 1959 at Sunshine Park.

In addition to several national races-won titles (1977 and 1978), Leatherbury also has taken numerous titles at Laurel and Pimlico.

He scored his 5,000th career winner on May 21, 1993.

RICHARD HAZELTON

Richard Hazelton (*The Thoroughbred Times*)

Though Thoroughbred racing does not yet have an official list of its all-time winningest trainers as it does for jockeys, one of the obstacles being "program trainer wins" (victories credited to a person who literally trained the horse in name only), fourth place on the list is believed to be held by Richard Hazelton, born September 2, 1930, in Glendale, Arizona.

Hazelton, who took his 4,000th career winner in April 1994 at Sportsman's Park in Chicago, had 4,125 victories as of April 15, 1996.

A former rider, Hazelton is generally acknowledged to be the winningest trainer in the history of Chicagoland racing, a circuit comprised of Arlington International Racecourse, Sportsman's Park, and Hawthorne Racecourse.

Like so many other great trainers, Hazelton gained his principal acclaim from his fine horsemanship with lower-level horses. However, his career incorporates horses of all kinds: stakes, allowance, claiming, and young prospects.

Long ago nicknamed King Richard for his domination at the three Chicago-area racetracks, where he has taken a slew of titles over the years, Hazelton considers multiple stakes winner Full Pocket to be the best horse he's ever trained.

Other good ones campaigned by Hazelton include 1981 American Derby hero Pocket Zipper (a son of Full Pocket) and the storied Maxwell G., who won 47 races, one of them at age 16.

Other craftsmen of this elite company (trainers known to have saddled 3,000 career winners or more) on this noninclusive list are:

FRANK MERRILL JR. (1919–1990)

The first Canadian trainer to lead the American list in wins (1955), Merrill took two more American races-won titles in 1958 and 1960. In his native Canada, Merrill topped the winningest-trainer list 22 times.

Born Frank Duco Marcello, Merrill—the son of Italian immigrants—began training in 1944.

Known as the Master of the Patch for his ability to transform crippled horses into winners, Frank Merrill Jr. polished off 3,968 winners during his distinguished career.

That life's work also included 62 stakes winners, including a pair of Canadian champions—Square Angel and Dance In Time. Other top horses handled by Merrill were Greek Answer, Hose, Lord Vancouver, Puss N Boots, No Parcado, One For All, Pas de Nom, and Sunny South.

His titles included championships at Arlington International Racecourse, Hawthorne, and Gulfstream Park, plus numerous crowns at tracks in Ontario.

HIRSCH JACOBS (1904–1970)

The winner of 11 national races-won titles (1933–39; 1941–44) and three national money-won crowns (1946, 1960, and 1965), Hall of Fame conditioner Hirsch Jacobs registered 3,596 lifetime victories.

His top runners included champions Stymie, Hail To Reason, and Personality.

Thoroughbred racing's winningest trainer at the time of his death, Jacobs became the first trainer to saddle 3,000 career winners when Blue Waters scored at Aqueduct on April 1, 1960.

Hirsch Jacobs (New York Racing Association/Adam Coglianese)

RICHARD DUTROW (BORN MARCH 8, 1937, IN HAGERSTOWN, MARYLAND)

A veteran of the New York circuit, Dutrow had 3,594 lifetime winners as of April 15, 1996, according to *Daily Racing Form* figures.

His career work includes one national races-won title (in 1975 with a then-record 352 victories) and such major stakes winners as Flawlessly, Shimatoree, Talakeno, and King's Swan.

Richard Dutrow (New York Racing Association/Adam Coglianese)

Trainer Grover "Buddy" Delp and his magnus opus—multiple champion Spectacular Bid (Keeneland Association)

GROVER "BUDDY" DELP (BORN SEPTEMBER 7, 1932, IN CRESWELL, MARYLAND)

Best known for his work with multiple titlist Spectacular Bid— champion two-year-old male in 1978, champion three-year-old male in 1979 off scores in the Kentucky Derby and the Preakness, and Horse-of-the-Year at age four in 1980 off a perfect nine-for-nine campaign—Delp notched his 3,000th career winner with Tangier at Arlington International Racecourse on June 26, 1990. It was reported at the time that he was the ninth trainer to have reached that plateau.

Through the end of the 1995 racing season, Delp had accrued approximately 3,300 victories.

Delp's other top runners include Dispersal, Truly Bound, Sunny Sunrise, Timeless Native, Aspro, Sweet Alliance, Western Echo, Take Heed, and Dancing Champ. His training crowns include Arlington, Delaware Park, Hawthorne, Monmouth Park, and Pimlico.

D. WAYNE LUKAS
(BORN SEPTEMBER 2, 1935,
IN ANTIGO, WISCONSIN)

The signature trainer of the present generation, D. Wayne Lukas—a former basketball coach and quarter-horse trainer—posted his 3,000th winner in late 1994. By the end of 1995, that total stood at 3,238 winners, and as of April 15, 1996, he was credited with 3,293 lifetime winners.

A four-time Eclipse Award winner who has won titles on both coasts and at points in between, that contingent including Santa Anita, Hollywood Park, Belmont, Saratoga, and Churchill Downs, Lukas had trained a record 18 champions

Trainer D. Wayne Lukas (Keeneland Association/Bill Straus)

through 1995, two of them Horse-of-the-Year titlists: Lady's Secret (1986) and Criminal Type (1990).

In 1990, Lukas became the second trainer in history to reach the $100 million mark in career purse earnings (Charlie Whittingham was the first), passing that mark with Criminal Type's victory in the Pimlico Special.

This nation's money-winningest conditioner a record 12 times (1983–92, 1994, and 1995), in 1986 Lukas became the first trainer to earn more purse money than the nation's money-winningest rider. In 1987, he set a national record with 92 stakes wins.

The winner of virtually every major stake in this country, he has won three Kentucky Derbies (his most recent this year with Grindstone), four Preaknesses, two Belmonts, and a record 12 Breeders' Cup events. He also has four national races-won titles to his credit (1987–90).

The list of his outstanding horses is staggering. Besides Lady's Secret and Criminal Type, it includes Althea, Badger Land, Capote, Codex,

Family Style, Farma Way, Golden Attraction, Grand Canyon, Gulch, Is It True, Landaluce, Lucky Lucky Lucky, Marfa, Mountain Cat, Open Mind, Sacahuista, Saratoga Six, Serena's Song, Stalwart, Steinlen, Tabasco Cat, Talinum, Tank's Prospect, Tejano, Terlingua, Thunder Gulch, Timber Country, Twilight Agenda, and Winning Colors.

WILLIAM HAL BISHOP (1900–1981)

This fabled trainer, a longtime regular on the Chicagoland circuit and namesake of a stakes race at Arlington International Racecourse, took his 3,150th and last lifetime winner with the aptly named Fairytale Ending at old Arlington Park on September 3, 1976.

His career work included two national races-won crowns, in 1949 (a tie with Bill Molter) and 1962.

HARRY ALLEN JERKENS (BORN APRIL 21, 1929, IN ISLIP, NEW YORK)

Sometime late last year, Hall of Famer Allen Jerkens—legendary for his ability to topple the "heavy heads"—passed the career 3,000-winner mark.

This is particularly interesting when you consider that Jerkens had his biggest career season, wins-wise, in 1994, at age 65 no less (is this really a young man's game?), when he registered 111 victories.

All of which proves two things.

First, the Giant Killer has been around for some time, steadily and consistently cranking out a slew of winners year after year. Nothing glamorous, just workmanlike.

Allen Jerkens (New York Racing Association/Adam Coglianese)

Second, after a while all those victories mount up, and it was only a matter of time before Jerkens, whose first winner was Populace at Aqueduct on July 4, 1950, reached the promised land of 3,000 victories.

It should be noted at this juncture that the standards of racing and baseball are remarkably similar. Both sports measure greatness by certain statistical milestones. To wit: 300 major-league wins by a pitcher is considered an automatic pass into baseball's Valhalla, the National Baseball Hall of Fame, which like its Thoroughbred racing counterpart, the National Racing Hall of Fame, is located in upstate New York—the former in Cooperstown, the latter in Saratoga Springs.

Thus, you can see, the aforementioned Cy Young, with 511 career victories, had no trouble getting into Cooperstown; indeed, he was a charter member.

Likewise, 3,000 career hits is considered an automatic, no-questions-asked admission pass to Cooperstown, much like 3,000 career winners by a trainer is a straightaway ticket to Saratoga Springs.

Certainly, if there was ever a trainer whose life story should be put on film by Hollywood, it is Jerkens.

His career work includes three upsets of five-time Horse-of-the-Year Kelso with Beau Purple, two defeats of Triple Crown winner and two-time Horse-of-the-Year champion Secretariat (with Onion and Prove Out), a conquering of Horse-of-the-Year Buckpasser (with Handsome Boy), and an underdog triumph over three-time filly champion Cicada (with Pocosaba).

Though much of his fame, and his moniker, can be traced to these wondrous wins, there is more to Jerkens, the youngest trainer ever elected to the National Racing Hall of Fame in Saratoga Springs (at age 45 in 1975).

His career work also includes an Eclipse Award (1975); a national money-won training crown (1983); and numerous titles on his longtime venue, the New York circuit. He has trained a slew of fine runners, including Devil His Due, Sky Beauty (the 1993 New York Filly Triple Crown victress and champion older female of 1994), Sensitive Prince, Aptostar, De Niro, Hechizado, Missy's Mirage, Poker Night, November Snow, and Virginia Rapids.

Through April 15, 1996, Jerkens had some 3,100 lifetime winners.

Based on "Requiem for a Pacer" in Hoofbeats magazine (March 1985)
Maywood Park Program (Friday, May 27, 1988)

The Ghost of Chicago

TWO-MINUTE MILES.

Once, they were the standard for the breed. Today, they serve as qualifiers of class. In the last several decades, the speed of the breed has accelerated so much that the real barrier now is 1:55. And it's getting lower.

Deuce miles, once the demigods of the sport, are now the products of hopeful two-year-olds on their way up, old horses on tired legs on their way down, and journeymen who have reached their peak in cheap company.

Progress is inevitable, but a natural by-product is what it leaves in its wake. Frequently, we find ourselves with stars that light up the night. Occasionally, we are left with ghosts that wander in darkness.

Like the ghost of Chicago—Star Pointer.

The sport's first two-minute miler, who was owned by a Chicagoan at the time of his extraordinary 1:59¼ time trial in 1897, Star Pointer has descended over the years into oblivion. So many others have replaced him that we can scarcely remember his name or his singular sporting deed.

At the top of that list is Niatross, the sport's fastest performer, who made time stand still eight years ago at the Red Mile with a 1:49⅕ time trial.

The mark stands there today, flashing like a neon sign at night. Drawn like moths to a flame, many have tried the mark on for size over

Star Pointer, the sport's first two-minute miler (United States Trotting Association)

the years. None have succeeded, and some have been permanently smoked up by their attempts.

Only one, a son named Nihilator, has ever made it into the same time zone, with a 1:49⅗ mark in 1985.

The progenitor of all this speed, by vivid contrast, barely lingers on.

The first racer to "push through the envelope" (as they said in *The Right Stuff*), the one who broke the sound barrier of the sport, the two-minute mark, Star Pointer endures today as a footnote in the same record book.

An obscure, antiquated racer from just before the turn of the century, he is just a freak item for maniacal trivia experts. Niatross lives and reigns in glory; Star Pointer is buried somewhere under a highway in Palatine, Illinois, a northwestern Chicago suburb.

His bizarre fate mirrors his life and times.

Picked up for a song as a yearling in 1890, he was not officially started until age five. During his career (1894–99), he passed through the hands of three trainers, two of them Hall of Famers. Five times during his life (1889–1910) he was sold.

At age eight (1897), he reigned as a world champion, but was retired a cripple two years later, ignominiously, in the face of a distance flag.

At stud, he spent a nomadic decade-long existence in three different states that saw him fail to pass along his speed, resulting in the end of the last true pacing line in America, the famed Hal family of Tennessee.

And, though he was elected to the Hall of Fame, it came not as a charter member but in their second year of inductions in 1954.

The wildest part of the story, however, belongs to Chicagoan James Murphy, who owned Star Pointer twice. Murphy, who had a farm near Park Ridge, Illinois, bought Star Pointer in February of 1897. Six months later, he was rewarded with the sport's first historic performer when Star Pointer turned a 1:59¼ mark on August 28, 1897, at Readville, Massachusetts (which in 1903 produced the game's first "deuce"—two-minute—trotter, Lou Dillon).

Murphy, however, was unable to stand the strain of owning such a celebrated star as Star Pointer, who was part of a group known as the Five Pacing Kings (an entourage that also included Joe Patchen, John R. Gentry, Robert J., and Frank Agan).

Thus, at the end of the 1898 season, he sold Star Pointer.

Their paths crossed again twice, once in life and once in death. In 1909, Murphy saw Star Pointer exhibited at the fall meeting in Lexington, Kentucky, and bought him for old times' sake. Murphy then shipped him to his birthplace in Columbia, Tennessee, where he stood the 1910 season. Several weeks before Christmas that year, Star Pointer died at age 21 of a stroke.

The chronology gets somewhat blurred after this, but the facts are clear.

Murphy, enamored of Star Pointer, had the horse stuffed and mounted. It was offered to a New York museum, which refused it, and Murphy had the three boxes containing Star Pointer's remains sent to his Park Ridge farm.

Following Murphy's death, the farm was sold. In 1921, it was subdivided. Two men there at the time were eventual Hall of Famer Charley Dean and his son Chase. The latter revealed the final chapter in Star Pointer's life a few years ago in a letter.

Well-known Illinois racing figures, Charley Dean and his son had come to pick up a horse and some equipment they had bought. Offered Star Pointer's remains, the elder Dean accepted, and took the remains back to his vast farm in Palatine, where he later buried them.

Like Murphy's farm, the Dean place was eventually sold to land developers, so Star Pointer's grave was lost forever. However, the general location remains fixed, since Dean's farm was near Baldwin Road and Northwest Highway in Palatine.

Is Star Pointer worth a remembrance?

Well, a wise man once said you have to know where you've been in order to know where you're going. In other words, never—ever—let go of your roots, your heritage. It tells who you are, and defines your future successes.

Naming a local stake after Star Pointer could help us all remember a Chicago star who became a ghost through no fault of his own.

Author's Note: Through 1998, the world record for a harness mile was 1:46⅕ set by the pacer Cambest on August 16, 1993, in Springfield, Ohio. The fastest mile by a trotter is the 1:51-flat mark of Pine Chip on October 1, 1994, at the Red Mile in Lexington, Kentucky. Both were time trials.

Giant: Cigar's Win Streak

W ITH EVERY RACE THAT the grand Cigar wins, his streak
continues to take on greater and greater significance. On July 13
at Arlington International Racecourse, he scored his 16th straight victory, tying the modern-era (twentieth-century) mark set by the immortal
Citation approximately a half century ago.

The skein, which, like a good horse, shows no sign of stopping, could
be extended to 17 straight if Cigar captures the August 10 Pacific Classic
at Del Mar.

A victory there would give the Seattle Slew grandson the modern-era
American record outright. However, that standard is only part of a much
larger mosaic that incorporates the all-time American record holder and,
at the very summit, the all-time world record holder.

In mothballs for years, the names of long-discarded racers are
now being brought out of the woodwork as Cigar continues his extraordinary win streak.

This has posed problems. Only recently has attention been drawn to
the number-one story of the year. It's not Cigar. It's his win streak. Where
does it stack up in the nature of things?

The first to open the door on Cigar's win streak and try to shed some
light on its place in the overall scheme of things was Gulfstream Park,
where the Bill Mott–trained and Allen Paulson–owned racer initiated his
1996 campaign with a repeat score in the Donn Handicap.

During the 1996 meet, a series of three articles appeared in *The Gulfstream Handicapper*, the racetrack's daily program. That trio of articles featured American and European win streaks of the eighteenth, nineteenth, and twentieth centuries, all manually compiled over the course of several weeks.

That triad of articles was subsequently followed by stories in this country's weekly turf journals—*The Blood-Horse* and *The Thoroughbred Times*—plus a piece in *Sports Illustrated*.

Which brings us to an interesting point. Note the absence from this list of the sport's official publication and record-keeper, the *Daily Racing Form*. Had the *Daily Racing Form* done its job, turfwriters wouldn't have been scrambling to hand-construct vital information or to obtain such from an unavailable European book.

In the arena of America's other great sport, baseball, that information would have been instantly available because of the game's insatiable thirst for statistics of all kinds and its relentless devotion to recording all the history of that sport. Not coincidentally, baseball is known as the National Pastime (and not Thoroughbred racing, though it has a much older, organized history).

Unquestionably, the greatest find on win streaks to date has been the mammoth win-streak list published in a 1988 British book, *Guinness Horse Racing Records, Facts and Champions*. Coauthored by Tony Morris and John Randall, the list from this out-of-print book was the basis for the article in *The Thoroughbred Times*.

However, that list is not without its flaws.

For instance, it is missing horses like the fabulous European racer Andreina—winner of the inaugural 1884 Italian Derby, part of a 17-race win streak—and the epic American runner Ten Broeck (15 consecutive wins in the 1870s).

And Boston's first win streak was 17, not 19.

Clearly, the last word has not been written on this fascinating subject yet; only the vain would believe otherwise. One major addition, perhaps *the* major addition, would be documenting the race records of every horse in question on this roster. That's the downside.

But, like excavating the ruins of some ancient civilization, the layers that have been unearthed to date are immensely fascinating. That's the upside.

Here's a look at them.

(23) LEVIATHAN

It just plain stands to reason that the racer who holds the all-time American record for most consecutive wins was a giant in name, appearance, and deed.

Described by one turfwriter as America's first unsexed champion, Leviathan (foaled 1793, raced 1796 through 1803) posted 24 wins and four seconds from 30 lifetime starts. No doubt that fine record was the product of his size, strength, and stride: according to one historian, Leviathan was over 16 hands tall, possessed Samson-like strength, and exhibited the longest stride of any racehorse of his time.

The propitiously named gray gelding, whose namesake is a monstrous sea creature mentioned in the Old Testament, was purchased in early October of 1798 for $1,125 by the renowned horseman Colonel John Tayloe III. In the early stages of his win streak, Leviathan was bought so that Tayloe could withdraw him from a prominent race he wished to take with Calypso, a high-class racer who in the absence of her new stablemate took the event with ease.

Beginning in 1797 and continuing through the fall of 1801, the Virginia-bred Leviathan (who was originally called Flagellator) reeled off 23 straight wins. That streak, which was snapped on October 24, 1801, at Fredericksburg, Virginia, by the filly Fairy, included a grueling match against Brimmer in the spring of 1801.

Locked together virtually the entire way of the five-mile contest, in which he gave 70 pounds to Brimmer, Leviathan—under an impost of 180 pounds—prevailed by inches. That was the beginning of the end for this extraordinary racer, who closed out his career with a string of losses.

Though well recorded in John Hervey's *Racing in America: 1665–1865*, Leviathan, because of his ranking, absolutely needs a complete set of past performances constructed for him.

(21) FIRST CONSUL AND LOTTERY

Tied for second place on the all-time American list at 21 straight triumphs are First Consul (foaled 1798) and Lottery (foaled 1803).

Considered by some to be the greatest horse seen on the American turf prior to the epic, undefeated racer American Eclipse (1814–47), First Consul (also known as Bond's First Consul) registered 21 wins and a trio of seconds from 25 lifetime forays.

A homebred campaigned by Philadelphian Joshua Bond, the well-named First Consul was undefeated from age three (his debut season) through seven. His sire, interestingly enough, was Flag Of Truce, also the sire of Leviathan.

Pennsylvania-bred First Consul has several rich stories attached to him. His granddam (Dian or Diana, a daughter of Eclipse) had been brought to America, saw duty during the Revolutionary War (as the personal charger of a British cavalry officer), and was captured at the surrender of Cornwallis.

First Consul's name was the product of Bond's admiration for Napoleon Bonaparte, who in 1779 had crowned himself master of France under the title of First Consul.

Commencing his career with 21 straight triumphs, First Consul was finally taken down to size in 1806 at Baltimore by Oscar (also known as Ogle's Oscar). What followed were three more defeats, the last being his career finale at Harlem, New York, on October 19, 1807.

Lottery, foaled in 1803, posted 21 wins from 22 starts. After a career-opening loss, the elegant-looking chestnut ran off 21 consecutive victories.

As with Leviathan, the only thing missing on these two antique stars are complete past-performance records to verify their places on the all-time American win-streak list.

(20) FASHION AND KENTUCKY

Tied in third place on the all-time American win-streak list at 20 each are Fashion and Kentucky, both of whom have been past-performanced (both their profiles contain abridged race records).

Foaled April 26, 1837, Fashion—a rich-coated chestnut distaffer with a star and a white left hind coronet—raced from age 3 through age 11 (1840–48), compiling a glistening lifetime ledger of 32 wins and four seconds from 36 starts.

Her 20-race win streak, spread over four campaigns, began with her last three starts at age four. The finale in late October of that season is of particular note. In that race, she bested the widely heralded Boston, a winner of 19 straight races.

Fashion's 20-race win streak ultimately encompassed unbeaten campaigns at age five (all four starts), age six (seven-for-seven), and age seven (all six forays). The streak, which included three walkovers, came to an end in her eighth-year debut on May 13, 1845, at Union Course in Long Island, when the six-year-old chestnut mare Peytona beat Fashion in straight heats (both at four miles).

Broken down, Fashion's career record reads thusly:

1839 (2)   Unraced

1840 (3)   2-2-0-0

1841 (4)   5-4-1-0

1842 (5)   4-4-0-0

1843 (6)   7-7-0-0

1844 (7)   6-6-0-0

1845 (8)   4-3-1-0

1846 (9)   3-3-0-0

1847 (10)   2-1-1-0

1848 (11)   3-2-1-0

Translated into past performances, her work looks like this:

1839 (2)

  – Unraced

1840 (3)

    Oct. 21/Camden, N.J./WON

    Oct. 27/Trenton, N.J./WON

1841 (4)

    May 6/Union Course, L.I. (Long Island)/WON

    May 19/Camden, N.J./2nd

    Oct. 7/Union Course, L.I./WON

    Oct. 20/Baltimore, Md./WON

    Oct. 28/Camden, N.J./WON

1842 (5)

    May 10/Union Course, L.I./WON

    Oct. 6/Union Course, L.I./WON (walkover)

Oct. 29/Camden, N.J./WON

Nov. 4/Trenton, N.J./WON

1843 (6)

May 11/Trenton, N.J./WON

May 26/Camden, N.J./WON

June 1/Union Course, L.I./WON (walkover)

Oct. 6/Alexandria, Va./WON (walkover)

Oct. 13/Washington, D.C./WON

Oct. 20/Baltimore, Md./WON

Oct. 26/Camden, N.J./WON

1844 (7)

May 10/Baltimore, Md./WON

June 6/Union Course, L.I./WON

Oct. 1/Union Course, L.I./WON

Oct. 18/Baltimore, Md./WON

Oct. 24/Beacon Course, N.J./WON

Oct. 31/Camden, N.J./WON

1845 (8)

May 13/Union Course, L.I./2nd

May 17/Union Course, L.I./WON

May 28/Camden, N.J./WON

Oct. 22/Union Course, L.I./WON

1846 (9)

May 14/Baltimore, Md./WON

June 2/Union Course, L.I./WON

Oct. 16/Baltimore, Md./WON

1847 (10)

May 29/Baltimore, Md./WON

Oct. 6/Union Course, L.I./2nd

1848 (11)

    May 19/Union Course, L.I./WON

    Oct. 6/Union Course, L.I./2nd

    Oct. 20/Baltimore, Md./WON

A great racer, Fashion was also a great-looking racer, according to an account of her by W. T. Porter in Hervey's classic, *Racing in America: 1665–1865*.

Fashion was about "15½ hands high under the standard, rising high on the withers, with a light head and neck, faultless legs, an oblique, well-shaped shoulder, and a roomy, deep capacious chest."

She also possessed well-developed hindquarters. This was her great strength, one that served to propel her entire body mass forward with tremendous power and velocity.

In closing, Porter sang this anthem to this long-forgotten American racing giant:

> She goes with a long, rating stroke, gathers well, and moves with the utmost ease to herself. What is rather singular, she runs with a loose rein; she is as true as steel, has a remarkable turn of speed, can be placed anywhere, and nothing can be finer than her disposition; a more bloodlike, honest mare was never brought to the post.

It is truly the sport's loss that we do not know her better today. This is not without cause.

As stated before, Thoroughbred racing is guilty of two sins. One is its abysmal record-keeping, particularly its premodern (pre-1900) time frame. Its other transgression is its complete and continuing failure to market its single biggest asset, its fabulous history. While baseball's history is its lifeblood, indeed its primary reason for its stature in this country, it is quite a different matter in Thoroughbred racing.

By vivid contrast, Thoroughbred racing seemingly regards its history with disdain and embarrassment, for the most part only recognizing its history when obligated to do so. As a result, Thoroughbred racing's history comes off looking a bit like the senile relative who occasionally wanders into the family gathering by accident. Because of the logistics involved, you are obligated to introduce them. That done, it's back to the attic for them as quickly as possible.

Kentucky (*The Thoroughbred Times*)

Though Fashion fortunately has escaped the first trap, she has become ensnared by the second. As a result, Fashion—a racing masterpiece of the highest order—survives today only as some sort of trivia freak.

Kentucky was part of the great triumvirate from the 1861 class. That trio included unbeaten Asteroid (1861–88, 12-for-12 lifetime) and undefeated Norfolk (5-for-5 career). All three champions were sons of Lexington, a brilliant racer who went on to lead America's sire list an unprecedented 16 times.

According to race records gleaned from H. G. Crickmore's racing calendars (the 1861–65, 1866–67, and the 1868–69 editions), Kentucky compiled a lifetime register of 21 victories from 22 starts, ending that illustrious career with 20 straight wins.

Kentucky began his career with a win in a one-mile race at Paterson, New Jersey, on October 7, 1863. His next start was a loss (a fourth-place finish) to Norfolk in the Jersey Derby on June 7, 1864. Following that defeat, Kentucky was never beaten again, closing out his career with a string of 20 successive victories that encompassed his last six starts at three in 1864 and a pair of seven-for-seven campaigns at four and five.

In 1867, Kentucky entered stud for the first time and was not raced. However, he was sent out against his sire's four-mile record of 7:19¾ at Jerome Park on October 17, 1867. Carrying 120 pounds (Charles Littlefield up), Kentucky finished well off the mark, coming home in 7:31¾ (this the product of a track unfavorable to fast times, according to the aforementioned Hervey volume).

In that same work, Hervey includes this item about Kentucky's stature as a racer, recounting that at the 1868 Narragansett Park meeting, the conditions of the sweepstakes read: "Kentucky to carry 10 pounds extra in all races." This requirement, according to the sport's greatest scholar, was "quite exceptional in the history of modern racing."

However, Crickmore has no 1868 racing records for Kentucky (one reason is that his connections may have spent the year, unsuccessfully, looking for challengers). If there be a question about the 1868 season and Kentucky's career totals, there is absolutely no question about the 20-race win skein of this great who was permanently retired to stud in 1869. His documented race record follows.

1863 (2)

    Oct. 7/Paterson, N.J./WON

1864 (3)

    June 7/Paterson, N.J./4th/Jersey Derby

    June 9/Paterson, N.J./WON/Sequel Stakes

    Aug. 2/Saratoga, N.Y./WON/Travers (first running)

    Aug. 5/Saratoga, N.Y./WON/Sequel Stakes

    Sept. 13/Paterson, N.J./WON/Jersey St. Leger

    Sept. 15/Paterson, N.J./WON/Sequel Stakes

    Sept. 17/Paterson, N.J./WON (match race)

1865 (4)

    June 6/Paterson, N.J./WON

    June 8/Paterson, N.J./WON

    Aug. 8/Saratoga, N.Y./WON/Saratoga Cup

    Aug. 12/Saratoga, N.Y./WON

    Oct. 10/Paterson, N.J./WON

Oct. 11/Paterson, N.J./WON

Oct. 12/Paterson, N.J./WON

1866 (5)

June 5/Paterson, N.J./WON

June 6/Paterson, N.J./WON

June 7/Paterson, N.J./WON

July 25/Saratoga, N.Y./WON/Saratoga Cup

July 29/Saratoga, N.Y./WON

Sept. 25/Jerome Park, N.Y./WON/Inaugural Stakes

Oct. 3/Jerome Park, N.Y./WON/Grand National Handicap

Boston (*The Thoroughbred Times*)

(19) BOSTON AND SWEETMEAT

Deadlocked for fourth place at 19 successive victories on the American winning-streak list are Boston and Sweetmeat, though there is a question about the latter.

A lifetime 45-40-2-1 performer over eight seasons (1836–43), Boston (1833–50) ran off two major win streaks during his stellar career. The second and largest was a 19-race skein, comprised of his last eight starts at age six, all seven at seven, and his first four ventures at age eight in 1841. It ended on October 28, 1841, in Camden, New Jersey, when the previously profiled Fashion bested Old White Nose (a reference to Boston's blaze face).

As for Sweetmeat, she is identified on Morris and Randall's list as having raced in the 1840s in America. However, there is no mention of this runner in either of the two standard American racing histories— Hervey's *Racing in America: 1665–1865* and W. H. P. Robertson's *The History of Thoroughbred Racing in America*.

Perhaps the list could have made an error in the racing country involved, since there is a British racer named Sweetmeat. A foal of 1842 (Gladiator-Lollypop), that brown runner—according to British race records—ran off a perfect 19-for-19 campaign at age three in 1845.

Obviously, this horse requires more research.

VOL. 191 No. 17.
No. 202 CHAMBERS STREET

NEW YORK, SATURDAY, MAY 28, 1881.

SUBSCRIPTION
FIVE DOLLARS A YE

HINDOO:
THE WINNER OF THE KENTUCKY DERBY.

Hindoo (*The Thoroughbred Times*)

(18) SALLY HOPE AND HINDOO

Tied for fifth-place honors on the all-time American win-streak list at 18 straight wins are Sally Hope and Hindoo.

Foaled in 1822, Virginia-bred Sally Hope raced from 1826 through 1829, registering 22 wins from 27 starts. The conclusion of her streak and career was simultaneous, and had a taste of Hollywood to it.

In the spring of 1829, Sally Hope won a three-mile race at Belfield, Virginia. That was her 18th straight victory. It also was the end of her as a runner, as Sally Hope came out of the race lame and was retired to the breeding shed.

Winner of the 1881 Kentucky Derby, Hindoo took 30 of 35 career starts and never missed a check in his life (his work included three seconds and a pair of thirds).

His win streak totaled his first 18 starts at age three, one of them notably the Kentucky Derby. As an interesting sidebar, this stellar racer sired another win-streak craftsman in Hanover (the owner of a 17-race win streak).

(17) BEESWING, ALICE HAWTHORNE, BOSTON, AND HANOVER

Tenants of the 17-straight-win spot, the next landing place for Cigar, include Alice Hawthorne, Beeswing, Boston, and Hanover, though one of the quartet is under question.

According to Hervey's *Racing in America: 1665–1865*, Beeswing's 17-victory streak came to an end during the spring 1840 meet at Metairie, Louisiana, when she broke down in a race.

Regarding Alice Hawthorne, she may be another case of mistaken identity, like Sweetmeat. On the Morris/Randall list, she is posted as being an 1840s American racer. However, Hervey's volume identifies her as a British distaffer.

There is a good chance that Morris and Randall are referring to the aforementioned English racer. A bay foal of 1838 (Muley Moloch–Rebecca), this magnificent runner—whose name occasionally shows up as "Alice Hawthorne"—ran off a string of 15 consecutive victories during her six-year-old season in 1844.

The only runner with two streaks on the list, Boston first ran off 17 straight wins, then 19 successive victories.

Hanover (*The Thoroughbred Times*)

His 17-race streak was comprised of his last two starts at age three, all four at age four, and all eleven at age five. This streak came to an end in Boston's debut at age six in 1839 at the hands of Portsmouth. After the loss, the vicious-tempered racer commenced his 19-race win streak.

The kingly Hanover (1884–99), a son of the previously discussed Hindoo, posted career totals of 50-32-14-2 during a four-year career (1886–89). He was a product of the 1884 class, considered by authorities to be one of the greatest crops ever turned out by this country.

Other great crops include the 1928 contingent of Twenty Grand, Equipoise, Mate, Johnstown, and Vander Pool, the latter on the list with a 15-race win streak, and the 1954 class of Bold Ruler, Gallant Man, Round Table, and Gen. Duke.

Hanover's class included the meteoric Tremont (13-for-13, all at age two); the brilliant distaffer Firenze (82-47-21-9); and the sturdy Kingston (138-89-33-12), who still holds the American record for most wins by a Thoroughbred.

Hanover's streak was accomplished at ages two and three. Undefeated in three juvenile starts, he took his first 14 outings the following season, including such fixtures as the Withers, Belmont, and Brooklyn Derby (now the Dwyer).

Miss Woodford (*The Thoroughbred Times*)

(16) LUKE BLACKBURN, MISS WOODFORD, CITATION, AND CIGAR

A quartet now occupies the realm of 16 straight wins, the most recent addition being Cigar. His work of the last three seasons, in whole or in part, is reminiscent of Joe DiMaggio's record 56-game hitting streak in 1941. It is daily news, at rest or at work. Moreover, it has kept a sport desperately in need of a signature name (perhaps its first since John Henry) on the sporting pages on a regular basis.

Cigar's streak incorporates his last two starts in 1994 at age four; all ten in 1995, when he earned Horse-of-the-Year laurels off a campaign that concluded with a visceral triumph in the Breeders' Cup Classic; and all four to date this year—his second straight Donn Handicap, the inaugural Dubai World Cup (which enabled him to supplant Alysheba as North America's richest racehorse), a repeat in the Massachusetts

Cigar (Gulfstream Park/Equi-Photo)

Handicap, and the Arlington Citation Challenge at Arlington International Racecourse in Chicago.

By the way, a slight editorial correction is long overdue, and here it is. Many consider Cigar to be one of the great runners of this century. That's too restrictive. He is one of the sport's all-time great runners. Look at the list. It encompasses runners—Cigar one of them—from three different centuries.

The coholder of the twentieth-century American win-streak record, Citation took his last 15 starts at age three (that ledger including the 1948 Triple Crown) and his first start at age five in 1950 (he missed the 1949 season because of an osselet). It was his modern-era record that Cigar tied in Chicago and seeks to break in the Pacific Classic in California.

Luke Blackburn (1877–1904) took his last 15 starts at age three and his first outing at four. This mighty runner raced from 1879 through 1881, and from 39 ventures compiled lifetime totals of 25 wins, six seconds, and a pair of thirds. Without a doubt, the bulk of his greatness was exhibited at three, when he won 22 of 24 starts.

Trainer Jimmy Jones leads in the brilliant Citation (Eddie Arcaro up) after his victory in the 1948 Belmont Stakes and a sweep of that year's Triple Crown. (New York Racing Association/Mike Sirico; promotional gift from Eddie Arcaro to the author)

A 48-37-7-2 lifetime racer, Miss Woodford (1880–99) put her streak together by taking her last five starts at age three, going undefeated in nine starts at age four, and garnering her first two ventures at age five. The first horse in American Thoroughbred racing history to earn $100,000, she concluded her five-year racing career (1882–86) as this country's richest racehorse, with a $118,270 bankroll.

One sidebar to the 16-win group—Florida-bred Mister Frisky (foaled 1987) accumulated 16 straight wins in 1989 and 1990. However, the first thirteen were recorded in Puerto Rico (all twelve at age two, and his first start there at three). A winner of his next three starts, all in America, Mister Frisky had his 16-race skein broken in the 1990 Kentucky Derby; he finished eighth in that edition, won by Unbridled.

(15) RATTLER, TEN BROECK, COLIN, VANDER POOL, AND BUCKPASSER

In at 15 wins each, the last level Cigar occupied before ascending to record heights, is the quintet of Rattler, Ten Broeck, Colin, Vander Pool, and Buckpasser.

According to the Hervey volume, the blue-blooded Rattler (foaled 1816, Sir Archy–Robin Mare) garnered "15 consecutive races and (was) never beaten until injured." Also known as Thornton's Rattler (he was owned for some time by Dr. William Thornton of Washington, D.C.), this Virginia-bred racer stood stud in at least three states—Kentucky, Tennessee, and Indiana.

Ten Broeck concluded his racing career (1874–78) with 23 victories and three seconds from 29 forays. This epic nineteenth-century racer put together his win streak via his last seven starts at age four and his first eight at five.

Interestingly, Ten Broeck (1872–87) is not posted on the Morris/Randall win-streak list. However, that roster does include the celebrated mare Mollie McCarthy, whose 13-race win skein was soundly snapped by Ten Broeck in a much-publicized match race on July 4, 1878, at Churchill Downs. That battle, which saw him distance the California distaffer, was Ten Broeck's last and richest race.

Put together a roster of the top ten racers in America's history, and Colin (1905–32) would have to be on it. This fabulous, turn-of-the-century giant was undefeated in 15 lifetime starts—12-for-12 at two, and 3-for-3 as a sophomore.

Colin (*The Thoroughbred Times*)

A member of one of this country's three greatest crops (previously detailed in the Hanover profile), Vander Pool (foaled 1928) took all 11 ventures at two (one of them a win by disqualification over the mighty Equipoise), then followed up by winning his first four outings at age three.

According to one source, Vander Pool would have been regarded as something more than a great sprinter had his underpinning and constitution been sturdier. A winner of 19 of 32 lifetime starts, the Campfire son ended up as a Government Remount stallion.

One of the great racers of the twentieth century, Buckpasser captured his last 13 races as a three-year-old in 1966, when he earned Horse-of-the-Year laurels, then won his first two starts in 1967. He concluded his magnificent career with 25 victories, four seconds, and one third from 31 starts.

Man o' War (*The Thoroughbred Times*)

(14) PLANET, HARRY BASSETT, AND MAN O' WAR

This figure rates a look because it includes the signature name of Thoroughbred racing—Man o' War.

Still the yardstick many use today to measure great racehorses, the much-storied Man o' War, a winner of 20 of 21 lifetime starts, would be higher on the list if not for a loss at the hands of the aptly named Upset in the 1919 Sanford Memorial Stakes (run on August 13 that year, by the way).

Turn that loss—the result of an atrocious start and then being boxed in nearly the entire way around—into a victory, and Man o' War would have retired unbeaten in 21 lifetime forays. Any idea that Upset was Man o' War's equal is quickly dispelled by the fact that Man o' War met that little colt on six other occasions and beat him every time.

Incidentally, Man o' War's fate mirrors that of another great horse, Native Dancer, television's first racing star.

A victor of 21 of 22 career starts, Native Dancer (11 straight wins) might have retired undefeated in 22 outings had he not had to contend with several problems in the 1953 Kentucky Derby, not the least of which was a first-turn mugging by Money Broker.

Finally getting free in the stretch, the Gray Ghost (so nicknamed because of his color) landed up losing by a head to the ominously named Dark Star. Such was Native Dancer's stature that the chart of the race, in a rare editorial comment, stated that he "could not overtake the winner, although probably best."

The other occupants of the 14-straight-win level are premodern-era racers Planet (1855–75) and Harry Bassett (1868–78).

A grandson of Boston, Planet (28-24-4-0 career) copped his last nine victories at age four in 1859 and his first five starts at age five in 1860.

Harry Bassett took his last three starts at two, all nine forays at three, and his first two races at age four. Finally stopped by the great Longfellow, Harry Bassett logged 23 wins, five seconds, and a trio of thirds from 36 starts during a five-year career (1870–74).

Man o' War, Planet, and Harry Bassett are the last entries on the recompiled American list that follows.

ALL-TIME AMERICAN WIN-STREAK LIST

23: Leviathan

21: First Consul, Lottery

20: Fashion, Kentucky

19: Boston, Sweetmeat

18: Sally Hope, Hindoo

17: Beeswing, Alice Hawthorne, Boston, Hanover

16: Luke Blackburn, Miss Woodford, Citation, Cigar

15: Rattler, Ten Broeck, Colin, Vander Pool, Buckpasser

14: Harry Bassett, Man o' War, Planet

This list could also include early-nineteenth-century American champions Lady Lightfoot (1812–34) and Haynie's Maria (foaled 1808), who, according to one article, were reportedly undefeated until their final starts at ages eleven and nine, respectively.

In the case of the former, who raced from 1815 through 1823, this definitely is in error, the prime source being Hervey's *Racing in America: 1665–1865*.

According to that book, Lady Lightfoot raced but once at four, her campaign that year limited due to a severe case of distemper. That one start occurred in the late fall at Tarboro, North Carolina, where Lady Lightfoot ran second to stablemate Timoleon.

Other recorded losses included one to Hermaphrodite in November of 1817 at Hagerstown, Maryland; one to Beggar Girl in late fall of 1819 at Broad Rock, Virginia; one to American Eclipse in 1821 at Union Course in New York (this verified by Kent Hollingsworth's *The Great Ones*); and her career finale, in June of 1823 at Baltimore, where she was easily beaten by Betsey Richards.

The Hervey book estimates that Lady Lightfoot won between 30 and 40 races (of which 23 are documented in Hervey's profile, with no mention of a specific (and lengthy) win streak. Obviously, here is another racer in major need of past-performancing. As a broodmare, incidentally, Lady Lightfoot proved to be a distinguished producer of high-class foals.

(Regarding her career wins, several of her documented victories came in 1820 over a horse named Rattler, perhaps the same, mysterious horse mentioned before in the 15-straight-wins section.)

As for Haynie's Maria, Robertson's peerless work says she did indeed not lose until her final career start at age nine. However, no number is given for her victories, and therefore a search for her complete race records is in order to determine her place (if any) on the all-time American win-streak list.

To be sure, she was some horse, about whom it was said that she was the only thing, equine or human, that ever got the best of Andrew Jackson.

Owned by Captain Jess Haynie, she easily took her debut at Nashville in 1811, distancing five of her six rivals (one of them a colt owned by the future War of 1812 hero and American president).

She busted up Jackson's horses at least seven other times before the irrepressible general finally got the message and gave up, proclaiming, "She can beat anything in God's whole creation."

One final point on the all-time American list.

It includes horses who compiled their win streaks in one of two ways: "heat" racing and "dash" racing. Prior to the Civil War, heat racing was the norm in this country, a typical fare being best-two-out-of-three heats at four miles each. After the Civil War, the emphasis shifted to speed, and thus dash racing was born, a dash being a single event contested at a variety of distances ranging from a few furlongs to several miles.

As impressive as the American list is, it still falls far short of the two world-record holders: Puerto Rican star Camarero and Hungarian demigoddess Kincsem.

Foaled in 1951, Camarero, who debuted on April 19, 1953, won the first 56 starts of his career. He did not suffer his first loss until August 17, 1955, and he eventually won 73 of 77 ventures (all there on the island) from five furlongs to 1⅛ miles.

A pony-sized racer (14 hands, 750 pounds) with a wrong-side-of-the-tracks pedigree, Camarero made up for his shortcomings with a heart that was bigger than his stall. When he died prematurely in August 1956, all of Puerto Rico mourned his passing.

Kincsem, foaled March 17, 1874, in Hungary, won all 54 of her career starts. That included all 10 starts at age two, all 17 at three, all 15 at four, and all 12 at five. Her career finale was on October 21, 1879, in Budapest.

Broken down by country, her career work entailed 22 wins in Hungary, 16 in Austria, 14 in Germany (her career debut was made there on June 21, 1876), and one each in England and France (the Goodwood Cup and the Grand Prix de Deauville, respectively). Her other major career victories were the Baden-Baden Grand Prize (three times), the Austrian Derby, and the Hungarian St. Leger.

Sixteen–Race Win Streak of Cigar

Win #	Date	Track	Race	Distance
1	10-28-94	Aqueduct	Allowance	1 mile
2	11-26-94	Aqueduct	NYRA Mile Handicap (G1)	1 mile
3	1-22-95	Gulfstream Park	Allowance	1 1/16 miles
4	2-11-95	Gulfstream Park	Donn Handicap (G1)	1 1/8 miles
5	3-5-95	Gulfstream Park	Gulfstream Park Handicap (G1)	1 1/4 miles
6	4-15-95	Oaklawn Park	Oaklawn Handicap (G1)	1 1/8 miles
7	5-13-95	Pimlico	Pimlico Special (G1)	1 1/16 miles
8	6-3-95	Suffolk Downs	Massachusetts Handicap	1 1/8 miles
9	7-2-95	Hollywood Park	Hollywood Gold Cup Handicap (G1)	1 1/4 miles
10	9-16-95	Belmont Park	Woodward Handicap (G1)	1 1/8 miles
11	10-7-95	Belmont Park	Jockey Club Gold Cup (G1)	1 1/4 miles
12	10-28-95	Belmont Park	Breeders' Cup Classic (G1)	1 1/4 miles
13	2-10-96	Gulfstream Park	Donn Handicap (G1)	1 1/8 miles
14	3-27-96	Nad Al Sheba	Dubai World Cup	1 1/4 miles
15	6-1-96	Suffolk Downs	Massachusetts Handicap	1 1/8 miles
16	7-13-96	Arlington International Racecourse	Arlington Citation Challenge Cup	1 1/8 miles

Note: Cigar, who tied Citation's twentieth-century record of 16 straight wins, preceded his skein with a third-place finish in an October 7, 1994, turf-allowance race at Belmont and ended it on August 10, 1996, at Del Mar, when he ran second to Dare and Go in the Pacific Classic (Grade 1).

The Road Warrior

T HE NUMBERS JUST DIDN'T add up.
When the last of 4,161 fans finished piling into the Red Mile on Kentucky Futurity Day, Friday, October 7, all the recipients of a special poster distributed free for the other major occasion of the sunny and mild afternoon—the retirement of Rambling Willie—only a few posters remained.

Even allowing for future publicity needs, hard-core race fans, historical opportunists, and perhaps a few shady, glue-fingered black marketeers, the Lexington, Kentucky, oval should have found itself with hundreds of posters left over from an original press run of 5,000.

Instead, by day's end, it was virtually broke.

The situation once again proved that even in a simple matter of souvenir posters, Rambling Willie defied mathematical calculation.

If the quantity of that crowd that afternoon will forever remain in dispute, its quality was unquestionable. To a person, they all rose as Rambling Willie was escorted down the lane by Parade Marshall and Outrider Shelly Shrum promptly at 1:30 P.M., as advertised, between the fourth and fifth races of the day.

Passing a message on the tote board that read "Welcome to Kentucky, Rambling Willie," the pair split directions suddenly. Shrum kept to the

Rambling Willie, Bob Farrington in the bike (United States Trotting Association/George Smallsreed)

rail, moving behind a cadre of drivers standing at attention dressed in their driving colors, while Rambling Willie was wheeled to the right by trainer-driver and Hall of Famer Bob Farrington and disappeared into a circle of photographers, reporters, camera crews, racetrack officials, old friends, and his own connections.

As Red Mile General Manager Curt Greene began the bittersweet ceremonies, a sizable group of backstretchers up the lane, cordoned off by a rope that stretched the width of the track and was held intact by racetrack security, pressed slightly forward to see and hear better.

That brought back memories, vivid and rich.

Slightly more than three years before, on a track that draws harness-racing history with the flourish of a George Claxton, Niatross had become the sport's fastest horse ever when he passed down the same lane and into a new time dimension with an electrifying 1:49⅕ time trial that demolished the old world record by nearly three full seconds.

His impact on the sport, and well beyond, was permanent and overpowering.

Not only did he grab harness racing by its lapels and violently wrench it free of its long-standing and well-known inferiority complex, Niatross even made outsiders stand up and take notice, one of them a "running man" who had come expecting a simple afternoon's entertainment and left with tears streaming down his face, shaken to the very fiber of his being by what he called "the greatest single performance by any horse I've ever seen in all my life, regardless of the breed."

Having transcended his own sport like no other harness horse before him, Niatross then had gone back up the track after special ceremonies in front of the main crowd, threaded his way slowly through another crowd of well-wishers at the head of the lane, and left forever.

He had no time to wait or lose.

His job was only half done. The other half, the most important half, after a few more perfunctory races, including a win in the Messenger Stakes and a sweep of the Pacing Triple Crown series, lay just a few months ahead in the breeding shed, where it was hoped he would breed on.

And now, the crowd was up there again, awaiting another giant.

But this giant was a horse of a different color. Even their one common link—that both had beat time at its own game—separated them, since each had done it in an immensely different fashion.

Niatross had been measured in minutes and seconds. Rambling Willie was measured in years.

If Niatross was a sleek and powerful Mercedes-Benz, Rambling Willie was the good, old-fashioned, solid 283-cubic-inch Chevrolet Impala that just kept going and going and going.

If Niatross was the sport's first superstar, one whose feats marked him as harness racing's answer to Man o' War and the standard by which all harness horses would be measured in the future, Rambling Willie was the sport's ultimate journeyman, whose sheer grit and longevity smacked deliciously of Forego, the greatest gelding campaigner in the modern history of Thoroughbred racing and perhaps of all time.

Rambling Willie, of course, will not breed on like Niatross. But, even without the benefit of a breeding shed, his mark on the sport is just as indelible as that of Niatross.

As Greene would note in his ceremonial remarks, his voice seeming to crack for just an instant, "many people who would never have known the sport of harness racing otherwise, now do because of Rambling Willie."

You don't have to take his word for it: even a cursory look at Rambling Willie's records and itinerary shows a horse who is truly the classic embodiment of the American Dream and American work ethic.

Raced an even dozen years at countless tracks all across the North American continent before hundreds of thousands of fans, this son of an undistinguished sire and a crippled mare started out on the fair circuits, the gut-heart of a 175-year-old-plus sport that only in recent decades has learned about such matters as million-dollar syndication and race plants like The Meadowlands.

In Rambling Willie's peak years, from 1975 to 1977, he was voted Aged Pacer of the Year three consecutive times, but his rags-to-riches story was hardly over.

It continued until this year, when he had earned the last dollar of his $2,038,219 bankroll, establishing him as the world's richest pacer and North America's greatest money-earner; when he had scored the last of his 128 lifetime victories, a modern-day world record, as was his 305 lifetime starts; and when he had tallied his 79th and final sub-two-minute mile, also a world record.

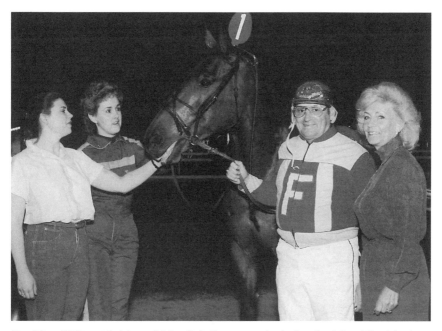

Rambling Willie with Mr. and Mrs. Bob Farrington (right-hand side) at The Meadow-lands (United States Trotting Association)

The blue-blooded Niatross had gone faster, but his blue-collar colleague, the People's Horse, who will democratically spend his retirement years at the Kentucky Horse Park as a major attraction in its annual Parade of Breeds show, had gone much farther.

Much farther. On much less.

It had not been easy for Rambling Willie, who hit the track seven years before Niatross and who was still racing three years after the latter's retirement, at the same time that wunderkind's yearlings were being auctioned on the Kentucky market for the first time.

And yet he had raced all that time, enduring four bowed tendons, an equal number of broken splints, a bad right suspensory, hazardous laser surgery that could just as easily have ended his career as prolonged it, and an epic joust with death.

At the very end, he raced basically on only one healthy leg—his left hind.

If occasionally the tree bent under the weight of time and physical strain, still it never broke.

That durability, as much as his courage off the track and his heart on it, which produced an array of world, American, track, and stakes records, indicated a quality of goods that far outstripped its original investment price.

Americans in general love durability, because in recent years, about the only thing solidly made on American products is the "union-made" tag.

But the majority of Americans do not make their living on a racetrack, where such durability, cherished because of its rareness, often means survival for a struggling stable trying to please an impatient clientele.

It is a certain bet that trainer-driver Bob Farrington and Rambling Willie's co-owners, Bob's wife, Vivian, and the late Paul Siebert, never found themselves in such desperate straits during Rambling Willie's career.

But that does not change the texture of the overall facts in the least.

Over a span of more than a decade, an initial $15,000 purchase price was parlayed into a mother lode of $2 million. Like Forego, Rambling Willie always carried his weight—even when it hurt—paid his way, and allowed his connections to eat well, regularly, and without fear of hunger.

Right up to the end, the buffet continued unabated.

In a legendary manner, he passed the ultimate test of any racehorse with flying colors: can he get you the dinner check and a little something else?

Always, he had.

Unlike the bulk of his comrades in both Standardbred and Thoroughbred racing, he never went on the dole or applied for food stamps, asking that the stable carry him. Always, the table was full, and it was a veritable feast.

Besides his sport, his many fans and connections, Rambling Willie enriched others, notably a number of people who probably never went near a racetrack.

Like the parishioners who attended the church run by Vivian Farrington's father in Mansfield, Ohio, the recipients of her generous tithing of her share of Rambling Willie's earnings.

After her father retired, the tithing did not end, as it conveniently could have. Instead, it simply relocated, the 10 percent going to other churches. Thus, it was only natural that when a best-selling book within the industry and sport came out several years ago, it was entitled *Rambling Willie: The Horse That God Loved.*

On at least one memorable occasion, in February of 1982 at Hollywood Park, where Rambling Willie was tied up with a twisted intestine, his Master had a chance to prove it.

The Church of Christ in Richwood, Ohio, where Rambling Willie's tithe was sent (United States Trotting Association)

In recounting the incident, some say that Death not only knocked on his stall door, but boldly opened it, walked in, unfolded his favorite chair when he learned that surgery was planned, made coffee, sent out for sandwiches, sat down, and waited.

And waited. And waited. Until finally he dozed off. That was all the opening that Rambling Willie needed.

Awakening from his Rip Van Winkle sleep approximately five months later, Death found the stall empty, and assuming the logical had occurred, confidently headed home.

On his way, perhaps out of spite, he passed over Chicago, Rambling Willie's home. To his amazement and consternation, he looked down and saw Rambling Willie gearing up for a morning qualifier at Sportsman's Park.

Death had been taken completely to the cleaners. Rambling Willie was back.

For those eccentrics who desire a less "rich" version of that episode, preferring instead that the facts be presented without any trace of evangelical fervor, they should consider the blunt but simple explanation

Red Mile General Manager Curt Greene (standing, far right) conducts the retirement ceremonies of Rambling Willie. (United States Trotting Association/George Smallsreed)

offered several years ago by a groom who watched his lightly regarded charge upset a highly regarded celebrity, a media horse whose publicity easily exceeded his talent.

"It don't take no damn genius to figure this situation out at all," he said to an amazed press gathering at his barn after the race.

"He ship in where he ain't wanted, we whip his tail good, then send his ugly ass apackin' down the road."

Within seconds, an era ended.

Microphone in hand once again, Curt Greene concluded the ceremonies by announcing that Rambling Willie, his final appearance on a racetrack almost over, was going to be unhitched and unharnessed for the last time in his illustrious career.

All eyes turned toward Rambling Willie.

For a few moments, an eerie silence hung over the track; only the sounds of leather popping and metal being unsnapped broke the stillness.

At last it was done, the final act completed. Part of the equipment hung on the arms of Rambling Willie's 37-year-old groom, Joe Campbell, the rest in the arms of Ed Brice, the equine operations manager at the Kentucky Horse Park outside Lexington.

It was history, all of it, including Rambling Willie's bike. Its final destination said so loudly: the Hall of Fame of the Trotter in Goshen, New York.

Amidst restrained applause, Campbell began to lead Rambling Willie up the track as Brice followed on the opposite side, nearest the rail, the pair helping to obscure Rambling Willie's naked awkwardness. As the trio moved toward the center of the track and away from the grandstand area, a fan in the railbird section leaned over the concrete abutment and yelled fiercely, "You're the best, Red Man, you're the best! We won't forget you."

Brice turned his head and smiled; Campbell never broke stride.

Walking quickly, Campbell maintained his steady pace up the lane. Tight-lipped and clench-faced, he walked all the way back to the unnumbered and unlettered receiving barn in silent partnership with Brice, responding to his questions or remarks with a nod of his head or short sentences.

Only once did Campbell slacken his speed, when he passed through a small group of well-wishers near the tunnel, halfway between the grandstand and the trio's anonymous destination. They were all Campbell's people—backstretchers. Then he moved on, rapidly.

Campbell and Brice were living proof that one man's meat is another man's poison.

A versatile and complete horseman who had trained both harness and running horses, but whose heart clearly lay with the former, Brice knew that his gain would soon be Campbell's loss, his ecstasy counterbalanced by the latter's agony.

Sensitive to the delicacy of the situation, which had in effect put Brice in the unenviable but official position of "claiming" Rambling Willie for the Kentucky Horse Park, Brice had spent the few days' time since Rambling Willie's arrival making that transition as easy as he could for Campbell, Rambling Willie's groom since early 1981 and now his last remaining connection.

It was a tall order of diplomacy, considering Brice's own intense desire for Rambling Willie, which bordered on outright coveting. And with good reason: in Brice's mind, the legendary pacer would fill a substantial void at the Kentucky Horse Park.

Once back at the nondescript receiving barn, Brice smiled and talked with a small group of photographers and reporters while Campbell completed final preparations for Rambling Willie's transferral to the Kentucky Horse Park, Brice's affable way helping to break the tense silence that hung in the air.

Repeatedly, he tried to open up Campbell for the press, but to no avail, as the latter sought refuge in the stall with the horse, or on his infrequent trips outside the stall kept his back turned to those assembled around him and his answers very short.

When the work was at last done, Campbell headed over to an adjoining barn, letting Brice know as he walked by that when he came back, they would leave.

Returning after a half hour, more than enough time for Brice to fully explain the situation to all assembled, including several camera crews who wanted to film Rambling Willie's departure, Campbell appeared more than anxious to load him and the equipment on the truck that had been provided free of charge by Paxton Van Service. Red eyes and all.

First Rambling Willie, then his equipment bag, and finally his bike were loaded on the small van, the last causing some temporary delay since the sulky's tall shafts barely fit inside the truck.

Brice offered Campbell a seat in the front, which he declined. The door slammed shut, with Campbell inside, squeezed between the bike and Rambling Willie. As the truck drove down the road that ran between the main track and the backstretch, its dull colors flared up brilliantly in the sunlit dust.

Scarlet and gray—the same colors as Rambling Willie's.

The silence was awkward.

Joe Campbell knelt in Rambling Willie's new stall outside the Hall of Champions barn at the rear of the Kentucky Horse Park, bandaging the 13-year-old gelding's legs, which legally under the rules of harness racing were entitled to one more year on the racetrack.

His operatives had declined, and Rambling Willie took an early retirement. He was in good company: his running (Thoroughbred) counterpart, Forego, stood idly across the way.

Campbell, who was now just minutes away from relinquishing his prized charge forever, came out briefly for some more equipment. I was the only writer out there; for that matter, I was the only person out there besides him.

If I made him angry, I might make myself very unhappy. I decided to ask the questions; I needed his answers.

"How has this day been for you?" I asked stupidly.

"Terrible," he said softly. "I'd sooner give up my right arm than give up this horse, you know."

He tried to go on, but couldn't. His eyes watered as his jaws tightened visibly, choking his words to pieces. Stepping back inside the stall, he closed the door diplomatically but completely, and went back to work on Rambling Willie.

Five or ten minutes passed by, then he came out again. I rephrased the question, asking him if he planned to visit Rambling Willie much at his new home.

"Every chance I get," he replied as he began to choke up again. Finally, his eyes stopped watering, and with perfect composure, he fielded a raft of questions I threw at him as the two of us stood there looking at Rambling Willie.

As is the case with most grooms, Campbell has been with horses all his life. Tall and slim in build, he had been a rodeo cowboy once, a calf roper, when in his own words, "I was young and foolish."

That memory brought the first smile I had seen all day to his face. It broadened farther when he recounted Rambling Willie's national tour several years before, a sojourn made in conjunction with the book that covered 16 tracks in 17 cities and included three unscheduled stops in Toledo, Audubon, and The Meadowlands.

That was a glory year for the Greenville, Ohio, native, who now calls Chicago, the Farringtons' main racing base, his home.

Finally, I had all the information I needed and I thanked him for his time.

"Glad to do it," he said. "I'm surprised that someone asked me what I thought. Newspeople never do talk to the grooms. I guess they don't realize a groom is important, too; he can make a lot of difference in a horse. After all, he's the one that takes care of him every day."

As we left the barn together, I took a long shot, hoping to repay the favor he had done me.

I asked if he had gotten a copy of the souvenir poster commemorating Rambling Willie's retirement. His surprised look told me instantly that he knew nothing about the poster. *Bingo*, I thought.

I reached inside the trunk of my car and handed him one. Noticing that I had a few to spare, he asked if he could have several more for his kids and assorted family members.

I gestured to him to take all he wanted.

We talked on a few more minutes. Then, suddenly, he dropped a bombshell.

"I'll tell you something," he said. "Two years, that's what I give this horse. Two years, tops. It's nobody's fault, but retiring this horse is the same as signing its death certificate. This horse can't live without the roar of the crowd. He's just got to have it."

When he finally left, I felt a cold, icy fear. But not for long.

A half hour later, at four o'clock, two employees from the Kentucky Horse Museum and Park's art department arrived at the barn with a newly painted sign for Rambling Willie's stall.

Ed Brice hadn't wasted any time. He had planned well and in advance. Right then, I knew that the old road warrior had passed into the best hands possible.

His Master had seen to that personally.

A young Isaac Murphy, this country's first great black athlete and the first riding dynasty in Kentucky Derby history (Keeneland Library)

Silver Lines, Golden Rider

Isaac Murphy
January 1, 1861—Fayette County, KY
February 12, 1896—Lexington, KY

Tell the world that Isaac Murphy is alive. We saw him yesterday at a race meet in Kentucky. And Chicago. And California. And New York. And Florida. And all the other great racing palaces around the country.

It is true.

For as long as good men and women race good horses anywhere, he will be alive in the hearts of those people.

FEBRUARY 12, 1996, MARKS the centennial of the passing of America's first great black athlete and Thoroughbred racing's first great rider—Isaac Murphy.

A charter member of the National Racing Hall of Fame, Murphy died of pneumonia at age 35 on February 12, 1896, a victim of strenuous weight reducing over the years that had virtually destroyed his health.

A century later, however, his glistening work lives on.

One of Murphy's greatest prizes was the American Derby, an event he took an incredible four of the first five times it was run, that quartet including the inaugural 1884 edition with a champion chestnut filly named Modesty.

Murphy's sensational American Derby performances helped that race quickly become *the* derby in America.

Isaac Murphy (third from right) at a clambake in upstate New York in August of 1890 (Keeneland Library)

But Murphy's saddle élan was not restricted to this giant Chicago race (now run at Arlington International Racecourse, also the site of a stake race named in his honor).

The winner of nearly every major stake in America during his epic career, Murphy also left an enormous imprint on America's most heralded classic—the Kentucky Derby.

He was the first man to win three Kentucky Derbies, a record not equaled until 1930 by Earl Sande and not broken until 1948 by another Hall of Famer, the fabulous Eddie Arcaro.

Murphy was also the first of four men (to date) to take consecutive renewals of the Kentucky Derby. A winner in 1884 with a rogue named Buchanan (a riding commitment he was forced to honor by the stewards), Murphy followed up with Riley in 1890 and Kinsman in 1891.

And to the end, Murphy—who was literally destined for Thoroughbred racing, being born on January 1, the birthday for all Thoroughbreds in the Northern Hemisphere—remained a winner.

The last mount of his fabled 20-year career came on Wednesday, November 13, 1895, at the old Kentucky Association Racetrack in his

Eddie Arcaro is featured here in a handsome portrait shot. The autograph at top is that of fellow Hall of Famer and trainer H. A. "Jimmy" Jones. (Philip Von Borries Collection)

hometown of Lexington, Kentucky, where he nursed a notorious quitter named Tupto to a glorious and well-appreciated victory.

Considered the finest rider of the nineteenth century, and by some of all time, Murphy certainly had the numbers to back it all up.

By his own personal accounts, he had a 44 percent win mark. Existing but incomplete historical records put it at 34 percent. Either way, one

Isaac Murphy (Keeneland Library)

This haunting and rare panoramic action shot shows Isaac Murphy (inside, aboard Salvator) narrowly defeating Tenny (Snapper Garrison up) in the epic 1890 match race that electrified the sporting world and the nation. Close finishes like this were Murphy's forte. His premier talent lay in exactly measuring his opponents. If possible, he always tried to "leave some horse for the next race," rather than gutting them.

Needless to say, this photograph is considered to be one of the greatest ever taken in the history of American Thoroughbred racing. (Keeneland Library)

thing is certain: his lifetime win-percentage rate still stands as the all-time record, far ahead of his closest competitors.

Clearly, Murphy was a money rider in every sense of the word.

A native of Fayette County (whose capital seat is Lexington, centerpiece of the world-famous central Kentucky bluegrass area), his major career victories included a remarkable total of *14 derbies*: five editions of the long-defunct Latonia Derby (at one time, one of the great races in this country), four American Derbies, three Kentucky Derbies, one St. Louis Derby, and one Brooklyn Derby (now the Dwyer).

Other noteworthy career stakes wins included the Suburban, the Travers, the Kentucky Oaks, the Clark (four times), the Phoenix (this country's oldest Thoroughbred stakes race, three times), and the Alabama (twice).

Frank B. Borries Jr., the writer who found Isaac Murphy's long-lost grave after a relentless three-year search (Photo courtesy of Mrs. Frank B. Borries Jr.)

The son of a freeman who died during the Civil War in a Confederate prison camp, Murphy was a brilliant finesse rider who rarely used the whip and who possessed an uncanny sense of pace.

As a man, Murphy was carved in gold, too.

Impeccable in dress, gentle in nature, and socially prominent, Murphy was—above all else—known for his absolute integrity, an almost childlike incorruptibility that drew and kept a large legion of friends of all backgrounds at his side all his life.

Indeed, Murphy's honesty on the turf was as well-known as his consummate riding skills, which were utilized by all the top stables of his time and upon such great racers as Salvator, Firenze, Emperor of Norfolk, Kingston, and many others.

For all that, though, Murphy might well have been lost to the ages had not Lexington, Kentucky, journalist Frank B. Borries Jr. discovered Murphy's lost grave after a torturous three-year search.

Borries's subsequent articles, which began with an exclusive 1961 story in *The Thoroughbred Times*, slowly but surely drew widespread attention to Murphy.

They eventually culminated in Murphy being reinterred at old Man o' War Park in early May of 1967 alongside that racing immortal. Honorary chairman of the event, held shortly before that year's Kentucky Derby, was Eddie Arcaro, the man who had supplanted the duo of Murphy and Earl Sande as the Kentucky Derby's winningest rider.

"I'm certain that had he been born in my time or I in his, we would have been the very best of friends," Arcaro was moved to say at the ceremonies. Coming from the ferociously competitive rider who had once spent a year on the ground due to rough riding, this was indeed a remarkable testament.

A man who wound up having as many graves as he did Kentucky Derby winners, Murphy was buried for the third and final time—alongside Man o' War and some of his famed progeny—outside the front entrance of the Kentucky Horse Park in Lexington, in 1978.

He is a giant who lives on in name and deed.

Saddlemaster of the World

He always honored the challenge.
(Old racing adage)

THOUGH FEW KNOW IT, the rider with the best winning aver-age in Kentucky Derby history is the redoubtable Jimmy "the Wink" Winkfield, who from four turn-of-the-century mounts produced two wins, a second, and a third.

Also the second man to win consecutive runnings of the Run for the Roses, Winkfield was born on April 12, 1882, in Chilesburg, Kentucky, the product of the southern rural-agrarian society of that era that turned out high-caliber riders as a matter of course.

He was a natural from the get-go, a prodigy, a glistening talent who legendary horse trader Colonel Phil Chinn said "just sat up there like a piece of gold." Winkfield also was a man possessed, a situation best described by another horseman: "On the ground, Winkfield was a perfect gentleman, but in the saddle, he was a demon."

The career debut of the voraciously competitive rider, according to his own account, produced monumental trouble.

Aboard a horse aptly named Jockey Joe at Chicago's venerable Hawthorne Racetrack on August 10, 1898, Winkfield gunned his mount out of the four hole and across the path of the inside three horses. His mission was to get to the rail in the five-furlong race.

No one made it, however, and
Winkfield's part in the resulting
"demolition derby"—which combined
the daring of a cat burglar in broad
daylight with the innate recklessness of
a raw but talented rookie—earned him
a trip to the stewards.

Decades later, Winkfield recounted
his hell-bent-for-leather beginning in
a *Sports Illustrated* article entitled
"Around the World in Eighty Years":

> *When the barrier broke, I took him right
> to the rail, right across in front of the
> three inside horses, and we all four went
> down. So the stewards had me up, and
> they asked me where I had been riding.
> "I just rode," I told them. "Ain't you
> never rode before?" they asked me. "No
> sir," I said. So they looked at one
> another for a while, and they put me
> afoot for a year.*

Winkfield's version, however, may
be subject to some modification.

According to volume 2, 1898, of
Goodwin's Official Turf Guide, Winkfield finished second in the August 10
contest by two lengths after a fair start,
and only one horse in the field fell. Further muddying the waters is the fact
that about a month later, on September
6, 1898, he again finished second with
Jockey Joe at Hawthorne.

Jimmy "the Wink" Winkfield: for
twenty cents in wooden nickels, he'd
drop you . . . and never look back. A
fierce competitor, he was also worldly
beyond description, riding in such
faraway places as Russia and France.
(Keeneland Library/C. C. Cook)

Regardless of which account is the correct one, one thing is indis-
putable: When Winkfield returned to riding approximately a year later
(his first winner, according to several sources, was Avenstoke at old
Harlem Racetrack near Chicago on September 18, 1899), all the fire was

still there, perhaps more so. He was just more circumspect about it all, carefully picking his spots. After all, he was a professional rider, and he couldn't do what he did best on the ground.

His attitude thus adjusted to incorporate an ever-so-slight degree of safety, responsibility, and seeming repentance, Winkfield commenced one of the finest and most storied riding careers in the history of Thoroughbred racing.

Occupying the highest echelon of that fabled career is Winkfield's remarkable work in the Kentucky Derby. Long America's most coveted racing prize, Winkfield made his first appearance in 1900, running third with 7-to-1 outsider Thrive.

In 1901, the Wink earned his first Kentucky Derby win with an around-the-horn triumph aboard His Eminence, shaking him up at the eighth pole en route to a 1½-length victory. Last in that edition, which required two starts, was prohibitive 7-to-10 favorite Alard Sheck.

The 1901 campaign was easily Winkfield's best here in America.

Later that season, Winkfield scored another major win there at Churchill Downs with His Eminence, taking the venerable Clark Handicap. Winkfield that same year also garnered a pair of now long-defunct—but at that time grand—racing fixtures: the Tennessee Derby with Royal Victor and the Latonia Derby with Hernando. Coupled with the Kentucky Derby, those scores gave Winkfield a total of three derbies for the season, substantial saddle work in anyone's book.

The next year, Winkfield took another Kentucky Derby. This one came with Alan-a-Dale, and it was a virtual duplicate of the 1901 win, as Winkfield again scored in wire-to-wire fashion and again victimized an odds-on choice (3-to-5 shot Abe Frank, who also ran last).

However, the road home to the 1902 Kentucky Derby roses was anything but easy for Winkfield and his horse.

According to the racing-chart notes, the poetically named Alan-a-Dale, who "outclassed the field, was in front by three lengths after a quarter mile. He widened it to six [lengths] after a half, went lame in the stretch, but carried on with flawless courage to win by a nose."

The back-to-back Kentucky Derby victories thrust Winkfield into an elite company. To date, the pantheon of riders to have taken consecutive Kentucky Derbies numbers four, and when Winkfield turned out his magic, it duplicated the work of just one other, an even more widely heralded black rider.

That was the peerless Isaac Murphy, America's first great black athlete and a charter member of the National Racing Hall of Fame. Considered by a number of historians to be the greatest rider in the history of the sport, Murphy had taken the 1890 and 1891 renewals with Riley and Kingman, respectively.

The difficulty of this feat by first Murphy, then Winkfield, is almost incomprehensible. Some seventy years later, Ron Turcotte became only the third man to score a straight Derby double, accomplishing it via champion Riva Ridge in 1972 and Triple Crown winner/two-time Horse-of-the-Year titlist Secretariat in 1973.

The trio became a quartet in the early 1980s when Eddie Delahoussaye triumphed with Gato del Sol in 1982 and with Sunny's Halo in 1983.

This list is equally remarkable for the jockies it *doesn't* include, the notable absentees being Hall of Famers Eddie Arcaro and Bill Hartack, who share the Kentucky Derby riding record with five wins apiece. It also doesn't include the sport's all-time winningest rider, Bill Shoemaker, whose 8,833 career victories included four Kentucky Derbies (good enough for second-place honors behind Arcaro and Hartack).

Incredible as it may seem, however, Winkfield blew a chance to make it *three* straight Kentucky Derby wins in 1903, and thus move into a riding dimension all by himself.

Displaying uncharacteristically bad judgment, Winkfield made his move too soon with a runner propitiously named Early, and came up empty in the stretch aboard the 3-to-5 odds-on favorite as 10-to-1 outsider Judge Himes rolled on by. In later years, Winkfield would describe Early's second-place Kentucky Derby finish as his greatest regret in racing.

An impulsive and somewhat peripatetic figure, Winkfield left America shortly after his last Kentucky Derby appearance (1903) when a lucrative offer from abroad beckoned him.

Riding until 1930, the multilingual Winkfield rode in a number of countries, including Russia (riding for Czar Nicholas II at one point, so the story goes), Germany, Austria-Hungary, Poland, Spain, and France.

His victories overseas, according to one source, included the Moscow Derby twice (1907 and 1908), a pair of Polish Derbies (1904 and 1905), and the Russian Derby three straight years (1914–16). After his retirement, this self-made man of the world settled down in France, where he trained for a number of years with solid success.

A true Kentucky Derby legend who escaped the Bolsheviks in World War I and the Nazis in World War II, Winkfield died at age 91 on March 23, 1974, just weeks before the centennial running of the Kentucky Derby.

Baseball scouts have a particular phrase in their parlance reserved for the mega-talented marvels they occasionally stumble on and discover. They call such wonders "a complete package" or "a real piece of work."

Historians would go the diamond guys one better. They would call Jimmy Winkfield an American original, a man who gave as good as he got, and in many cases, rendered better than he got.

Had he strode among artistic circles, he would have been hailed as a masterpiece, a classic for all times.

Racing people would remind you that the only color that counts on the racetrack is the color green. Thus, by extension, Winkfield's pronounced ability to bring home that "green" on a regular basis made him worthy of the single highest accolade his colleagues could pay him:

When you are hungry, call on him. He will feed you. Well, and often.

Simple people would just call him a winner—both at his craft and at the even harder task of living—and leave it at that. It's a simple, genuine compliment. It's also an understatement, which under the circumstances cannot be helped.

The lions of life—the true, untarnished giants—are never easily described.

In point of fact, Jimmy Winkfield was all of these and more. Occasionally, the powers above feel compelled to send us mortals down below an example to sustain us all through the rough goings of everyday life.

Possessed of a white-heat talent, viscerally competitive, single-minded in purpose, fiercely courageous and proud, widely respected, inherently decent, and a beloved national racing treasure at the end, Jimmy Winkfield continues to serve us today as a constant reminder that giants of all sizes and colors walk among us.

It was our good fortune to have him with us for as long as we did.

Lost Giants

AMONG THE LOST GIANTS of American Thoroughbred racing are late-nineteenth-century black reinsmen Anthony "Tony" Hamilton and Shelby "Pike" Barnes.

Born in 1866 in South Carolina, Hamilton rode for some of the greatest owners of his era, notably August Belmont Sr. and Jr., Pierre Lorillard, Billy Lakeland, Mike Dwyer, and J. R. Keene.

Hamilton's list of major career victories and mounts includes the 1895 Suburban Handicap astride Lazzarone; the 1887 American Derby with C. H. Todd; the 1881 Phoenix Handicap aboard Sligo; the 1896 Metropolitan Handicap on Counter Tenor; the Brooklyn Handicap twice, in 1889 with Exile and in 1895 on Hornpipe; the 1890 (Belmont) Futurity and the 1891 Lawrence Realization Stakes with Potomac; the inaugural 1887 running of the Gazelle Handicap with Hall of Fame race mare Firenze and the 1890 edition of that race with Amazon; the 1889 and 1890 Monmouth Oaks with Senorita and Her Highness, respectively; the 1891 Sapling Stakes with Air Plant; and the 1892 Swift Stakes on Vestibule.

Other top-level scores by Hamilton were the old St. Louis Derby in 1888 with Falcon, the inaugural 1890 Toboggan Handicap on Fides, and five runnings of the Twin City Handicap at old Sheepshead Bay

Tony Hamilton aboard Pickpocket in 1893 (Keeneland Library)

Racetrack (Louisette in 1886, Exile in 1888 and 1889, Lamplighter in 1892, and Dorian in 1894).

Though he never won a riding title, Hamilton was a consistently top-ranked reinsman. His best year was a second-place tie with Fred Taral in 1891; both had 154 wins behind champion Hugh Penny.

Hamilton, whose date and location of death are unknown, also rode overseas. According to a 1902 news item, he rode five winners out of seven mounts in Warsaw, Poland, in May of 1902.

The roster of ace triumphs by Barnes is equally staggering.

His saddle work included the 1890 Belmont Stakes and the 1890 Brooklyn Derby (now known as the Dwyer) on Burlington, the 1890 Alabama Stakes on Sinaloa II, the 1889 Travers Stakes on Long Dance, the 1890 Sheridan Stakes on Santiago, the 1891 Brooklyn Handicap aboard Tenny, the 1889 Champagne Stakes with June Day, the inaugural 1888

Futurity at Belmont aboard the notorious Proctor Knott, and the fabled Latonia Derby in 1888 with White (in a dead heat with Los Angeles).

Barnes's most famous losing effort may have been in the 1889 Kentucky Derby.

Astride the aforementioned Proctor Knott, Barnes had his hands full from start to finish with the 1-to-2 favorite. Wildly fractious at the gate, Proctor Knott broke away twice (once galloping off for an eighth of a mile) and almost unseated his rider both times.

From there, matters only got worse.

Finally getting away with the field, Proctor Knott fought Barnes for his head and got the lead a quarter of a mile into the race. Approaching the backstretch turn, the horse had accrued a five-length lead, which he then proceeded to waste as he bolted for the outside rail.

Regaining control, Barnes kept the tiring Proctor Knott on the far outside for the stretch run, while 16-to-1 long shot Spokane, who had been steadily advancing all the while on the rail, reached second place and a good striking position at the stretch call.

Fighting tooth and nail to the wire, Spokane emerged the winner by a nose (following a protracted review by the stewards). Capping off the whole affair was the fact that the winner had come home in stakes-record time, meaning that if Proctor Knott had maintained his manners and a reasonably straight course, he—and not Spokane—would have been the record-setting victor of the 15th Kentucky Derby.

Among the major owners that patronized Barnes were such renowned turf giants as Lucky Baldwin, Marcus Daly, and J. B. Haggin.

According to *Goodwin's Official Turf Guide*, Barnes's sterling career work also included consecutive national riding crowns in 1888 and 1889. The 1888 campaign was a monster season for Barnes, who piloted a gargantuan 206 triumphs from 626 mounts. It is significant to note that his closest pursuer for riding honors that year did not even tally 100 wins.

Barnes posted numbers almost as good in 1889, bagging 170 winners from 661 mounts for his second straight American saddle title.

A little more is known about Barnes's life than Hamilton's, though the origin of his moniker "Pike" remains a mystery.

Born in 1871 in Beaver Dam, New York, Barnes died of lung trouble at age 37 on January 7, 1908, in Columbus, Ohio (where he is buried). It was reported at the time of his death that though Barnes had earned substantial money during his fine career, he nonetheless died penniless.

Kentucky Kings

ONLY ONCE SINCE 1895,
when the *Daily Racing Form*
began keeping formal statistical
records on American Thoroughbred
racing, has a family turned out both
a national champion rider and a
national champion trainer.

That extraordinary distinction
belongs to a black family, the heralded Perkins family of Lexington,
Kentucky, that produced brothers
James "Soup" Perkins (1880–1911)
and Will Perkins (1875–1927).

James "Soup" Perkins, who
gained his nickname from his
favorite food, was this country's first
officially recognized national riding
champion (that is, by the *Daily
Racing Form*). In that year, 1895, he
bagged 192 wins from 762 mounts.

James Perkins (Keeneland Library)

Pictured here is James "Soup" Perkins (jauntily holding cane, and possibly "holding court" as well) with friends. Eighteen-ninty-five was a blockbuster year for Perkins. At the ripe old age of 15, he bagged this country's first official national riding championship. That work also included the 1895 Kentucky Derby with Halma. (Keeneland Library)

One of those victories was aboard Halma in the Kentucky Derby. Perkins was all of 15 at the time of his 1895 Kentucky Derby triumph, making him one of the two youngest winning riders in Kentucky Derby history (the other is yet another black reinsman, Alonzo "Lonnie" Clayton, who won the 1892 Kentucky Derby with Azra).

Perkins, who was classed a good finisher with nerve and judgment, later that season took another major fixture at Churchill Downs with Halma—the Clark Handicap.

Besides Kentucky Derby–Clark hero Halma, other top career mounts piloted by Soup Perkins included Hall of Fame champion Henry of Navarre; Orinda, victress of the 1894 Latonia Oaks; Lady Inez, the 1896 Tennessee Oaks heroine; and Prince Lief, winner of the St. Louis Derby and Phoenix Handicap in 1896.

Perkins's career work also included a five-for-six performance at the old Kentucky Association Racetrack on October 30, 1893 (overall, he

Trainer Will Perkins (left), the national champion trainer of 1926, and his brother, Eddie Perkins, his longtime stable agent (Keeneland Library)

tallied five wins and a second that day); four of the first seven races at Saratoga on August 13, 1894; and another five-for-six day, this one at Saratoga on August 23, 1894, that quintet including a nice stake called the Californian.

Weight, the age-old nemesis of jockeys, curtailed the riding career of Soup Perkins in the late 1890s. He then turned to training horses, but died prematurely at age 31 in mid-August 1911 while at a race meet in Hamilton, Ontario, Canada. Heart failure was reported as the cause of death.

The second half of the Perkins family's unique record was written in 1926, when Soup Perkins's brother, Will Perkins, took the national training championship with 82 winners.

Unlike his younger brother, Will Perkins never did win a Kentucky Derby. Still, he fared well in that race, with a pair of thirds (John Finn in 1922 and Son of John in 1925) from the six starters he sent out between 1915 and 1925.

Perhaps the best racehorse Will Perkins ever handled was the superb Billy Kelly. A winner of 39 of 69 races whose forte was sprinting, Billy Kelly was trained by Perkins until August of his two-year-old season (1919), when he was sold to other interests.

While under the care of Perkins, Billy Kelly won such prestigious stakes as the Bashford Manor Stakes, the Idle Hour Stakes, the Flash Stakes, and the United States Hotel Stakes (all under the hands of black jockey Roscoe Simpson).

Will Perkins's solid foundation work showed the following season when Billy Kelly ran second in the 1919 Kentucky Derby to stablemate Sir Barton, America's first Triple Crown winner.

Blood poisoning, the result of a bruised toe, claimed the life of Will Perkins in 1927 at age 52.

James "Soup" Perkins and Will Perkins, two Kentucky kings of yesteryear, are both buried in Lexington, Kentucky. James "Soup" Perkins is in the old No. 2 Cemetery on East Seventh Street (where legendary Hall of Famer Isaac Murphy was once interred); Will Perkins is buried in Cove Haven Cemetery (formerly Greenwood Cemetery).

Interestingly enough, within sight of Will Perkins's grave is the final resting place of another great black horse trainer, Raleigh Colston Jr. (circa 1862–1928), a longtime friend who shared a racetrack barn with Will Perkins for many a racing season.

Good King Edward

THE CENTERPIECE OF THE 1877 Kentucky Derby won by Baden-Baden was the legendary black trainer Ed "Brown Dick" Brown, who along with riders Isaac Murphy and Willie Simms, is one of three black Thoroughbred racing sportsmen enshrined in the National Racing Hall of Fame at Saratoga Springs, New York.

Reputedly one of the wealthiest racing personalities in the country during his lifetime, the thrifty Brown—so the stories go—usually carried a bankroll of $75,000 cash. His success in racing, however, which culminated in his election to the Hall of Fame in 1984, thoroughly belied his roots.

Born into slavery in 1850 in Lexington, Kentucky, Brown began working at age seven for R. A. Alexander, who stood the famed racehorse and fabulous sire Lexington at his Woodburn Farm.

One of Lexington's many champions was the sensational colt Asteroid, undefeated in 12 lifetime starts, including 9 forays at three, when Brown became his regular rider.

Following Alexander's death in 1867, Brown went to work for Baden-Baden's owner, Daniel Swigert, a breeder of three Kentucky Derby winners in a six-year span (1881 through 1886).

One horse that Brown rode was a sprinter named Brown Dick, and because Brown was an excellent footracer, people said he was almost as

Hall of Fame trainer Ed Brown (Keeneland Library)

fast as the horse he was riding. In time, he acquired the runner's name as his nickname (Ed "Brown Dick" Brown).

Brown's greatest success in the irons came when he rode Swigert's Kingfisher to victory in the 1870 Belmont Stakes.

By then, however, Brown was beginning to put on weight, and two years later he became the trainer of Swigert's stable. Between that time and his death in 1906, Brown developed a number of outstanding runners.

Directly or indirectly, Brown was connected with four Kentucky Derby winners.

He saddled the aforementioned Baden-Baden—the winner of the third Kentucky Derby, in 1877—and put the foundation on three others who went on to capture The Run for the Roses in someone else's hands: Hindoo (1881), Ben Brush (1896), and Plaudit (1898).

Brown is buried in Midway, Kentucky, which is part of central Kentucky's famed bluegrass horse region.

Author's Note: The group of black turfmen in the Racing Hall of Fame currently numbers four, trainer Ansel Williamson having been elected in 1998.

Little Big Man

THIS YEAR MARKS THE centennial of the first Kentucky Derby win by Hall of Fame reinsman Willie Simms, one of this country's greatest riders, who was a star jockey on both sides of the Atlantic.

Born in Augusta, Georgia, in 1870, Simms as a young man was attracted to the bright colors of the racing silks that he saw at various county fairs. He determined then to become a rider, and without the consent of his parents, set out for New York.

The first American reinsman to win in England, Simms gained notice there for his "short-stirrup" style: riding far forward, crouched over the neck and the withers of the horse, his feet tucked into short stirrups.

Though some credit the epic Tod Sloan with introducing the short-stirrup style (long the American way of riding) to the British turf, most historians today agree that Sloan only popularized the method. Simms, they say, was the one who showed it to the English turf first.

Following his overseas success in the early 1890s, Simms returned home and won both Kentucky Derbies in which he competed.

The first came in 1896 with the brilliant champion Ben Brush, a memorable victory called the Bloody Spurs Derby because it left the winner's flanks dripping with blood following a grueling stretch drive and the rider beside himself for having so punished the horse.

Handsome, articulate, and talented, Hall of Fame reinsman Willie Simms endures today as one of the sport's brightest—and truest—stars. (Keeneland Library)

Simms took his other Kentucky Derby triumph with Plaudit in 1898. That same year, Simms piloted Sly Fox to a score in the Preakness.

His work in a series of races that are today called the Triple Crown included back-to-back Belmont Stakes wins in 1893 and 1894 with Comanche and Henry Of Navarre, respectively.

For the record, Simms remains today the only black competitor (jockey, trainer, or owner) ever to have won all three legs of the American Triple Crown series (though not in the same year).

Following a highly successful career as a jockey, one that saw Simms win nearly every major stakes race in America, Simms turned to training in 1902.

A wealthy man because of wise investments, Simms never married and lived with his widowed mother in Asbury, New Jersey, where he died of pneumonia in 1927 at age 57.

Willie Simms was elected to the National Racing Hall of Fame in 1977.

Willie Simms (Keeneland Library)

Black Triple Crown History Chart

The following is a list of all known and possible American Triple Crown–event wins by black jockeys and trainers.

KENTUCKY DERBY (Inaugurated 1875)

Jockeys

> Oliver Lewis (Aristides, 1875)
>
> William "Billy" Walker (Baden-Baden, 1877)
>
> George Garrett Lewis (Fonso, 1880)
>
> Babe Hurd (Apollo, 1882)
>
> Isaac Murphy (Buchanan, 1884; Riley, 1890; Kingman, 1891)
>
> Erskine Henderson (Joe Cotton, 1885)
>
> Isaac Lewis (Montrose, 1887)
>
> Alonzo "Lonnie" Clayton (Azra, 1892)
>
> James "Soup" Perkins (Halma, 1895)
>
> Willie Simms (Ben Brush, 1896; Plaudit, 1898)
>
> Jimmy "the Wink" Winkfield (His Eminence, 1901; Alan-a-Dale, 1902)

Kansas City, Missouri, native Alonzo "Lonnie" Clayton was the winner of the 1892 Kentucky Derby aboard Azra at age 15. He and Soup Perkins are the youngest winning jockeys in Kentucky Derby history. (Keeneland Library)

Trainers

Ansel Williamson (Aristides, 1875)

James Williams (Vagrant, 1876)* *[His race is not specifically known.]*

Ed "Brown Dick" Brown (Baden-Baden, 1877)

Raleigh Colston Sr. (Leonatus, 1883)* *[Some sources list John McGinty.]*

William "Billy" Bird (Buchanan, 1884)

Alex Perry (Joe Cotton, 1885)

Dud Allen (Kingman, 1891)

Winning Kentucky Derby Black Rider-Trainer Tandems

Oliver Lewis–Ansel Williamson (Aristides, 1875), inaugural running

Billy Walker–Ed Brown (Baden-Baden, 1877)

Isaac Murphy–William "Billy" Bird (Buchanan, 1884)

Erskine Henderson–Alex Perry (Joe Cotton, 1885)

Isaac Murphy–Dud Allen (Kingman, 1891)

PREAKNESS (Inaugurated 1873)

Jockeys

Willie Simms (Sly Fox, 1898)

BELMONT (Inaugurated 1867)

Jockeys

Ed "Brown Dick" Brown (Kingfisher, 1870)

Shelby "Pike" Barnes (Burlington, 1890)

Willie Simms (Comanche, 1893; Henry Of Navarre, 1894)

Trainers

Raleigh Colston Sr. (Kingfisher, 1870)

*Presently under historical review

Hall of Fame trainer Ansel Williamson, whose many stars included the winner of the inaugural 1875 Kentucky Derby—Aristides (National Museum of Racing and Hall of Fame)

Ansel Williamson (Calvin, 1875)
Albert Cooper (Burlington, 1890)

Winning Belmont Black Rider-Trainer Tandems

Ed Brown–Raleigh Colston Sr. (Kingfisher, 1870)
Shelby "Pike" Barnes–Albert Cooper (Burlington, 1890)

HALL OF FAMERS

Jockeys: Isaac Murphy, Willie Simms
Trainers: Ed Brown, Ansel Williamson

VI

PORTRAITS, TRIBUTES, AND FEATURES

The Niatross Trilogy

The Twilight Zone Pacer
Reflections in Purple
Lost in Time

The "Twilight Zone Pacer" himself, the incomparable Niatross: Clint Galbraith behind the wheels of this mighty racer (United States Trotting Association)

Hoofbeats magazine (March 1984, Part 1 of a three-part series) Originally published in The Standardbred (November 5, 1980)

The Twilight Zone Pacer

NORMALLY, THE JUDGES' STAND high above the Red Mile racetrack in Lexington, Kentucky, is about the last place you want to be during a race. After you've seen a few hundred races, the horses and the results all tend to blur together and the novelty of having the "best seat in the house" wears thin.

In the three years I've worked as a judge's assistant, posting photos and the call numbers, I've developed claustrophobia, acrophobia, and severe frustration at not being able to bet, occasionally sip a cold beer, or pathologically lie about my winning and losing streaks.

Worst of all, never at any time have I been able to socialize with the beautiful ladies who frequently stroll the grounds, because when you're located 125 feet up in the air, it's dangerous to fly, gauche to yell, and impossible to cover that much distance on the ground without losing them. The only thing that makes it all worthwhile is how well you're getting paid.

But on the afternoon of October 1, 1980, my assessment of that seat radically changed as I watched a gargantuan pacer named Niatross time-trial in 1:49.1, shattering the previous world record of 1:52 set by Steady Star in 1971.

When Niatross set foot on the track shortly after the seventh race, he was already the fastest horse around in a race. Earlier in the season, he

had come in at 1:52.4 in Syracuse, knocking down Abercrombie's rela‑
tively new record of 1:53.

His appearance was more than eagerly expected and in sharp contrast
to his previous outing. On the Saturday before, a crowd of over 6,000 fans
had surged through the Red Mile gates, filling the tiny plant, eagerly antic‑
ipating the assault on Steady Star's mark. They all left disappointed some
hours later when trainer‑driver Clint Galbraith decided that both the tem‑
perature and the wind were less than optimum.

To racing officials and knowledgeable racing fans alike, the decision
was easy to understand. Galbraith was looking for minimum wind resis‑
tance and high heat.

While the wind factor is obvious, the temperature factor is a subtle
nuance of harness racing based upon many horsemen's belief that a colt or
stallion will go faster when it's hot, a filly or mare when it's cooler. In short,
Galbraith was looking for a clean, hot Kentucky summer day at the top of
October; he might as well have asked that Niatross go in 1:49 and change.

That apprehension about the volatility of Grand Circuit weather
explained why, briefly, management and racing officials tried to talk
Galbraith into going. He might not have a better day. Still, they under‑
stood and backed his decision.

Downstairs, the capacity crowd reacted differently when the
announcement was made that no assault would be made that day on the
record. A perfunctory parade down the track scarcely placated the crowd,
which began, on a restrained level, to murmur, hiss, and even boo at the
1979 harness Horse‑of‑the‑Year and the sport's all‑time leading money
winner with earnings of over $1.7 million.

Clearly, they wanted more than just a look at the great champion.

Four days later, on a sunny Wednesday that produced a perfect 79‑
degree temperature and still winds that saw the flag wrapped around the
pole behind the winner's circle like two homely blind dates embracing
each other, the crowd got what they wanted and more.

Official attendance records listed the crowd that day as exactly 4,132,
no doubt including some hard‑core faithful and returnees from the previ‑
ous Saturday's aborted effort. In the years to come, I'm certain I will meet,
read about, or hear from at least twice that number who will all claim to
have been there that day. It doesn't bother me; that's the hallmark of a
great sporting achievement. It makes believers out of the nonbelievers, and
liars out of both.

Incredibly, I damn near missed it all. At 4:19 in the afternoon, the blooded son of Albatross out of Niagara Dream came with a rush toward the start just as I was beginning the long descent to post the seventh-race photo in the clubhouse and grandstand photo boxes.

Instantly realizing what was about to happen, the presiding judge, Bob Steele, yelled to me, "Forget the photo, Phil. History's coming!"

Getting no immediate response, the door flew open and he came out to find me frozen on the stairs, photo in hand. Unable to explain to me in detail in the few seconds that were left that Niatross was coming in a hurry, he simply grabbed me by the arm and hauled me back into the judges' stand to the best seat in the house. It would prove to be the first of two major dents that my right arm incurred that day.

Clearly, the man did not want me to miss this piece of history. Pushing me rapidly to the front of the stand, I caught sight of the track and then the horses not more than 100 feet from the start.

If there had been fanfare on the previous Saturday, it was all business four days later. Quickly gaining momentum, Niatross moved with swiftness past the starting wire; at the same time, the two Thoroughbred prompters moved square into position, one at his side, one directly behind him.

To his credit, veteran track announcer Carl Becker left no stone unturned in his call. Most would have been satisfied to simply and routinely call out the times at every position, as is usually done in most time trials.

But this was not your ordinary time trial, with the horse simply racing against time. For Niatross was in effect racing against Steady Star, and the fractions given on a comparative basis would tell an entirely different story.

Shrewdly, Becker had done his research before the race, getting the fractions of Steady Star's own record, which he compared to Niatross's at every call. Any idiot could read the time on the tote board, but with Becker's help, no one at the track that day was left in the dark about how well Niatross was doing.

Shortly before Niatross hit the quarter pole, Becker reminded the crowd that Steady Star's first fraction was $28\frac{2}{5}$. An instant later, Niatross motored past in $27\frac{3}{5}$ as the crowd roared. At the half, Niatross and the invisible Steady Star were on even terms, as both hit the pole in $54\frac{3}{5}$.

There was an audible groan. Steady Star was gaining ground, Niatross was losing. Little did they know it, but that would be the last time that Steady Star was ever in the race.

Announcer Carl Becker, one of the great names—and personalities—in the harness racing sport (Courtesy of Kurt Becker)

Coming to the three-quarters pole, Becker told the audience that Steady Star's time was 1:23 flat, a call that was never heard as Niatross reached it in 1:21.4 and a deafening roar consumed the entire track.

Then all hell broke loose.

The crowd didn't need Becker anymore to tell them what was obvious. Niatross was going to get the record, smash through the 1:50 barrier, and perhaps into the twilight zone of the unthinkable time: less than 1:50, and on into the 1:40s.

Like father, like son. Carl Becker's equally gifted son, Kurt Becker, is a seasoned harness racing caller whose Thoroughbred racing résumé includes a prestigious trio—Arlington International Racecourse, Churchill Downs, and Keeneland Racecourse. (Courtesy of Kurt Becker)

Louder and louder they seemed to cry, vibrating the entire rickety wooden stands that housed all the officials. Long before Galbraith and Niatross hit the wire, the crowd knew what was later confirmed: that at the three-quarters pole, Niatross had the record.

It was just a matter now of by how much.

Coming into the stretch, Galbraith daringly allowed the horse to drift out a shade, carrying the outside prompter, Freddie Bach, with him. The intent was to allow the rear prompter, Dennis Lacey, to come up on the

Niatross lights up the board with his world-record mile, going where no one had gone before. (United States Trotting Association)

inside, delude Niatross into thinking that a horse was gaining on him, and thereby further push the pace.

Reflecting on that then, I found it hard to believe that you would have to push a horse who merely needs to come home in a tick under 30 seconds to have the world record after going three different quarters in almost identical 27-second patterns. Looking back on it now, I realize what Galbraith meant. He was not pushing for the record, he was pushing Niatross for the greatest suspension of time he could get, by his own admission around 1:50 and change.

He got more than he bargained for.

At the wire, Galbraith turned to see it flash up 1:49.1, which sent the crowd wild with ecstasy, continuing to drown out Carl Becker (who had not been heard from since the three-quarters pole).

Becker finally gave up amidst the swell.

Steady Star's 1:52 was not just a ghost. Time had stood still, if only for an instant, and it was all Niatross had needed to shatter the record by nearly three full seconds.

Events like this affect everyone differently, producing an eccentric variety of madness and euphoria. As Galbraith continued around the first turn, all the while talking to his prompters, that variety began to manifest itself.

The judges were the first set I noticed. Over in the left-hand corner, Associate Judge John Jenuine smiled as I had never seen him smile before, from ear to ear, his face seeming to say that Jenuine's Thoroughbred competitors had nothing on him this day. Bob Steele, the presiding judge, whose physical presence would awe anyone, kept saying one line over and over: "You'll never see a better day of racing in your life—NEVER."

The kid of the group, Billy Emerson, just looked out at the track, absolutely transfixed. There was nothing for him to say. It had all been done. All had one thing in common. For five solid minutes, they clapped. In all the time I had known them, I had never seen this kind of display of emotion.

But then, I had never seen a race like this.

Down on the track, I could see starter Greg Coon, acknowledged by many as perhaps the best track man in the country. He had prepared the track, and now it begged the question: Who was faster, the track or Niatross? Or had they both been equal to each other and the occasion?

Briefly, the greatness of the moment was interrupted when the TV man stormed in the door, adjusted the color monitor for the replay, then viciously delivered another dent to my shoulder. I knew what for.

Earlier in the afternoon, a group of us had formed a pool, betting on Niatross's final time. Originally, he had spotted Niatross at 1:49 and change, then had been talked out of it, only to lose to the owner of C&J Harness Publications, Carmen Guzzetta. In addition to publishing all the programs at the Red Mile and Louisville Downs, Carmen had spotted Niatross shrewdly at 1:50.2, well off the record but more than close enough to win the $10 pool.

"You bastard," he swore at me, "you don't know nothing about harness racing. I don't know why the hell I ever listened to you. Damn, I could have won the whole pool. But, oh no. I listened to that crap of yours about a slightly-less-than-fast track, and now someone's got my money. I just don't believe it."

As the door slammed behind him, I went back over to the edge of the judges' stand and looked out. The real madness was down there, and started to increase as Galbraith slowly worked his way back down the track toward us.

Below, I could see the grandstand crowd pressed against the concrete abutments. The clubhouse clientele was pressed up against the window, all trying to catch a glimpse of the pacer as he went by.

But the biggest scene was at the three-quarters pole down through the stretch.

By the scores, the fans had come out on the track even before the race was over, unable to resist the temptation to see if what had happened was real. They had been the first to realize something big was happening when the three-quarters time of 1:21⅘ flashed up on the board.

Under normal circumstances, they would have been ejected, but these were not normal circumstances. Briefly, they had seen immortality come by, and it was real. Shrewdly, they knew Galbraith would have to come back with the great horse and they could share that moment over again. No one could blame them for standing there where they had no right to be. Their right to be there had been defined and secured when Niatross had passed them in 1:21⅘.

Not surprisingly, Galbraith and Niatross would pass that way again much slower. Lined up on each side, like a wedding party welcoming the bride and groom, Galbraith would part them like Moses parting the Red Sea. They would let him through, but only after he had shook all of their hands or allowed them to either touch the horse, slap him on the back, or both.

That was the last of Galbraith's obstacles before he finally left the track for the day with the great pacer who wasn't even distressed by the world-record effort.

It proved to be more difficult than standing at attention for several minutes while the crowd continued to applaud, then being taken incredibly into the winner's circle for more photographs, then out for more applause and quotes, and finally up the track toward the three-quarter-mile well-wishers.

On his way, he passed a group of surveyors who earlier had recorded Niatross's stride in the stretch. Now they were at the finish line, and they looked just as pleased at the results as they did at the final time of Niatross. And that in itself produced a few more facts about the great pacer who several weeks earlier had set six records in winning the prestigious Little Brown Jug.

Those facts I later learned at the barn, the kind that make, to quote a cliché, giant legends.

Niatross's stride had been measured at 23 feet, 5 inches. Steady Star's was an even 22 feet.

And while the normal pacer took a 55- to 58-inch hobble (completely extended), Niatross measured out at a full 61½ inches.

There was no comparison there with Steady Star, who went free-legged, but clearly the point was made. Niatross was different to say the least, and big, a shade over 16 hands high. There was absolutely nothing average about him.

And there was more.

As I watched his groom, Marie Carson, hotwalk him in the background, I listened to the banter of a few brave souls who wanted to enjoy the magic of the moment forever. Forget the fact that it was getting nippy, the temperature was dropping, and it was getting dark. The sun was almost gone, and like it or not, the day had to end.

From the Red Mile, Niatross would go to Roosevelt to triumph in the Messenger Stakes, the last leg in pacing's Triple Crown. Niatross had already won the first two legs, the Cane at Yonkers and the Little Brown Jug at Delaware, Ohio. Still, whatever he did after this performance almost seemed anticlimactic. He would easily repeat as harness Horse-of-the-Year.

Then possibly on to California. Someone else added that Niatross might still go faster. Even with a jacket on, I felt a chill go up my spine. There was also talk that he would compete as a four-year-old, which would be an entirely moot point, because ownership of the horse was now locked up in litigation.

Knowing lawyers, the third hardy groom allowed that if they didn't have it settled by January at the latest, Niatross would have to stay in training because by then it would be too late to stand him at stud.

Out of the corner of my eye, I spotted Milo Folley, his wife, Marsha, and their new baby daughter, Brooke, just taking it all in like me. I introduced myself and congratulated Milo on one of his award-winning pieces that had recently appeared in *Hub Rail* magazine.

For a few minutes we exchanged pleasantries, each trying to hone Niatross's achievement down to mere mortal terms. We couldn't. All we could do was stand there and enjoy the euphoria of it all.

Distressingly late for work, I finally had to take my leave of them. As I turned, I noticed Milo's daughter yawning. Yes, it had been a long day, and we were all more tired than we realized.

I walked away, then turned to see Niatross one more time. Marie Carson was still walking him, even though the afternoon had become a chilly dusk.

By God, I thought, we know how fast you can go. Now if we just knew who owned you, maybe we could create another one like you.

Hoofbeats magazine (April 1984, Part 2 of a three-part series) Originally published in The Standardbred (December 17, 1980)

Reflections in Purple

TIME WILL SOON HAVE established the ownership and future stallion quarters of Niatross, with prodding from the American legal system, but it has not in the least diminished the aura of his world record 1:49⅕ pace at Lexington's Red Mile on October 1 of this year, which secured for him the title of the fastest Standardbred ever in the history of harness racing.

An event like this always produces intelligent reflections, but only long after the fact. This is the natural course of human behavior, in the main due to the vulnerability of the human heart.

The human heart is a fragile, high-strung instrument that is utterly without guile. Caught up in and transfixed by a moment like Niatross's record, it responded quickly and without proper regard for the consequences in a wild profusion and rapid succession of love, shock, joy, bewilderment, and ecstasy.

In self-defense, the mind retreated automatically, refusing to be seen in public once again with its idiot sibling, who nakedly showered affection on a mere pacer without even so much as a formal introduction.

Now that the heart has composed itself, the mind can return to that record-setting day to objectively translate what the heart felt and saw as Niatross changed the mad illusion of a sub-1:50 mile into a glittering reality.

Flying Locomotion: Niatross, with Clint Galbraith in the sulky, shows the exquisite and powerful stride that earned him records, championships, and quasi-immortality. (United States Trotting Association)

In the process, the mind has joined with the heart to clarify facts, revive memories, and in short order methodically justify every damn bit of the wild emotion and passion that flowed that wonderful fall day, from the judges' stand to the three-quarter pole, where stood a standing-room-only crowd, down past the grandstand railbirds to the elite clubhouse gallery.

Some of these reflections are simple, others are subtle and complex, and a few simply serve to separate fact from fiction. Nonetheless, they all provide us with delicious little vignettes and insights that solely entrusted to the heart would surely be lost forever.

Shortly after the time trial, I heard a railbird casually remark that the Thoroughbred prompters seemed to have trouble keeping up with Niatross.

Thankfully, they never chose to exert their "superiority" by running past him and aborting a historic effort.

Trainer/driver Clint Galbraith and "King Purple"—the brilliant Niatross (United States Trotting Association)

Yet unwittingly this racing fan corroborated a later remark in the barn area that Niatross's time for the mile roughly equaled that of a Thoroughbred leisurely galloping the same distance.

Watching Niatross cool out at the barn, I could not believe his condition. He was not distressed in the least. No sweat, no lather, no nothing. As he passed me for the tenth time, my stare must have caught him.

He returned it with a calm look in his eyes that seemed to say, "Yes, I just went in 1:49 and change, and I could do it again if I had to."

I could believe it.

I do not believe, however, that the tote board actually melted from the intense heat of his fractions that day or the report that Red Mile security several days later arrested a trespasser named Father Time, who was found wandering aimlessly around the track, mumbling incoherently, carrying a broken stopwatch in his hand.

That kind of romance belongs in a Harlequin novel.

However, a good case for incarceration could be made for another individual—who shall remain nameless for reasons of his own personal safety—who questioned what was so special about Niatross's "run" of 1:49.1. One has a feeling that if this idiot were to view the Venus de Milo in the Louvre at Paris, he would ask what was so special about a broad with no arms.

And at least one informed source failed to see the beauty of Niatross's moment at the Red Mile in October. Several weeks after the effort, *Sports Illustrated* carried a story on Niatross sweeping the pacing Triple Crown with a win in the Messenger, while briefly mentioning his Red Mile mark as an aside.

At this point, I could be accused of being self-serving, since that magazine had rejected my account of the event. But I am not a small person. I have the facts on my side.

It is now safe to say that never in the history of harness racing in particular, and racing in general, has a sweep of the Triple Crown ever meant so little.

In the Messenger, Niatross vanquished routinely (as is his habit) all competition.

At the Red Mile, he challenged the greatest foe of all—time itself— and spread his remains all over the red-clay track like so many losing tickets.

It is equally safe to state that there has not been a better performance by a horse anywhere in the world this year in any form of racing, possibly for all time. In setting the record, Niatross stamped an indelible trademark on the very sport of harness racing itself, giving it a standard of quality no one will ever again question.

If Thoroughbred racing has its Man o' War, harness racing now has its Niatross, and only the very ignorant or very prejudiced can fail to understand the import of that statement.

Literally, as well as figuratively, Niatross enriched everyone he came in contact with.

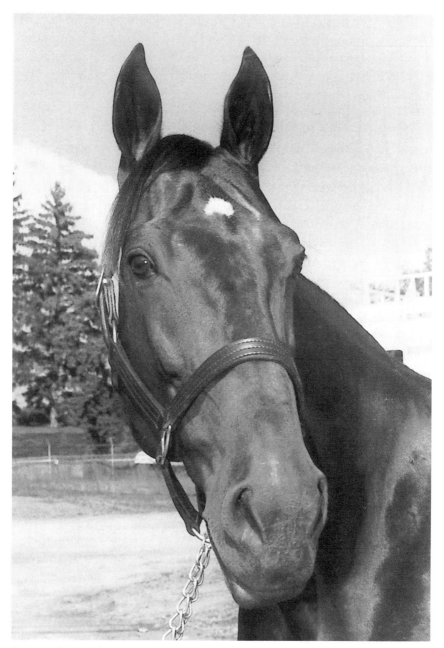

Portrait of a Wunderkind in His Golden Years—Niatross at Delaware, Ohio, in 1996 at age 19 (United States Trotting Association)

On the day after his record feat, the photo-finish man at the Red Mile, Bob Nash, casually asked me to help him print an additional 250 copies of Niatross crossing the wire in 1:49⅕.

The initial printing of 75 copies had completely sold out on Thursday afternoon, and Nash planned a marathon printing session beginning at 11 that night and ending at 6:30 on Friday morning.

It was the only way to meet the huge public demand.

For me, it meant 36 hours without sleep, as I was working two jobs. I demurred slightly, until Nash told me that I would be getting $15 an hour. At that point, greed prevailed over common sense.

Thus, it came to be at 6:30 the next morning I found myself more than $100 richer, eight hours poorer in sleep, and sucking on wood like a common cribber, the last a result of myself alternately drying prints, then laying my head down on the rickety wooden stand in the announcer's booth for occasional rest.

In the weeks that have passed since all these events, I have tried to figure out rationally and intelligently why Niatross's record pace affected me so profoundly.

It's really not so hard to figure out, if you just stop and think about it.

And best of all, you don't need a USTA license, a subscription to a harness journal, or a degree from Harvard. Just a basic ability to both see and observe, as Sherlock Holmes habitually admonished Dr. Watson to do.

Simply put, Niatross appealed to all that is good and noble and decent in life itself. In an age of antiheroes, he had resurrected the rare personage of a true hero who could endure and overcome all challenges.

In an age of cheap hype, despair, cynicism, insensitivity, shoddy workmanship, and inferior goods, he had delivered unparalleled quality.

He enabled us to forget, for at least one brief moment, all our fears, shortcomings, and failures, and forced us to take stock of our assets.

He had reaffirmed basic human values, exalted the beat of life, and sanctified the pursuit of excellence. Freed temporarily from our natural reserve, we dared to live and dream.

And yes, if we felt somewhat small in the presence of Niatross and the magnificence of his achievement, he nonetheless revealed to us all there that day that locked deep within our own souls lies the spirit for our kind of 1:49-and-change performance.

All we have to do is turn the key.

Ironically, this basic lesson in life had not come from a fellow human being, but from a horse. And, incredibly, he had taught the lesson in the purest form possible. In a time trial, with no money or championships on the line, with no betting possible, and no competition eligible except time itself.

Clearly, he was everything his Maker intended him to be: a champion pacer who could make the human heart believe in wondrous things again.

Small wonder, then, that his racing colors are purple. Purple. As in royalty. You'd expect nothing less from a king.

Originally published in *Trot!* magazine (December 1981)
Hoofbeats magazine (May 1984, Part 3 of a three-part series)

Lost in Time

A FIRE CAN WARM OR it can burn; it just depends on where the hell you sit. For proof of that fact, you need look no further than the world-record 1:49.1 performance of Niatross at the Red Mile in October of last year.

Immediately, the pair of Niatross and trainer-driver Clint Galbraith began to glow (and continues to) with an aura of immortality unmatched in the history of the sport of harness racing.

At the same time, the white heat of that achievement scorched prompters Freddie Bach and Dennis Lacey, relegating them almost instantly to figures of mere triviality.

On what had to be their greatest moment in the sport, Bach and Lacey were the first two to leave the track that day and the last, absolutely the last, remembered by a media more enamored of the obvious than aware of the sublime.

To be sure, no one could have outshone Niatross or Galbraith on that day, even if they had wanted to. Yet every star must have a supporting cast that forces and elicits the best out of him or her. And in prompting a pace that led to a record that made one person say (and many others agree) that Niatross had apparently skipped one, possibly two generations of the Standardbred strain, it was obvious that Bach and Lacey had followed Galbraith's instructions to the letter.

Freddie Bach (United States Trotting Association)

Most importantly, outside of Galbraith himself, no two people on the track that day were closer to the feel and pulse of that record than Bach and Lacey. Somewhere, though, shortly after they passed the finish line, they got lost in the shuffle.

The fire of October had now turned to the bitter cold of a mid-March morning at the Red Mile, where the bite of the air cut through to the bone, ridiculing everything that expensive lined windbreakers, heavy sweatshirts, and thick wool socks are supposed to stand for, especially in the face of a winter that had more than worn out its welcome.

Still, it was all home to 34-year-old Dennis Lacey, who was wintering his modest stable there at Barn 12, directly facing the red-clay track where his greatest moment in the bike had occurred.

Inside the small cubicle of an office that adjoined the barn, I began to suffer manic depression at the sight of an empty coffeepot, a felony compounded by the pathetic bleating of a minuscule heater that was no more a threat to the invading cold than any opponent ever had been to Niatross.

All that was quickly forgotten as the amicable Lacey began to explain the nature of time trials in general and to analyze the performance of Niatross in particular.

Lacey and Bach go back a long way, to the mid- and late 1960s, when Lacey was a pre-vet student at the University of Kentucky. Looking for a part-time job, Lacey wandered over to the Red Mile, where he quickly found work rubbing horses for Bach. From that time forward, Lacey knew he never wanted to do anything else except work with horses.

Though a successful driver in his own right, Bach now divides his time between his New York farm and his prompting business, which he got into last year on a full-time basis with Lacey.

This season, as usual, the pair will split the prompting duties. Bach will work the north at Syracuse, Vernon Downs, and for the first time this year, at The Meadowlands, while Lacey handles Du Quoin, Indianapolis, and Springfield. If one gets overloaded, the other helps out.

Then it's down to the Red Mile for both of them during Grand Circuit week, where last year they hooked up for more than 100 time trials. The season is short but furious, bets conducted on mile tracks where the turns are wide, sweeping, and minimal in number (two).

Time trials aren't cheap, either.

If you don't beat two minutes, it costs $200 for one driver, $400 for two drivers. If you *do* beat two minutes, it's $250 and $500 respectively. And that doesn't include fees to the track, which are less expensive before the meet actually begins than during it.

To be sure, both men more than earn their money. By the time the Red Mile's Grand Circuit season ended last year, they could hardly feel their arms.

Over the years, both Bach and Lacey have developed the kind of arms and shoulders that would rival those of many Olympic weight lifters. At the same time, they've developed a widespread reputation, since they may be the only two men in North America engaged in prompting on a full-time basis.

"For obvious reasons," Dennis Lacey explained, "time trials used to be called 'breeders records' for horses who couldn't or didn't race well. Definitely, a career mark is more impressive than a time trial because of the competition involved in a race, but in at least one instance, time trials serve a valuable purpose. Say a horse is unlucky enough to follow an Albatross or a Bret Hanover, or yes, a Niatross. That time trial is the only way to get a true measure of his speed."

Having spoken the magical name, it was only natural that Lacey would get specific and analyze the time trial that beat all time trials.

"Ironically, the Niatross drive was easier than you'd think, in at least one way," he continued. "The faster drives are easier on the drivers because those Thoroughbreds are born to run, and in that case, we can let 'em out. The slow drives are harder on me and Freddie because we're constantly having to pull the reins.

"When we hit the first turn, the track seemed tacky [heavy], and between the quarter and the half, Niatross was playing around. I was behind him, with Freddie on Clint's head, and from where I sat, I could see Niatross turning his head and ducking shadows. Just playing around.

"I knew we weren't out there playing around, we were going after the record, but my main concern was not to run up on him. That little blaze-faced mare of mine, Lugar, can be skittish at times.

"When we hit the three-quarters, the crowd went wild and I knew something was up. I didn't realize how much until we passed the finish line and I saw those times. Somewhere between the three-quarter and the tunnel, Niatross hit another gear and we were all really flying.

"I was glad to see Clint finally get the record. The pressure was tremendous on him and had really built up when bad weather stopped him at Syracuse. And we were getting short on time, too, at the Red Mile.

"The day of the time trial, Clint took Freddie and me out under that tree over there [close to Barn 12] and made it simple. He wanted to go every quarter in twenty-seven [seconds] or twenty-seven and a piece, and when we hit the top of the stretch, he would bear out slightly to let me come up inside and force Niatross a little more.

"Freddie and me knew what we were about to do, and what was expected of us both. I tell you, if either one of us had messed up, run into him or up on him or past him, voiding the time trial, we had an emergency escape route all planned out. We were both going to head for the nearest exit, go straight down Broadway, and head outta town."

Then he roared with laughter. He was still living in Lexington, and the time limit for being serious was obviously up, fully expired.

Writers tend to make complex issues out of the simplest things, using superlatives and adjectives when mere monosyllable verbs will suffice. To Lacey (and to Bach, for whom Lacey spoke in absentia), it was simple. Either they did it or they didn't do it. The world wouldn't end either way.

Outside of some fleeting publicity, neither Lacey's nor Bach's life has changed dramatically, particularly for Lacey. He has no pretense or illusions about his greatness, no regrets that more coverage was not directed toward the prompters.

He doesn't even bear any ill feeling toward several writers who suggested, incredibly enough, that the pair couldn't keep up with the blooded Albatross son.

The good-humor man can laugh at it all.

He's doing the only thing he ever wanted to do. He's as happy with his small stable now as he was the day Niatross hit out the record. To him, they both have an equal value. Clearly, Lacey has his feet on the ground, knows what he wants, and loves what he has. I envy him for that.

It was time to go. I had looked at an empty coffeepot in a semi-frostbitten state long enough; still, I wanted to ask a forbidden question, one which had bothered me since I had first run across the term.

I wanted to know why they called harness horses "jugheads."

The silence hung so long in the air I thought I had actually succeeded in achieving the impossible. I had insulted and angered Lacey.

Then I realized it was all a hoax, staged for my benefit. The eyes lit up first, then his whole face widened into a huge grin, punctuated by a loud roar of laughter that bounced around the walls like a basketball.

"Well," he said, "in the old days they used to call them that because they were so ugly. But they've gotten a lot better looking over the years. . . ."

As his voice trailed off, I looked at him and instantly realized we were both thinking of the same thing: the beauty of Niatross that October day in 1980 when he changed the face of the sport, literally and figuratively, forever. Great minds tend to think in the same channels. Enough said.

Author's Note: Niatross was humanely destroyed at age 22 on June 7, 1999.

Combo Man

Hey man, I like you. I've always liked you.
(Attributed to Elvis Presley)

If you have to say you're great, you ain't.
(Old Italian saying)

R OUND TABLE, THAT MESMERIZING ghost from the past that everybody's heard about but few remember, was the consummate horse. He left everything on the racetrack. He didn't take nothing home at all with him. He was a horse who enriched all whom he touched. This is not opinion. Rather, it is opinion based upon fact.

His work at Gulfstream Park was reflective of his overall greatness. He raced just twice there, but he didn't hold anything back. Everybody got their money's worth, and then some, from this giant who left a big Grand Canyon–sized mark on the sport.

His first Gulfstream foray came on March 14, 1958, when he took a tune-up—the Challenge Purse—with Bill Hartack up in the irons for a track-record time of 1:41⅗ for 1¹⁄₁₆ miles.

His farewell came on March 22 under Bill Shoemaker, when he hauled down the venerable Gulfstream Park Handicap—at 1¼ miles—in a track-record-equaling time of 1:59⅘. You love to see that type of horse come, and you hate to see them go.

The races were copycat performances, Round Table laying in third in the early goings, then moving and holding the lead by the stretch call, and finally drawing off to win easily over five anonymous horses. Only

Round Table, Eddie Arcaro up, comes out on the track for the 1958 Woodward Stakes. The event was won by Clem, with Round Table running an uncharacteristically poor fifth. (Keeneland Library/Bert Morgan)

the margins were different—3½ lengths in the prep, 4 lengths in the 100-grander stake.

You can't prove it, but you get the feeling he never even broke a sweat in either of these races. They were *fait accompli*, a $50 Latin phrase meaning that the race was for second and beyond because you could take it to the bank that Round Table was going to win. (There's no such thing as a "lock" in racing, it's true, but at times Round Table was about as close as you could come to that ageless and shimmering mirage.)

A pair of real tough races, so tough that his only legitimate foe both occasions was time, and he beat that one once and tied it the other.

So who is this ageless demigod from the mid- and late 1950s called Round Table, this mercurially blended banquet who never truly failed at any time during his four-year career (1956–59)?

Put in quick terms, he was this country's first great "combo" (combination) racer, a "jamming" racer who cut it well on both the dirt and the turf.

This is not idle street talk; this is money fact backed up by statistics in a sport where such numbers mean everything.

Look at any part of his résumé. Look all you want. You won't find any short-stacking anywhere at all in the record of this pony-sized, regally bred runner (1954–87/Princequillo–Knight's Daughter, by Sir Cosmo).

Here are the pertinent details, and in no particular order.

MULTIPLE TITLIST

Horse-of-the-Year (1958); unprecedented three straight national grass titles (1957–59); and champion handicap male (1958).

MEMBER OF THE LEGENDARY 1954 CROP

Considered one of the three greatest crops ever produced in this country (and, by some, *the greatest* crop ever produced in this nation), the 1954 class included the likes of Bold Ruler, Gallant Man, Round Table, Iron Liege, Federal Hill, Clem, Barbizon, and Vertex.

Those ranks also included the precocious but ill-fated Gen. Duke, the 1957 Florida Derby hero who died of the wobbles (incoordination) at age four.

The 1954 class shares its epic stature with the 1884 class (Tremont, 13-for-13; Firenze, 82-47-21-9; Hanover, 50-32-14-2; and Kingston, 138-89-33-12) and the 1928 crop of Twenty Grand, Equipoise, Mate, and Jamestown.

NOTABLE RECORDS

Round Table retired as the world's richest racehorse, with a career bankroll of $1,749,869. Perhaps that seems a laughable figure today, until you consider that at the time the "100-grander" (the $100,000 stakes race) was the game's trademark.

Adjust for inflation, and you get a true gauge of Round Table's worth. He was like an ATM gone wild, a cash-and-carry horse who brought in the money like some people bring in the morning newspaper and the day's mail.

Besides the title and the money, Round Table also exited the sport having equaled or set one world record, three American marks, and 12 track or course standards.

In short, he was the perfect combination: rich and fast.

CAREER LEDGER

Handled for the bulk of his career by Hall of Fame trainer William "Bill" Molter Jr. (1910–1960), whose top career charges also included 1954 Kentucky Derby victor Determine, Round Table won 43 of 66 lifetime starts, ran second eight times, and finished third five times.

That overall record included 31 stakes wins—22 on the dirt and 9 on the turf. And, on 25 occasions, he shouldered 130 pounds or more.

Broken down, Round Table's dirt record is an eye-catching 50-29-7-5 ledger that had room for only nine off-the-board finishes.

Brilliant on the dirt, he was damn-near invincible on the grass, posting 14 wins and one second from 16 lifetime grass starts. Round Table did not suffer his first career turf defeat until he was four years old. Carrying 130 pounds, he ran a narrow second to Clem in the 1958 United Nations Handicap at old Atlantic City, the winner using a 17-pound advantage to pull off a new course record.

Round Table's other losing turf effort came at age five in the 1959 Washington's Birthday Handicap, where he floundered over the soft going ("off" surfaces were his one, true weak point) and finished last in the 16-horse field.

More than just the surface, however, played a factor in this poor run. After the race, it was discovered that Round Table had suffered a quarter crack. Such was the gravity of the injury that he did not race again for four months. That injury, by the way, was the only major one ever sustained by this racer, who was one of the soundest and most durable runners ever to appear on the American racing scene (according to W. H. P. Robertson's classic, *The History of Thoroughbred Racing in America*).

No discussion of Round Table's turf work, incidentally, would be complete without a mention of the position he enjoys today with many

Bill Molter (right), trainer of Round Table, and Eddie Arcaro at Belmont in late
September of 1958 (Keeneland Library/Bert Morgan)

Round Table (#1) holds off Manassas (on the rail) to win the 1959 Arlington Handicap in track and American record time (1:53⅖ for 1³⁄₁₆ miles over the lawn). Third was Noureddin (#5). (*The Thoroughbred Times*)

knowledgeable racing people as the greatest grass racer ever turned out by this country.

There are plenty of people who will challenge that statement. That's okay. That's what makes America and racing. But beware. There are a cadre of old-timers left who swear that there hasn't been a turf horse before or since in this country that could have even warmed up Round Table.

They detail that opinion by speaking of his action.

Possessed of a fluid, economical stride, Round Table devoured ground in his grass forays, seemingly gliding over the surface, inhibited by nothing (at least one old racing film backs this up emphatically).

Factor in the other available data, and you've got a pretty strong case, best summed up by a hero in another type of film, a western: "Go ahead and draw, Mister. I'll *wait* for you."

I couldn't have said it better myself.

This glamorous old "three-way" dutifully records one of Round Table's great turf wins—the 1957 American Derby at Old Washington Park in Chicago. (*The Thoroughbred Times*)

RACETRACKS AND RACECOURSES

Round Table didn't carry his racetrack or racecourse around with him. He was well-traveled and scored major victories anywhere and everywhere—Florida, Kentucky, New York, California, and Chicago.

Round Table winning on the dirt, a six-length demolition job in the 1957 Blue Grass Stakes at Keeneland (Keeneland Library/J. C. "Skeets" Meadors)

In addition to the Gulfstream Park Handicap, his list of major career stakes wins includes the United Nations Handicap, the Hawthorne Gold Cup, and the Arlington Handicap (all twice), plus the Hollywood Gold Cup, the Manhattan Handicap, the Blue Grass Stakes, the Santa Anita Handicap, the American Derby, the Westerner Stakes, the Santa Anita Maturity, and the Washington Park Handicap.

THE KARMA FACTOR

Every great horse has this, and Round Table had it in spades.

Literally from the beginning, he was a special being in the cosmos, touched by the stars, being born on the same day and at the same farm as Bold Ruler—April 6, 1954, at Claiborne Farm in Paris, Kentucky.

This is not destiny; it is major-league manifest destiny, the kind that in retrospect makes your teeth sweat and the hair on the back of your neck stand up, because it's a sign that we're not alone in the universe (you know what I mean). The upside is that it makes you feel smug about the future of agnostics and atheists.

Nearly three years later, on the afternoon of February 9, 1957, Round Table was the focal point of one of the most memorable sales in Thoroughbred racing history.

Shortly before the gates opened for the fifth race at Hialeah, two men shook hands, and the ownership of Round Table passed from the colt's breeder—A. B. "Bull" Hancock Jr., the longtime master of Claiborne Farm—to Oklahoma oilman Travis M. Kerr.

The principals were Hancock and Dr. John Peters (Kerr's agent), and the price was $175,000. It proved to be a bargain for Kerr, in whose colors Round Table raced the majority of his career (Hancock, however, shrewdly maintained a 20 percent interest in Round Table as a stallion).

Finally, there was Round Table's gargantuan walk, one of several things that had caught the attention of Peters. When Round Table put his feet down at a walk, Peters had noticed, he overstepped his front hoof-prints by approximately a foot.

Such action suggested a powerful thrust, and as events later proved, the looks were for real as Round Table repeatedly decked opponents with it during his career.

The one rival that consistently—and successfully—challenged that explosive kick were "off" surfaces, which prevented Round Table from getting a secure grip.

Although solid and consistent at stud, in his last years Round Table wasn't a fancy sight. He showed his age (as they all do). His back sagged, and he had a basket on his halter to keep him from biting himself (this habit dated back to his early stud days).

But he also had some remnants of a hard-guy look in his eyes, a kind of lean-and-mean look that told you that though the body was weary and worn out, the racing flame was still there, burning like a brushfire out of control.

To the end, this sturdy little giant—who lasted to age 33 and broke bread with the very best of them—stayed hungry.

Of all the qualities that separate champs from chumps, this is the greatest one.

Grey Star

Home is the heart.
(Old saying)

Let us now sing for the famous of life.
(Old saying)

FOR ONE MAGNIFICENT SEASON, Holy Bull—in whose honor today's feature race is named—was the heart, mind, body, and soul of Thoroughbred racing.

Voted Horse-of-the-Year in 1994, his victories en route to the grandest of American championships included one of the most powerful performances ever witnessed in the Florida Derby—the foremost preview of the Triple Crown.

A winner of 13 of 16 career ventures, the precocious and sturdy front-runner was unbeaten in four starts at two. Highlighting that campaign was a score over the then-unbeaten Dehere in the Futurity at Belmont and a rousing triumph in the In Reality Stakes, the final leg of the open division of the Florida Stallion Stakes.

Despite his stellar work as a juvenile, the epically named colt ran a distant and virtually anonymous third in that year's Eclipse Award balloting for the nation's 1993 two-year-old male title.

The champion was the aforementioned Dehere (unplaced in the 1993 Breeders' Cup Juvenile at Santa Anita), the runner-up Brocco, the winner of that million-dollar race.

It was a mistake, however, that if it had been a movie, would have been entitled: "While you were in California at the Breeders' Cup

Holy Bull winning the 1993 In Reality Stakes, one of America's top juvenile events, at Calder Race Course (Calder Race Course/Jean Raftery Photos)

worshiping false idols, we were in south Florida crowning the once and future king."

Besides his mammoth talent, the magnetic gray colt had the stuff of which legends are made.

There was his name. There was the matter of his unfashionable pedigree. And then there was the matter of his ownership, which like his name seemed to have a providential quality about it.

On the day he made his first career start, Holy Bull's owner—Mrs. Rachel Carpenter—passed away. Several days later, her attorneys informed trainer Jimmy Croll that all her horses had been willed to him, a shining example of her inherent sporting class and abiding loyalty to her longtime trainer.

The inheritance proved to be a mother lode, as well, for a sport that historically can never get too much of a good thing.

Hall of Fame conditioner Jimmy Croll, the trainer of Holy Bull. (Calder Race Course/Jean Raftery Photos)

By the time the 1994 year was done, the situation was reversed. Holy Bull, who had secured a permanent niche for himself in Thoroughbred racing's history book, held center stage while Dehere and Brocco were merely part of his supporting cast.

His list of early wins included two of Gulfstream's classic three-year-old races—the Hutcheson and the Florida Derby—and the Blue Grass at Keeneland, in which his foes followed him around the track single file, the one serious challenge to him coming at the top of the stretch, which he dispelled with frightening ease, like that of a person swatting away a worrisome fly.

Installed as the favorite for the Kentucky Derby, he struggled with a squeezed break, an off track, and unfavorable position.

Meanwhile, Go For Gin turned out a career race (it would be his fifth and last career victory) in winning the Kentucky Derby.

Though Holy Bull lost a lot of followers with that Kentucky Derby loss—a situation that got worse when Tabasco Cat took the final two legs of the Triple Crown, the Preakness and the Belmont—he was not out of the picture.

In rapid succession, he made his comeback for three-year-old male honors and Horse-of-the-Year laurels, polishing off the Metropolitan Mile (in which he beat eventual champion sprinter Cherokee Run); the Dwyer; the Haskell Invitational; the Travers (in which he defeated Tabasco Cat); and the Woodward (another triumph against older horses, that field including Suburban victor Devil His Due, Pacific Classic winner Tinners

Mighty, mighty Holy Bull easily winning the 1994 Blue Grass Stakes at Keeneland Race-course, with Mike Smith in the irons (Keeneland Association/Bill Straus)

Holy Bull taking the 1994 Travers (New York Racing Association/Adam Coglianese)

Way, Whitney Handicap conqueror Colonial Affair, Donn Handicap victor Pistols and Roses, 1993 champion older male Bertrando, and 1994 Kentucky Derby winner Go For Gin).

Of all of them, no victory was more emotion-drenched than his giant-heart Travers victory, in which he proved he could handle a fast pace set by someone else; proved that he was more than just a sprinter or a miler, rather that he was a classic racehorse who could go 1¼ miles; and most spectacularly of all, proved his courage and gameness once and for all by holding off Concern to win by a neck over a wet-fast track.

It was proof paramount that you can measure everything in Thoroughbred racing except heart.

Retired in early 1995, Holy Bull stands at stud at Jonabell Farm in Lexington, Kentucky. The possibility of his racetrack magic being duplicated is one more glimmering facet of this megastar who shook the entire sporting world to its core.

No friend of the jaded, cynical, or lovers of the antihero, Holy Bull gave us unparalleled brilliance and mesmerizing devotion to the only duty

A look at a topflight racing machine: Holy Bull prior to winning the 1993 In Reality Stakes at Calder, with Mike Smith up (Calder Race Course/Jean Raftery Photos)

he ever knew—that of a champion racehorse and high-class product in a time when overhyped junk is a way of life.

He knew his lot in life and he carried himself well. He was more than just an example; he was the original mold.

He also woke our hearts to the majesty of living and doing the best we can at all times. (All you have to do is, as the song says, walk through that open door and fly.)

He also gave us hope, optimism, and the unfailing belief that there would be many tomorrows, and that all of them—in some way or another—would be as good and rich as his Travers performance (which that night saw his fans chanting his name in the streets of Saratoga Springs).

For all that and more, Holy Bull ranks as one of the greatest songs ever sung in the history of Gulfstream Park and one of the two greatest sports in the universe.

He is righteous, and let no one question it.

Silver Boy

TWENTY-FIVE YEARS LATER, it stands there, shimmering and glittering in the record book, like an oasis on the desert. But this is no mirage.

Dr. Fager—the greatest miler this country ever turned out—still reigns supreme for the epic 1:32⅕ world record he registered on August 24, 1968, in the Washington Park Handicap at old Arlington Park in Chicago.

Certainly, it wasn't easy.

Dr. Fager carried a bone-jarring 134 pounds, by 8 pounds the heaviest impost ever carried by any of the thirteen horses to date to have done the mile in 1:33 flat or better.

In the race itself, the weight differential was even more substantial, Dr. Fager giving from 16 to 23 pounds to his nine foes. That field included Hedevar, principally known as the "rabbit horse" for his stablemate, the great Damascus, a part of the famed Dr. Fager–Damascus–Buckpasser rivalry.

---

*Also ran as "A Day Unequaled and Unmatched" in *The Thoroughbred Times*, August 20, 1993. American Racetrack Series title: "Silver Streak."

Dr. Fager winning the 1968 Washington Park Handicap in world-record time (*The Thoroughbred Times*)

Also in the field was Kentucky Sherry, who had run in that year's controversial Kentucky Derby (in which original winner Dancer's Image was disqualified for the presence of an illegal medication and runner-up Forward Pass was awarded the victory).

Bet down to thirty cents on the dollar, Dr. Fager was in a financial class all by himself; the other nine competitors were all priced in double figures, the lowest of them Racing Room, the eventual runner-up, at $10.40-to-$1 odds.

The early leaders were a mere formality, play toys for Dr. Fager. After a quarter of a mile, run in 22⅘, Angelico led the field, then faded into oblivion. At the half, contested in 44 seconds flat, R. Thomas was the new leader.

Then, as suddenly as it had begun, it was over. For R. Thomas. For all of them.

Sent "away alertly" according to the chart notes, Dr. Fager was "hard held to be reserved just off the lead" in the early stages. Somewhere after the halfway point of the race, though, the speedy four-year-old bay colt "moved with a rush while still under restraint," and that was it.

The regal Braulio Baeza was no longer the jockey, just a passenger. The train and the passenger were one and the same, traveling flawlessly at near-light speed over a "fast" track underneath picture-perfect weather conditions—86 degrees and clear.

Clocked in 1:07⅗ for the three-quarters, Dr. Fager disposed of Racing Room on the turn for home, then drew off through the stretch, hurtling home a ten-length winner in a new world-record time of 1:32⅕, a time that eclipsed Buckpasser's old standard (set just two years prior in the Arlington Classic) by two-fifths of a second.

If the performance was awesome, it nonetheless had a frightening quality to it, too. According to the chart notes, Dr. Fager had "won with something left." By implication, this meant he could have gone even faster. The thought chills the soul, boggles the mind, melts the best of watches.

In the years since, the sport has thrown everything it has had at the Good Doctor, and failed. The Tartan Farm homebred is still the king, and perhaps most richly, Dr. Fager—named after Dr. Louis Fager, the Boston neurosurgeon who had performed lifesaving brain surgery on the racer's trainer, John Nerud—belongs first and foremost to his native state of Florida.

As to be expected, Dr. Fager—off a smashing record of seven wins from eight starts, his lone loss to the mighty Damascus in the Brooklyn

Handicap—took 1968 Horse-of-the-Year laurels, his work highlighted by the Washington Park Handicap score in which he vanquished both mortal foes and time alike.

Considered one of the greatest seasons ever enjoyed by an American racer, the 1968 finale campaign of Dr. Fager (Rough 'n Tumble–Aspidistra, by Better Self) entailed another feat that has yet to be duplicated—an unprecedented *four titles in one season* (besides Horse-of-the-Year honors, Dr. Fager also earned champion sprinter, older-male, and grass honors in 1968).

That phenomenal 1968 season ran Dr. Fager's magnificent career totals to 18 wins from 22 starts. The lifetime ledger of the stellar Florida-bred also includes a pair of seconds and a third, glittering work that enabled him to leave the racetrack a millionaire in an era when that financial term carried weight. (For the record, Dr. Fager's career slate—technically—is even better than it looks. His lone career unplacing came as the result of a disqualification in the 1967 Jersey Derby. Though he won the race by 6½ lengths, he was placed fourth and last for interference.)

Today, Dr. Fager lives on mightily because his competition that historic afternoon in the 1968 Washington Park Handicap at old Arlington Park in Chicago, quite simply put, was not of this world.

A living entity who did the unthinkable—facing time on its own terms and shutting it down completely for a brief moment, smoking it with a white-heat performance that made time flinch and stand still literally in its own tracks—Dr. Fager came as close to immortality that day as any living, breathing thing ever will.

Such magnificence is the lifeblood not only of racing and its greatest stake events, but life itself, a fervent affirmation that humankind—in William Faulkner's words—must not merely survive, but prevail on the highest level possible.

In his world-record-setting performance in the 1968 Washington Park Handicap, Dr. Fager—an extraordinary giant and a visceral competitor who was part literature, part good medicine, and all racehorse—gave us the very best he had, and in doing so, made us all the better for it.

MIGHTY MILERS

1. Dr. Fager (1:32⅕, 1968 Washington Park Handicap)

2. Easy Goer (1:32⅖, 1989 Gotham Stakes)

3. Buckpasser ($1:32\frac{3}{5}$, 1966 Arlington Classic)
   Greinton ($1:32\frac{3}{5}$, 1985 Californian)
   Williamstown ($1:32\frac{3}{5}$, 1993 Withers)

4. Bold Bidder ($1:32\frac{4}{5}$, 1966 Washington Park Handicap)
   Precisionist ($1:32\frac{4}{5}$, 1985 Mervyn Leroy Handicap)
   Melair ($1:32\frac{4}{5}$, 1986 Silver Screen Handicap)
   Bayakoa ($1:32\frac{4}{5}$, 1989 Hawthorne Handicap)
   Quiet American ($1:32\frac{4}{5}$, 1990 NYRA Mile)

5. Conquistador Cielo ($1:33$ flat, 1982 Metropolitan)
   Caros Love ($1:33$ flat, a 1988 overnight handicap)
   Grand Canyon ($1:33$ flat, 1989 Hollywood Futurity)

Author's Note: This chapter is dedicated to two Chicago aces—David Zenner and Joe Kristufek.

The Chocolate Soldier

TO BE CONTESTED THIS YEAR for the 43rd time, the Equipoise Mile (G3) honors the 1932 and 1933 Horse-of-the-Year champion who placed an indelible stamp on both Chicago and American racing.

Nicknamed Ekky for obvious reasons and the Chocolate Soldier because of his liver chestnut color, Equipoise was owned by the late C. V. Whitney.

One of the sport's great patrons, Whitney took over the talented racer late in his juvenile season following the death of his father, H. P. Whitney, in whose colors the homebred had raced initially.

Despite being plagued by shelly feet (he raced with a chronic quarter crack virtually his entire career, from 1930 through 1935), Equipoise posted a 51-29-10-4 career slate that included $338,610 in purse earnings. Though a modest figure today, his money earnings at that time were astonishing, coming during the heights of the Great Depression.

A multiple stakes winner whose major career victories included the Metropolitan (twice), the Suburban, and the Saratoga Cup, Equipoise earned lasting demigod status in Chicago—and old Arlington Park— when he won *three stakes within the span of ten days* in the summer of 1932.

The streak began with the Delavan Handicap on June 30, when he set a then world record for the mile with a clocking of 1:34⅖; continued with the July 4 Stars & Stripes Handicap; and concluded with the July 9 Arlington Gold Cup (so great was Equipoise's strength that the streak's finale saw only three runners go postward, four runners being scratched from the Arlington Gold Cup).

Other Chicago victories by Equipoise, in whose honor the mile chute at Arlington is named, included the Arlington Handicap and the Hawthorne Gold Cup. And notably, he did his work in a time when the competition was uncommonly keen.

His class, the 1928 crop, is considered by many racing historians to be one of the three greatest ever produced in American racing history. That contingent included Twenty Grand, who took the 1931 Kentucky Derby and Belmont Stakes in the absence of an injured Equipoise; 1931 Preakness victor Mate; and Jamestown.

Only the 1884 crop (Tremont, 13-for-13; Firenze, 82-47-21-9; Hanover, 50-32-14-2; and Kingston, 138-89-33-12) and the 1954 class (Bold Ruler, Round Table, Gallant Man, and Gen. Duke) stand in equal comparison.

Though Equipoise raced six seasons, his finest career performance came early on, as a two-year-old in the 1930 Pimlico Futurity, where he displayed in gold the indefinable tangent that separates champion runners from run-of-the-mill racers.

Turned sideways at the start and left at the post, he grabbed a quarter and literally ran out of his shoes. It made no difference in the end, though.

Encased from head to toe in blood, slop, and glory (the result of having sheared off both front plates over the muddy track), he returned with a gallant win under the hands of eventual Hall of Fame reinsman Raymond "Sonny" Workman over archrivals Twenty Grand and Mate, who ran second and third, respectively.

A premature death at age 10 in 1938 ended the road of this brilliant Hall of Fame racer, but the four racing crops sired by him notably included 1942 Kentucky Derby winner Shut Out and 1941 inaugural Equipoise Mile victor Equifox, giving indication that had he lived, Equipoise would have been as great a stallion as he had been a racer.

Though long gone, Equipoise endures grandly today, a classic star of epic proportions. It is no accident.

Possessed of Herculean courage that more than matched his prodigious talent, Equipoise was proof paramount that when the heart runs true, any foe—regardless of size—can be taken.

Take a look at this pair of Hall of Famers—the incomparable Equipoise with Raymond "Sonny" Workman up. The top panel of this old "two-way" shows Equipoise winning the 1933 Suburban Handicap. (Keeneland Library/C. C. Cook)

Mr. Lucky

TODAY'S GRADE 3 SWOON'S Son Handicap at Arlington, a 1¹⁄₁₆-mile grass test for three-year-olds and up that is the second local prep for the Arlington Million, honors a giant from both Chicago's and Arlington's past.

A stellar Chicago-area racer of the mid- and late 1950s, Swoon's Son was retired just short of the magical million-dollar mark in career purse earnings, ironically the very figure for which he was syndicated.

Remarkably consistent, Swoon's Son earned over $200,000 every season he raced. He accrued the bulk of his career earnings (some 90 percent) in Chicago, where he annexed numerous stakes, including the 1955 Arlington and Washington Futurities (then the "two-year-old double," which was consolidated in 1962 as the Arlington-Washington Futurity), the 1956 Arlington Classic, and the 1956 American Derby (at that time the "three-year-old double"), and two editions of the Equipoise Mile (1957 and 1958).

Though his money totals may seem ludicrous today, it should be remembered that Swoon's Son (The Doge–Swoon, by Sweep) competed in a day when a dollar was really a dollar, a million dollars was a fortune, and the "100-grander" ($100,000) stake was the king of the hill.

A homebred owned by E. Gay Drake (1894–1974) and trained by A. G. "Lex" Wilson, the muscular bay racer—whose sculpted look

Swoon's Son (left), complete with trademark facial marking (*The Thoroughbred Times*)

appeared to have been done by Michelangelo himself—wasn't legitimately unplaced until he was four.

As a juvenile in 1955, he won 7 of 13 starts, including 6 in a row at one point. He finished off the board once when he ran third in the Hawthorne Juvenile but was disqualified.

At age three in 1956, he won 10 of 12 starts and ran second the other two times.

When he left the racetrack, he exited with four-year totals of 30 wins, 10 seconds, and three thirds from 51 starts for $970,605 in purse earnings.

A multiple stakes winner who set several track and course records during his fabulous career, Swoon's Son was a brilliantly versatile runner who could run short, long, on the dirt or on the grass, against older horses, and he could carry weight (he conceded *24 pounds* in one of his Equipoise wins).

At stud, Swoon's Son was also solid.

His 21 stakes winners included 1974 New York Filly Triple Crown victress and divisional champion Chris Evert—easily the best of his get—plus Sheldrake, Swoonalong, Swoonaway, Swoon's Flower, Loom, Kinsman Hope, and Mr. Washington.

Swoon's Son, who died of a twisted intestine at age 24 on February 22, 1977, was also the maternal grandsire of 18 stakes winners.

All in all, not bad for a horse foaled on Friday the 13th (Friday, February 13, 1953).

The King Is Gone
but Not Forgotten

THE PROGRAM FOR THE Keeneland race card of Thursday, October 18, 1956, its cover done in the bright orange long emblematic of the Lexington racecourse, hides its age well until one turns to the sections between the fifth and sixth races of that particular day.

Then it reveals the truth of its years.

The "special" pages are separated from the main body of the program, simultaneously tanning and flaking inexorably with age, the result of far too many years spent sequestered in an abandoned locker stored in the darkest corner of a musty basement.

Hauntingly, the program has managed to retain the majesty of its own being despite the loss of its own beauty years ago. That majesty was due to, as the top page proudly proclaims, the "Final Public Appearance of Nashua."

Below the banner headline are sketches of Nashua with Eddie Arcaro up; Leslie Combs II, the man who syndicated Nashua for a then-record $1,251,200; and James "Sunny Jim" Fitzsimmons, Nashua's trainer.

The next page shows Nashua's pedigree and his race record for 1954 and 1955, while the reverse side gives his 1956 racing record, a career summary, and a precise schedule for his afternoon activities at Keeneland: entering the walking ring at 4:05, parading and galloping on the racetrack

The cover of the program for Nashua's last public appearance—Thursday, October 18, 1956, at Keeneland (Philip Von Borries Collection)

beginning at 4:17, and concluding with special infield ceremonies at 4:24.

The ceremonies remain obscure in my memory. However, I still remember the reason for my presence that day on an afternoon ordinarily reserved for the primary education of a nine-year-old: a father who wanted me to witness a historic racing event and further sweetened the pot by facetiously adding that we would get to ride a "million-dollar horse."

That, my mother stated simply, was opening a can of worms for which he would pay dearly later. She turned out to be correct only on the timing.

Nashua's Breeding and Racing Record

Foaled April 14, 1952, at Claiborne Farm, Paris, Ky., Nashua raced for the late William Woodward, Jr.'s Belair Stud at 2 and 3. After Woodward's death, Nashua was sold by sealed bid to a syndicate headed by Leslie Combs II, of Lexington, for $1,251,200.

NASHUA Bay colt 1952			
	*Nasrullah	Nearco	Pharos
			Nogara
		Mumtaz Begum	Blenheim II
			Mumtaz Mahal
	Segula	Johnstown	Jamestown
			La France
		Sekhmet	Sardanapale
			Prosopopee

—1954—

	Dist.	Wt.	Fin.	Time	Value
May 5 Belmont Purse	4 1-2 wc	118	1^{3}	:52 3/5 ft	$ 2,600
May 12 Belmont The Juvenile	5-8 wc	117	$1^{1/2}$	:58 ft	12,150
May 19 Garden State The Cherry Hill Stakes	5-8	119	2^{5}	:58 3/5 ft	3,000
Aug 21 Saratoga Grand Union Hotel Stakes	3-4	122	$1^{1 3/4}$	1:12 3/5 ft	18,550
Aug 28 Saratoga The Hopeful	6 1-2	122	1^{nk}	1:17 4/5 ft	57,050
Sep 21 Aqueduct The Cowdin	6 1-2	124	$2^{3/4}$	1:15 ft	5,000
Oct 1 Belmont Anticipation Purse	3-4 wc	118	1^{1}	1:08 1/5 ft	6,500
Oct 9 Belmont The Futurity	6 1-2 wc	122	1^{hd}	1:15 3/5 ft	88,015

—1955—

	Dist.	Wt.	Fin.	Time	Value
Feb 21 Hialeah Spanish Moss Purse	1 1-16	126	$1^{1 1/2}$	1:44 1/5 ft	$ 4,875
Feb 26 Hialeah Flamingo Stakes	1 1-8	122	$1^{1 1/2}$	1:49 3/5 ft	104,600
Mar 26 Gulfstream Florida Derby	1 1-8	122	1^{nk}	1:53 1/5 sy	100,000
Apr 23 Jamaica Wood Memorial	1 1-8	126	1^{nk}	1:50 3/5 ft	75,100
May 7 Churchill Downs Kentucky Derby	1 1-4	126	$2^{1 1/2}$	2:01 4/5 ft	25,000
May 28 Pimlico Preakness Stakes	1 3-16	126	1^{1}	1:54 3/5 ft	67,550
Jun 11 Belmont Belmont Stakes	1 1-2	126	1^{9}	2:29 ft	83,700
Jly 2 Aqueduct Dwyer Stakes	1 1-4	126	1^{5}	2:03 4/5 ft	37,200
Jly 16 Arlington Arlington Classic	1	126	$1^{1/2}$	1:35 1/5 ft	91,675
Aug 31 Washington Wash. Park Match Race	1 1-4	126	$1^{6 1/2}$	2:04 1/5 gd	100,000
Sep 24 Belmont Sysonby Stakes	1 1-8	121	3^{4}	1:49 1/5 sy	10,000
Oct 15 Belmont Jockey Club Gold Cup	2	119	1^{5}	3:24 4/5 sy	52,850

(Philip Von Borries Collection)

Barely inside the gates at Keeneland, I began to question my father about the ride on Nashua, which he tolerantly endured, confident in the knowledge that if one facetious remark had gotten him into this mess, another one, even bigger, would extricate him.

"Okay, no problem," he replied. "Tell you what I'm going to do. I'll just stroll over to the jocks' room there and let Eddie Arcaro know he's been replaced by you today. Then I'll look Fitzsimmons up and tell him about the change and your marvelous riding record.

"You remember that, don't you?" he continued. "The only time in your life you've been on a horse was on the merry-go-round at Joyland, and you fell off three times in two minutes. That'll impress him for sure.

"And, if I've got any extra time left, I'll jaunt on up to Leslie Combs's box seat and see if he's interested in letting you into the million-dollar syndicate that just bought Nashua. I'm certain you two could work out something on your allowance of 25 cents a week. Would you like that?"

I nodded in the affirmative and watched his eyes practically roll out of his head. With that, my father grasped me firmly by the hand and kept me in tow the rest of the afternoon, until we left shortly after the ceremonies in order to beat the heavy traffic home.

—1956—

Feb 18 Hialeah Widener Handicap	1 1-4	127	1^{hd}	2:02	ft	$ 92,600
Mar 17 Gulfstream Gulfstream Park Handicap	1 1-4	129	5^{7}	2:00⅗	ft	2,500
May 5 Jamaica Grey Lag Handicap	1 1-8	128	1^{hd}	1:50⅗	ft	37,100
May 19 Garden State Camden Handicap	1 1-8	129	1^{2}	1:49⅕	ft	22,750
May 30 Belmont Metropolitan Handicap	1	130	4¾	1:35	ft	2,500
Jun 30 Belmont Carter Handicap	7-8	130	$7^{3½}$	1:23⅕	ft	—
Jul 4 Belmont Suburban Handicap	1 1-4	128	$1^{1¾}$	2:00⅘	ft	55,900
July 14 Monmouth Monmouth Handicap	1 1-4	129	$1^{3½}$	2:02⅘	m	78,200
Sep 29 Belmont Woodward	1 1-4	126	$2^{2½}$	2:03	gd	15,000
Oct 13 Belmont Jockey Club Gold Cup	2	124	$1^{2¼}$	3:20*	ft	36,600

*American Record

Recapitulation

Year	Age	Sts	1st	2nd	3rd	Unp.	Won
1954	2	8	6	2	0	0	$ 192,865
1955	3	12	10	1	1	0	752,550
1956	4	10	6	1	0	3	343,150
Totals		30	22	4	1	3	$1,288,565

As a juvenile, Nashua was voted Best Two-Year-Old Colt and Best Two-Year-Old in the annual championship polls conducted by the Daily Racing Form and the Thoroughbred Racing Associations.

Last year, Nashua made a clean sweep of honors when he was named Best Three-Year-Old Colt, Best Three-Year-Old, and Horse of the Year.

Nashua's Schedule for Final Public Appearance

4:05 P. M.—Enter walking ring.

4:17 P. M.—Enter track for parade and gallop.

4:24 P. M.—Enter infield for ceremony.

(Philip Von Borries Collection)

Insistent on knowing why I had been denied the mount on Nashua, I refused to leave until I got a serious answer. Sensing rapidly we would get caught in a traffic jam, my father improvised quickly.

"This is a million-dollar horse," he explained firmly, "and they're not about to give him to just anybody. Why, they paid a king's ransom for that horse. Now do you understand why you can't ride him—not today, not ever, never?"

I nodded that I did and finally agreed to leave peacefully. I had no conception of a million-plus dollars, but I did understand the meaning of the word *king*.

Nearly 15 years had elapsed since I had last seen Nashua when I found myself, after graduation from college, working as a staff writer for *The Thoroughbred Record*.

Armed with press credentials, I had brassed my way into Spendthrift Farm, ostensibly to do a story on Nashua. Secretly, I wanted a private look at the horse, unobstructed by tourists or farm personnel.

The situation changed instantly when Nashua's fabled groom, Clem Brooks, arrived on the scene.

"Today's my day off, usually," Brooks explained, "but when I heard there was a guy here from the *Record*, I thought it the right thing to come on up anyway."

Nashua is being led to post for his final racetrack appearance and action, with Eddie Arcaro up. Note the number on Nashua's saddlecloth. (Keeneland Library/J. C. "Skeets" Meadors)

Right on cue, I pulled out my pad and pencil.

"This horse here," Brooks began, "was retired in 1956 as the world's leading money winner with earnings of $1,288,565 and *no change*. He was also the first horse ever syndicated for a million dollars or more, $1,251,200 and *no change*. A champion at two and Horse-of-the-Year at three, when he set a single-season earnings record of $752,550 and *no change*, he won numerous classic events, that means fancy stakes races, including the Preakness in stakes record time, the Belmont, and the Jockey Club Gold Cup, the last in the American record time of 3:20⅖.

"But you probably already know that, don't you?" Brooks said as he opened Nashua's stall, sensing I wanted more. "Well, it's your lucky day, 'cause I'm gonna show him to you personally and tell you a few things about him that nobody knows except the people that work here on the farm.

"This horse here, Nashua," Brooks said as he calmly led the stallion out to the grassy area that fronted the stables, "is King with a capital K. He knows it, I know it, Mr. Combs knows it, everybody knows it.

"And a king don't talk to nobody he don't want to," Brooks continued. "That's why he didn't pay you no nevermind when you came up. He's king, he don't have to. You might have stood there all afternoon waitin'

Nashua roaring down the lane for the last time (Keeneland Library/J. C. "Skeets" Meadors)

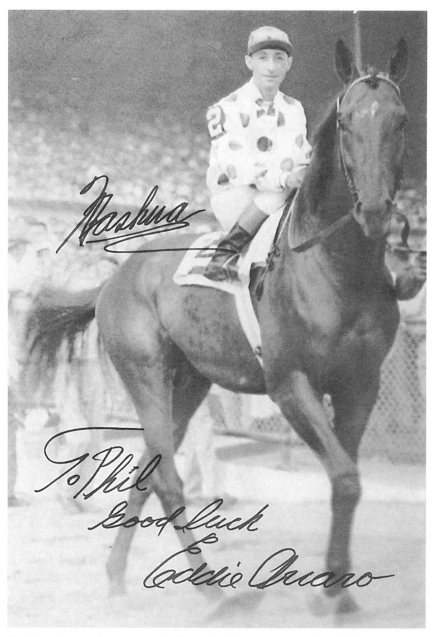

Don't let the smooth symmetry, fine lines, boyish innocence, and overall elegance of this photograph fool you; pictured here are two of the game's most ferocious competitors in sweet, but temporary, repose—Mr. George Edward Arcaro and his frequent running mate, Nashua. (Philip Von Borries Collection)

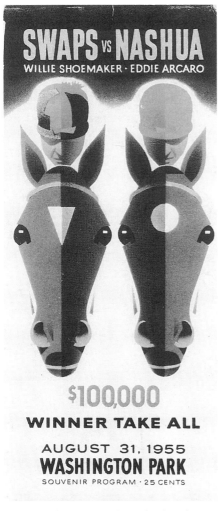

SWAPS vs NASHUA
WILLIE SHOEMAKER · EDDIE ARCARO

$100,000
WINNER TAKE ALL
AUGUST 31, 1955
WASHINGTON PARK
SOUVENIR PROGRAM · 25 CENTS

Cover of the program from the famed 1955 Swaps-Nashua match race (Philip Von Borries Collection)

for him to pay attention to you, unless I had come up.

"I figure I saved you from a highly embarrassing situation," Brooks said, winking at me. "A fine man like you being ignored by a horse, a king of a horse to be sure, but a horse all the same.

"Think about what your friends would say if they found out about that. Why, you'd never hear the end of it. I think it's the Nasrullah blood in him. All them Nasrullahs is just plain antisocial unless their good friends like me is around.

"The important thing to remember about this horse," Brooks continued, as he led Nashua back into his stall, "is that he only does four things. He eats, he sleeps, he runs in the paddock, and he makes love. That's it. Nothing more, nothing less. Bother him for anything else, and you got trouble with a . . . very . . . large . . . capital *T*.

"Can you imagine that? Eatin', sleepin', runnin', and making love all your life? You and I sure can, 'cause we sure ain't gonna do that 'cept occasionally, unless we both want to get fired from our jobs. This horse here, Nashua, he don't imagine it. He do it all the time. It's what he gets paid to do.

"Son," Brooks said as we headed away from Nashua's barn toward our cars, "this horse don't live like a king. He lives *better* than any damn king I ever heard of."

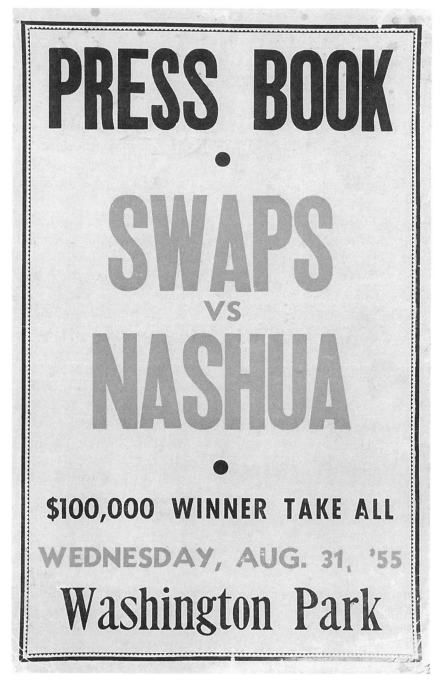

Cover of the media guide for the epic 1955 match race between Swaps and Nashua (Philip Von Borries Collection)

On a slow September afternoon near the end of the 1981 racing meet at Arlington Park, I made a routine trip downstairs from the press box to the main storage room in search of some old *Daily Racing Form* chart books.

I stepped into the room . . . and stepped back in time.

Straight ahead of me, lying on top of a heap of publicity scrapbooks and promotional materials that dated back to the track's opening in 1927, were two programs from the famed $100,000 winner-take-all match race between Nashua and Swaps, run at old Washington Park on the last day of August in 1955.

With trembling hands, I picked up the two programs, scarcely believing their mint condition. More than a quarter of a century old, they looked as new as the day they had been printed, and their clean, economical geometric design put to shame the vast majority of programs sold today at American racetracks.

Minutes later, this treasure officially became mine via the permission of a high-ranking track official.

Call it fate, or whatever, but no unusual circumstances prompted me to watch the January 31, 1982, broadcast of *The Winner's Circle* (hosted by Tom Hammond) on the minuscule television in the research department of *The Thoroughbred Record*.

The end of the regionally televised show made me glad I had.

On came a faded color film of the match race between Nashua and Swaps. The film was clearly dated. But something else emphatically dated the clip: how few of the race's participants were left.

Washington Park had burned down in the late 1970s. Swaps had died in 1972, Arcaro had retired in the early 1960s, Fitzsimmons was long since dead, and Mesh Tenny no longer actively trained. That left only Shoemaker and Nashua active in the sport.

Three days later, only Bill Shoemaker, the rider of Swaps, remained in the game.

Suffering from the infirmities of old age, Nashua was humanely destroyed on Wednesday, February 3, 1982, slightly more than one month after Spendthrift Farm had held special ceremonies commemorating his 30th birthday.

In a much simpler ceremony, he was buried close to his stall, which had come to be known as the Nashua Motel, a bronze sculpture placed on a headstone directly over the grave to be added later by Spendthrift Farm.

Nashua did well at stud right up to the last year of his life, when he was represented by Noble Nashua and Flying Nashua. He was particularly good with fillies, siring Shuvee, Producer, Bramalea, and Marshua.

Reduced to sheer statistics, through 1981 Nashua had sired 74 stakes winners with total crop earnings well in excess of $16 million. Moreover, 79 percent of his foals had raced, with 78 percent of those winning an average of $33,000-plus.

He was special in one more way, too, a subtle figure gained accidentally while, in 1981, I was researching the stud figures for the most expensive stallions in the country.

The overwhelming majority stand here in the central Kentucky area, including several at Nashua's residence for his entire career, Spendthrift Farm.

"Ballpark" figures, or estimated "open-market" figures, were relatively easy to arrive at on Affirmed, Seattle Slew, and Raise a Native. Nashua proved to be a different case.

"No matter what I tell you," said the friendly voice on the other end of the line, "it won't make any difference. His price is substantially lower than the others we talked about, but that's due to his advanced age. The problem is not money; it's getting to Nashua. His book is closed, absolutely closed.

"More so today than ever before because shareholders figure he won't be around much longer, and they want the last of his get. It's an irony, but it may be easier to get to a more expensive stallion than it is to get to him."

To the closing curtain of his life and career, Nashua had remained a king all unto himself.

Author's Note: This chapter is dedicated to Clem Brooks (1907–1998).

War and Peace

THIS AFTERNOON'S FEATURED Sheridan Stakes salutes General Philip Henry Sheridan (1831–1888), a hero in war and peace who was also the first president of the first racetrack in Illinois— old Washington Park Racetrack on the near-south side of Chicago, which opened its doors on Saturday, June 28, 1884.

A graduate of West Point, Sheridan was a brilliant Union general who earned his nickname—Fighting Phil—off ferocious successes in the Chattanooga, Wilderness, and Shenandoah Valley campaigns of the Civil War.

The man who helped to end the Civil War by cutting off General Robert E. Lee's retreat from Appomattox, Sheridan—according to historians—never lost a battle during his distinguished military career.

In addition to his country, Sheridan served the city of Chicago well during its greatest calamity—the Great Chicago Fire.

On the night of October 8, 1871, a blaze broke out in a barn at the rear of the O'Leary residence at 137 DeKoven Street on the west side of Chicago. Racing through the largely wooden-framed city, which was suffering through an unusually dry autumn, the conflagration destroyed everything in its path.

Indeed, the heat of the fire was so intense that it could be felt 100 miles away in Holland, Michigan.

General Philip H. Sheridan (Archive Photos)

Aided by a propitious rainfall, the fire ended the next night. In its wake, however, lay devastation of unbelievable magnitude. Whole sections of the city's south side had been destroyed; property damage was estimated at some $200 million; 100,000 people had been left homeless; 200 to 300 people had been killed; and 73 miles of streets and 17,500 buildings within a 4-mile radius had been destroyed.

Yet, despite that extraordinary destruction, historians one and all agree it could have been much worse had it not been for Sheridan.

Under his leadership, the fire was stopped before it leveled the entire city. And at the urging of frantic city officials—one of them Mayor R. W. Mason—Sheridan temporarily placed Chicago under martial law until the city got back on its feet.

In the matter of the fire, which had moved in a northeasterly direction, Sheridan had wasted little time in halting its deadly advance with a series of firebreaks.

One such firebreak was effected by blowing up every building on Harrison Street, from State Street on the west to the Wabash Avenue Methodist Church on the east.

In the course of this explosion and others, Sheridan almost became a casualty of the fire himself when he ran across a workman who was watching the city's gunpowder supply. Not recognizing Sheridan, the workman pulled a pistol on Sheridan, who quickly exited the scene and continued his demolition work at another location.

Unlike many others, Sheridan did not lose his home (on Michigan Avenue) to the fire. However, he did incur some substantial losses, including his divisional headquarters at LaSalle and Washington, and all of his professional and personal papers.

And, on a sentimental note, Sheridan's favorite horse—a gray pacer named Breckinridge—fell victim to the horrible fire.

Having resolved the issue of the fire, which he stopped like the great general he was, Sheridan put Chicago on the road to recovery as quickly as he could.

A notable example of his skills in the aftermath of the fire was his aid to 30,000 citizens who had sought refuge in Lincoln Park. To them, he sent tens of thousands of rations, tents, and blankets.

And for the panic-stricken city, whose streets were overrun with loose animals of all kinds—horses, dogs, and cats, also refugees from the fire—Sheridan imposed martial law.

It had two benefits. It restored peace and order to the battered city, and at the same time allayed fears of the citizens that their city would be plundered by looters and other types of lawbreakers (there had been rumors that out-of-town hoods and safecrackers planned to descend on the beleaguered city).

In the end, all those fears and worries proved to be groundless, as General Sheridan protected Chicago from enemies within and without until the city got its full health back.

When Sheridan died some 17 years later, he was remembered not only as a hero of the Civil War, but as the hero of the Great Chicago Fire—the man of the hour who had saved one of America's great cities.

Today's featured Sheridan Stakes more than matches its namesake in stature.

One of the two oldest races in Chicago (the American Derby, also run at Arlington, is the other), the Sheridan was inaugurated in 1884.

One of this country's oldest races, the Sheridan has been held at three different racetracks during its venerable existence: the original Washington Park Racetrack at 63rd and Cottage Grove; the second Washington Park Racetrack in Homewood, Illinois; and Arlington, where it has been contested since 1964.

A Million Memories

IT WAS A SEASON THAT literally lived up to its name. Billed as "1981: The Championship Season" and highlighted by the inaugural running of the Arlington Million, the glorious season—and dream of Arlington Park President Joe Joyce—reached its climactic apex in February 1982 with dramatic fanfare, farther south in Miami Beach.

There, the stars of Chicago's and Arlington Park's young crown jewel, the Arlington Million, at that time the world's richest Thoroughbred race, garnered all the major Eclipse Awards, Thoroughbred racing's highest accolades.

Most prominent was Arlington Million victor John Henry, the world's richest racehorse, who recently came out of retirement to make a bid again at a race he has won twice and finished second in once from three starts.

John Henry's honors include the much-coveted Horse-of-the-Year championship, plus divisional honors as champion older male and champion grass male.

Joining him were Sam and Dot Rubin, the owners of Dotsam Stable, under whose banner John Henry raced; trainer Ron McAnally; and rider Bill Shoemaker. All that was missing was the groom.

For Chicago, it meant the city's long-standing order for a major sports champion had been filled almost as richly as had Arlington Park's. It

John Henry (left) takes the inaugural 1981 Arlington Million by a photo-finish bob-of-a-nose over The Bart (right). (*The Thoroughbred Times*)

was, in short, redemption, recognition, and respect all rolled into one neat package.

This was, you understand, pre-Cubs (if only for 1984) and pre-Bears (ad infinitum?), and you didn't have to be a racing fan to love it, just from Chicago. (So we stretch the imagination; this is how the Million was built.)

As expected, some detractors questioned that "championship" claim, viewing it more as the product of good publicity than truth. The crux of their argument was this: John Henry was based in California, and on his rare jaunts outside that state patronized New York almost exclusively.

Yet that jaded and myopic viewpoint—and that's what it was, complete with geographical prejudice—conveniently focused on an entire year while simultaneously denying John Henry's greatest moment *during* the year.

Simply put, John Henry's finest hour had occurred in the hinterlands between those two coastal racing meccas—at Arlington Park. That hour, combined with a clean sweep of the 1981 Eclipse Awards, more than sustains the championship claim of Chicago.

And the numbers were there to back it up: loudly, boldly, and proudly.

Significantly, none of John Henry's races in 1981 were decided by a closer margin than his throw-of-a-nose victory in Arlington Million I, nor worth more than the gargantuan $600,000 he received for his brief excursion of a shade over two minutes (2:07⅗ to be precise), which equaled the course record.

Unlike 1982 winner Perrault, John Henry's first Million win came over a soft turf. Had the course been firm instead, no doubt John Henry would have set a stakes record in Million I, a mark somewhat muted by the technicality that the 1981 running was the inaugural running.

Nevertheless, the record belonged to John Henry for 12 months until a younger Perrault shattered it the next year by nearly ten seconds over a much firmer course.

As it was, the first Arlington Million marked the only time that year in ten starts that John Henry either equaled or set a time mark of any kind. In that particular race, he managed to do both.

And there was at least one subtle nuance to the race, missed by many observers who concentrated on the immediate impact of the race to the exclusion of the Million's future ramifications.

By year's end, however, it had become apparent to all just how well John Henry had cleaned up in Chicago.

The 1981 Million score had saved the veteran gelding a minimum of three races he surely would have needed to become the world's leading money-winning Thoroughbred. That was a plateau he reached in December that year when he became the first horse ever to win more than $3 million lifetime on the track.

In addition, his first Arlington Million triumph enabled John Henry to set what was then a single-season earnings mark of $1,798,030. Repeating his Horse-of-the-Year honors in 1984, when he won the Million for the second time, John Henry confirmed that his stature as Thoroughbred racing's all-time money winner (well over $6.5 million) is indeed deeply rooted in Chicago.

But there was more to the 1981 Arlington Million than just money. When the Eclipse Awards were announced in early 1982, they proved to be an encore performance for the first Arlington Million.

Two of the industry's top trade publications, the *Daily Racing Form* and *The Blood-Horse*, featured a photograph of the dramatic finish of Million I on the covers of their special Eclipse Awards editions. A third, *The Thoroughbred Record*, prominently displayed a reverse-angle photograph of that same Million finish inside their magazine next to their story on John Henry.

And, for good measure, the 1981 Arlington Million finish picture later made the cover of the sales catalogue for the January 1982 Mixed Sale at Keeneland, ironically the

An American epic—Bill Shoemaker (*The Thoroughbred Times*)

exact same sale where John Henry had been sold as a yearling in 1976 for $1,100, and then again as a juvenile in 1977 for $2,200.

It was almost as if no other winning picture of John Henry's 1981 campaign existed.

Many say that Bill Shoemaker—who sets a record every time he just dons his silks—has a patent on close finishes. Untrue. It just seems that way.

For technical purposes, the official winning margin of the first Arlington Million will be forever listed in the record books as a nose. In actuality, it was the "bob" of a nose thrown in the last stride by John Henry that proved to be just enough to nail his game and much-maligned rival, The Bart, at the wire.

That same bob caused The Bart's rider, Eddie Delahoussaye (later to become only the fourth man to win successive Kentucky Derbies, in 1982 with Gato del Sol and in 1983 with Sunny's Halo), to hurl an epithet partly in jest and partly in anger at Shoemaker shortly after they passed the wire.

Unlike the 30,367 fans there that final Sunday of August in 1981, and long before the placing judges were able to decide the outcome with the aid of a photo-finish print, Delahoussaye knew that he had lost.

For those familiar with Shoemaker and racing history, his dramatic finishes are remindful of Isaac Murphy, the famed nineteenth-century charter Hall of Fame black reinsman who won the American Derby—a Chicago fixture now run at Arlington Park—four of the first five times it was run.

Murphy's cardiac-arrest finishes were legendary, and on more than one occasion left his winning owners more exhausted than the winning horse.

Shoemaker did not affect his own connections that way in the inaugural running of the Million. Still, if there was one prime advantage to the deep and holding condition of the main track that day where the Arlington Million presentation ceremonies were held, a track made that way by a virtual Noah's ark flood that hit the week of the Million, it was that the mucky track provided everyone associated with John Henry with a perfect excuse for unsteady feet.

One could hardly tell whether the group was more the shaken product of the bad weather or the electrifying finish.

Included in that entranced company was Shoemaker himself, who earlier this year became the oldest rider (age 54) ever to win the Kentucky Derby when he scored with Ferdinand.

Mesmerized by the race itself, despite more than three decades in the saddle, Shoemaker elected to stay over the night and enjoy his richest success ever, financially, to its fullest.

He explained his action in the simplest terms possible, an understatement in a sport that scarcely knows the meaning of the word: "It isn't every day you win a million-dollar race."

No discussion of the first Million would be complete without a look at the game runner-up, The Bart, in particular, and the field of the inaugural Million in general.

Both before the Arlington Million and after it, The Bart suffered the slings and arrows of outrageous fortune.

The postrace episode, when television announcers mistakenly declared him the winner, can be passed off as the excitement of the moment. The prerace incident, however, when one announcer questioned his credentials as an Arlington Million starter, will forever beg for an explanation.

Though his record showed only one win at the time of the Million, The Bart's ledger was still solid and consistent. His record looked even better at year's end, showing three wins in eleven starts with seven additional placings for earnings of nearly $470,000.

Moreover, nine of his wins or placings came in stakes matches, the majority of those in the toughly competitive graded events.

Rested for nearly two months, The Bart was shipped across the country to Florida in late February of 1982. There, he took the rich Hialeah Turf Cup in the new course record time of 2:26 flat while carrying top impost of 124 pounds.

Simultaneously, he proved his worth emphatically as a superior racehorse and opened the door for history to repeat itself: Arlington Million winner John Henry had won the same race in 1980 en route to year-end laurels as best male grass horse.

In the same month, February of 1982, the inaugural Arlington Million field displayed their wares when *The Blood-Horse* magazine and the *Daily Racing Form* released their 1981 Free Handicap rankings.

Those rankings are expressed in weights assigned hypothetically to horses on the basis of their performances during the prior season. Thus, the higher the weight, the better the horse.

As expected, John Henry led the older-male lists for both publications, followed by a slew of Arlington Million horses who either raced in the lucrative event or were originally selected for it. Similarly, Arlington Million starter Kilijaro led the older-female lists for both journals.

In its first year of existence, the Arlington Million had managed to stand on equal footing and in the same class with some of America's longest-established classic races.

John Henry wasn't the only notable with the initials of "J.H." who attended the inaugural running of the Arlington Million in 1981. Several days before the race, word filtered out that Joe Hirsch, the executive columnist for the *Daily Racing Form*, was on his way up to the press box.

The "filterer" was my boss, Tom Rivera, who made it clear that whatever the Eclipse Award–winning acknowledged dean of American turfwriters wanted, he was to get.

"Philip," Hirsch said after quickly surveying the situation upon his arrival, "this won't do." My heart went up in my mouth.

"If you don't mind," he said with a pleasant smile beaming down from an Olympus that measured well over six feet in height, "I need to work alone rather than here in the press box. I know there's a room upstairs, and I'm going to take that. It's simple, but it will meet my needs. If you'll be so kind as to help me carry this typewriter and table upstairs, along with that chair over there, I would appreciate it."

Before I could explain that his eschewal of the plush press box facilities for a spartan existence upstairs between the track announcer and the television man running the pan camera threatened my future employment at Arlington Park, Hirsch had left.

By the time I arrived upstairs a few minutes later, Hirsch had already cheerfully set up his makeshift headquarters, with the exception of one "major" item.

"If you would be so kind as to obtain for me four two-by-fours," he said, "I would be eternally grateful."

In a flash, I headed down to the basement in search of the wood I was sure would ultimately decide whether I retained my job. In vain, I had tried to talk Hirsch out of his move. Now the least I could do for him was to get the wood.

Only one obstacle lay in the way of my heavenly redemption.

A complete stranger was wandering aimlessly around the very stack of two-by-fours I wanted. For a full five minutes, we both walked around the wood, looking at each other but never speaking.

Desperately, I tried to figure out who he was. Was he a union carpenter protecting his wood? Or an HBPA (Horsemen's Benevolent and Protective Association) official touring the facilities? An anonymous track executive I hadn't met? And, in a moment of (Million) madness, I considered that the individual could be a CIA agent sent incognito to thwart my procurement of wood.

Time was running out. I was desperate. What to do? Who was this guy, and what the hell did he want?

He must have heard me, must have read my mind, because in an instant I got my answer.

"Young man," he said politely, breaking his silence and finally revealing his sphinx-like identity and purpose, "I've been down here for an hour and I still have not yet found the Classic Club elevator. Could you help me?"

I looked toward the roof, shaking my head in disbelief.

Instantly, I consummated a deal. I would *personally* direct him to the Classic Club elevator (which I had to use to get back to the press box), provided he asked no stupid questions about the wood I was taking without following the proper procedures.

Minutes later, I found myself putting those valuable two-by-fours under the table that held Joe Hirsch's typewriter. He liked things to be steady when he worked, Hirsch explained.

"I know the feeling, Joe, I know the feeling," I said silently as I left.

During the first Arlington Million, class was exhibited off the track as well as on it. One morning, Pedro Medina and his connections greeted us at the gate of the security-laden Arlington Million Stakes Barn, which had been specially constructed for the rich event. The sad look in the trainer's eyes told us that what we had heard was true.

Premio Nobel, the Chilean Horse-of-the-Year, was going to be scratched because of a mild fever incurred while being shipped to Arlington Park. Now only the formalities remained as the news and publicity personnel surged through the gate to get the story. One more bit of business needed to be cleared up before the defection of Medina's horse became official.

He walked with us to the stall, all the while talking about how great the horse was. When he looked in, he saw his "baby," as he described Premio Nobel. Medina tried to talk, but instead began to visibly shake. His eyes moistened. He could not control it.

"I am so sorry," he began with a wave of his hands, "for all of you. My friends, I have disappointed you. I brought this horse here to run in Arlington's great race. You invited me to the Arlington Million, the first one, but as you can see, I cannot run him."

No one was writing, merely listening, trying to appreciate the irony of the situation. In circumstances like that, it was our province to console, to extend sympathy. The situation had become a paradox, the roles reversed.

"You have all been so good to me and his owners. Everyone . . . everyone, they smile and laugh and make me feel wanted and important. But I cannot help it. I must withdraw him, for his own sake. He has a temperature, and it would not be right."

Medina looked away again, unable to go on. We all looked at each other. There was a genuine majesty to the moment. You would have thought the man was scratching from the Kentucky Derby or the Arc de Triomphe.

As we walked away, we thought how well the name of the horse fit his trainer.

Premio Nobel. In English, it means "noble prize."

It was an ironic mix-up.

The field for the biggest race of the year at Arlington Park was just minutes away from the post, but we couldn't get into the paddock to perform our assigned publicity tasks.

Our way was blocked by a beefy security officer named Ebony, one half of a famous black-and-white, tag-team security tandem named Ebony and Ivory, whose names and gargantuan size were generally enough of an introduction for most people—at least the intelligent ones who liked living, even to the total exclusion of racing.

Their orders were precise: to keep the small paddock clear of all people with the exception of owners, trainers, jockeys, television crew members, and certain track officials.

The track's reasoning was simple: they wanted the saddling area to be kept clear so that all of the aforementioned people could do their jobs. That select group included me; Ebony continued to see it the other way as time began to run out.

"Pal," he intoned authoritatively, "it's going to take someone *very* important to get you in here today."

At exactly the same moment, my saving grace passed by.

"Mr. Trotter," I heard a security voice say pleasantly, "come right in."

My desperate eyes quickly met those of Tommy Trotter, Arlington Park's racing secretary and handicapper, who was getting ready to go into the paddock. Quickly realizing my predicament, he casually wondered out loud if I would like to join him.

Ebony hesitated, then stepped aside.

At last, I was inside the million-dollar paddock. As I walked in with Trotter, I couldn't help but think of Moses. I knew exactly how his followers must have felt when he parted the Red Sea.

The report was not the first mistaken account of Phil Georgeff's call of the 1981 inaugural Arlington Million, but it was easily the most inaccurate, bar none. It was, as they say in racing, "in a class all by itself."

Several days after the running of the inaugural Arlington Million, a *Variety* magazine columnist stated that Arlington Park's track announcer,

The calls of Phil Georgeff, the longtime "voice of Chicago racing," were as impeccable as his dress, manner, style, knowledge, and talent. His retirement a few years back brought the curtain down on an extraordinary career that encompassed some five decades. (*The Thoroughbred Times*)

Phil Georgeff, had mistakenly called The Bart the winner of the Arlington Million, an error that was subsequently transmitted over live national television.

The false charge proved to be the most grievous error in a column plagued by the same, including a repeated misidentification of The Bart;

an incorrect quotation of his odds; and a historical blunder that saw Georgeff compared to Clem McCarthy, who "miscalled" the 1947 Kentucky Derby (actually, it was that year's Preakness Stakes).

Incredibly, all those mistakes occurred in the opening paragraph of a column that took Georgeff to task for a "mistake" he never made.

All of it stood in direct contradiction to the main fact of the entire episode: soon after the race had been run, the network itself confirmed that Georgeff had *not* made any such mistaken call.

When the columnist was finally contacted, he blamed his erroneous column on typographical errors, a bad memory, and a tight deadline. The product of this country's "new journalism" was at a total loss to explain why he hadn't even bothered to call Georgeff to get his side of the story.

When shown the column, Georgeff was only too glad to comment.

"No way I ever called The Bart the winner of that race," he stated emphatically several weeks later in the announcer's booth high above the racetrack.

"Not with that 'Photo' sign hanging on the board right after the race. I've called thousands of races over the last 25 years, and there's no way I'd go out on a limb like that and try to guess—and that's what it is, guess-ing—a photo finish. You're just asking for trouble."

Georgeff—known as the Racing Voice of the Midwest for obvious reasons—sighed heavily, then looked me square in the eye. The consum-mate professional hadn't finished making his point.

"Boy, I wanted to call that race so bad I could taste it," he continued. "That's my job. From the time those horses hit the track until they leave it, I'm supposed to keep everyone informed, but there was nothing I could do during the Million except sign off the way I did ['Will it be The Bart or John Henry?'] and then wait for the official result like everybody else."

All the recordings from that day, including Georgeff's own personal recording, back that statement up.

"Chicago," my friend said over the phone, "I do surely *love* that city."

"I assume that means you watched the Arlington Million last week," I said, instantly instigating a conversation with one of Kentucky's favorite sons.

"It certainly does, my fine, young Kentucky hardboot. Up in Derby City itself. In Luvil."

"Lou-ie-ville," I quickly corrected him. "Listen to the sound of my voice. The town has three syllables in its name."

Ron McAnally, trainer of John Henry (*The Thoroughbred Times*)

"That ain't all it had last week. It had the Arlington Million, the big race—the world's first million-dollar Thoroughbred race, which is more than I can say for Lexington. They exempted it down there for a Cincinnati Reds game. Can you believe that? Right in the middle of Thoroughbred horse country, the capital of the world, and they exempted it. We had to drive to Louisville."

I duly noted his correct pronunciation of the city that was clearly first in his heart, but I knew I still had some more work to do.

"Since you haven't got the pronunciation of Louisville correct," I said, "perhaps you won't mind improving your vocabulary. They didn't 'exempt' the Million, they preempted it."

"Call it any way you want," he replied cheerfully. "The upshot of it all was that we landed up here in Louisville—I hope my pronunciation continues to meet with your extreme satisfaction—at one of those pizza places with the wide-screen television. It took us all of 15 seconds to convince everyone there—including fans and young children—that they should watch the Arlington Million."

"Well," I asked him, "what did you think of the race?"

"Top or bottom line?" he countered.

"Both," I said.

"Top line," he said quick as a shot, "is that I dearly love to see dreams come true, and yours did last Sunday. The finish of that race told me so. The ghosts are gone. The champions are really coming back to Chicago, just like in the old days. And not just from this country, but from around the world."

"And the bottom line?" I asked curiously.

"If you believe in that dream long enough and hard enough, with *your greatest heart*, someday soon, maybe sooner than you or I imagine, the last Sunday in August at Arlington Park is going to be as famous as the first Saturday in May at Churchill Downs. Think about that statement, *bucko*."

I still was an hour after he had hung up.

The Horsemen's Journal (May 1985)
(Original title: "The King and the Prince")

A Prince of a Derby

A T 5:39 ON THE afternoon of May 3, 1969, the field for the 95th Kentucky Derby broke cleanly from the gate. The conditions were perfect for a good Derby. The track was fast, the temperature an attention-getting 87 degrees, the day a sunshine-filled afternoon that carried no wind.

Still, there was little evidence to indicate that all in attendance were about to witness the greatest Kentucky Derby ever run.

With 110 runnings to the credit of America's premier classic and longest consecutively run stakes race, hailing one as number one would seem impossible.

Collectively and individually, there have been more famous fields: the 1957 crew included two Horse-of-the-Year champions in Bold Ruler (1957) and Round Table (1958), as well as record-breaking Belmont Stakes winner Gallant Man, and eleven other fields produced Triple Crown champions.

Faster times have been recorded, the best in 1973 when Triple Crown champion Secretariat blitzed his field with a 1:59⅖ clocking. The Derby has hosted bigger crowds, notably the record 163,268 that poured in to see Cannonade win the centennial running in 1974.

In terms of money, the 1969 Kentucky Derby scarcely compares to the 1984 Derby record $712,400 gross that yielded a record $537,400 net to the ill-fated victor Swale, or the 1983 Derby, which established mutuel records for total Derby Day handle ($11,851,527) and Derby wagering ($5,546,977).

There have been wilder finishes, such as the infamous 1933 Fighting Finish Derby and the 1959 Bumping Derby.

There have been richer historic sidebars that elevated the winning connections to the status of demigod legends and folk heroes and heroines. None is perhaps more haunting than the story of 1924 Kentucky Derby victor Black Gold, the product of a mating between a common mare (Useeit) and a prepotent sire (Black Toney) owned by Colonel E. R. Bradley.

The breeder and owner of four Kentucky Derby winners between 1921 and 1933, Bradley was yet superstitious enough to believe the story of an old Indian woman who claimed her late husband had dreamed on his deathbed that such a pairing would result in a Kentucky Derby winner.

And there have been horses who made an even bigger mark off the track than they did on it winning the sport's biggest race, such as 1977 Triple Crown champion Seattle Slew.

The 1969 Kentucky Derby, however, is not distinguished for or by any one part. Rather, it is remembered for a collection of parts that, when totaled, yielded a sum actually greater than the whole of its six major parts.

No Kentucky Derby ever put it all together like this one, producing what Kent Hollingsworth, editor of *The Blood-Horse*, triumphantly called "racing's finest hour."

QUANTITY OF FIELD

The pages of the Kentucky Derby history book are filled with accounts of horses who were blocked, checked, impeded, interfered with, knocked to their knees (as 1936 Kentucky Derby favorite Brevity was), fell, unseated their riders, or were forced to change their running styles because of heavy traffic.

The 1969 Kentucky Derby, however, left no excuses for racing luck. Cleanly broken and run without incident, it gave all eight starters an equal chance at the roses.

To a certain extent, field size is relative, but there are acceptable limits on both ends of the scale. Still the smallest field to go out since the Calumet tandem of Citation and Coaltown headlined a six-horse field in

1948, the 1969 Derby field historically falls almost in the middle in terms of quantity.

Certainly, it stands in vivid contrast to its successors.

Ten times since 1969, fields of 15 or more horses have been sent off, requiring the use of an auxiliary gate (the record is 23 horses in the centennial 1974 Derby).

What resulted on a number of those occasions was less a horse race and more a cavalry charge, devoid of racing strategy and predicated on the basic instinct of survival. Though the Derby has for some time been limited to 20 starters on the basis of career earnings in unrestricted events, the upper limit is really that which can be accommodated by the main starting gate: 14.

By the same token, the 1969 field did not deteriorate to the opposite end of the spectrum: a field that was too small.

In 1892 and again in 1905, only three runners were sent out, the two shortest fields in Kentucky Derby history. Besides generating little fan interest and limited betting opportunities, those fields also guaranteed at the very least a cheap stakes placing.

Worst of all, they resembled match races and came dangerously close to being walkovers.

QUALITY OF FIELD

It isn't every year that a Derby field can lose a future Horse-of-the-Year (Ack Ack, 1971), a Canadian Horse-of-the-Year from the previous season in Viceregal, and a top stakes winner like Al Hattab and still come up with quality. With four major stakes winners, though, the 1969 running was clearly no two-horse affair. And in more than one way.

Geographical rivalries in the Kentucky Derby are nothing new. In 1879, Tennessee and Kentucky partisans jammed into Louisville to back their respective choices—Lord Murphy and Falsetto, who finished one-two in that year's Derby.

That tradition was still running strong a century later when coastal rivals Affirmed and Alydar locked up in 1978, though the most famous geographical-rivalry matchup remains the 1955 East-West Derby, which Nashua lost to the California wonder Swaps. Unlike those biregional affairs, however, the 1969 running pulled representatives from all four corners of the country.

Majestic Prince working out under the hands of trainer Johnny Longden (Keeneland Library)

Heading the group was California invader Majestic Prince, undefeated in seven career starts, including the Los Feliz Stakes, San Vicente Stakes, San Jacinto Stakes, and the Santa Anita Derby.

Equally impressive was his average winning margin of 4½ lengths. Priced off as a mild $1.40–to–$1 favorite, the Best of the West had not even been weighted the year before on the Experimental Handicap.

That was no slight, but the result of trainer Johnny Longden's patient handling. Raced just twice toward the end of the season, a record that included no stakes competition, Majestic Prince came out too late to make the juvenile listings.

Posted as second choice at $2.30–to–$1 odds was the 1968 juvenile-male champion Top Knight, a Vertex colt who was the leading money-earner of the group with more than $500,000 in career earnings. A true son of the South, the Florida-bred came into the Kentucky Derby with solid back-to-back wins in the Flamingo Stakes and the Florida Derby, both over Arts and Letters.

Though no one knew it at the time, the physically unsound colt was starting to come apart and would win no more races that year.

From the north came Dike. The dominant horse in New York, Dike had reversed his early-spring form in Florida and entered the Derby with a three-race win skein that included two stakes.

Bred in Kentucky at Claiborne Farm, the colt carried the hopes of Claiborne master A. B. Hancock Jr., whose sons A. B. III (part owner of Gato del Sol in 1982) and Seth (Swale in 1984) would later win the racing prize that had eluded three previous generations of Hancocks.

Off the board in two of his first three sophomore starts, a division of the Bahamas Stakes won by Ack Ack and the Flamingo Stakes, Dike was then shipped to New York.

The change of scenery had the desired effect, as he quickly emerged as a horse to be reckoned with. After taking a six-length score in his initial outing, an allowance event, Dike then picked up the Gotham Stakes and the Wood Memorial. Though both were by slim margins, they were still impressive wins, Dike coming off the pace both times over an off track.

Rated as the $4.20-to-$1 third choice, Dike's chances were substantially boosted by Jorge Velasquez, who would end the year as the leading money-earning rider in the country. Though Dike was his first Kentucky Derby mount, Velasquez apparently had a way with the huge Herbager colt, who had gone through six riders in eight outings as a juvenile before Velasquez took over at the beginning of Dike's sophomore season.

Completing the major geographical boundaries was Arts and Letters, a dark horse who was the $4.40-to-$1 fourth choice. The star of the Middle Atlantic region by virtue of his Virginia breeding, Arts and Letters was owned by sportsman and philanthropist Paul Mellon, whose Rokeby Stable campaigned internationally.

Though he had won just two of six outings, Arts and Letters was a consistent check-getter, hitting the board the other four times. In his initial stakes outing of that year, he used a 10-pound weight advantage to defeat highly regarded Top Knight. What followed were seconds in three major Kentucky Derby preps, two of those losses at equal weights to Top Knight in the Flamingo Stakes and the Florida Derby.

Rested for a month, the Kentucky Derby stock of Arts and Letters rose dramatically when he took the Blue Grass Stakes at Keeneland in late April with a powerful 15-length and near wire-to-wire score just two ticks off the track record for the 1⅛-mile distance.

Arts and Letters (*The Thoroughbred Times*)

The Wednesday of Kentucky Derby week, however, the questions about Arts and Letters returned after regular rider Bill Shoemaker was seriously injured when a spooky filly reared up in the paddock at Hollywood Park and fell back on him.

The accident necessitated a change in riders, Braulio Baeza getting the call on a horse he had never ridden. Still, as *Sports Illustrated* later reported, "It is not every Derby that a trainer can lose his rider and come up with a Baeza as a substitute."

While the supporting cast rated no comparison in terms of quality, it served three useful functions: it gave the field balance, offered bettors a chance to cash in on long shots, and continued the Derby's romantic tradition as "the people's race," one where anyone in America could enter a horse and win.

Easily the best of the second-line quartet was Traffic Mark, the Arkansas Derby victor and Blue Grass runner-up entered over the objections of trainer Ronnie Warren, who felt the colt was too tired to run well.

A son of leading sire Traffic Judge and a stakes winner all three seasons he raced, Traffic Mark left the track with career totals of 10 wins and 13 placings in 42 starts and $187,738 in earnings.

Filling out the field was Del Mar Futurity winner Fleet Allied, a career earner of nearly $165,000 who like Rae Jet entered the Derby winless as a three-year-old; minor Ohio stakes winner Ocean Roar, a son of 1955 Kentucky Derby winner Swaps and at 28-to-1 odds the cheapest of the outsiders; and 71-to-1 long shot Rae Jet, the only gelding in the field, whose last-place Derby finish would reflect a six-year career that saw him fail to even place in a stake.

TIMING

It is said that greatness is often a product of its times, meaning that heroes frequently arise simply because the times demand that they must.

The 1969 Kentucky Derby was proof paramount of that adage. Forced to carry a weight heavier than that of any of its predecessors, it rose to the occasion and overcame the worst of adversities.

At the time, the 1968 Kentucky Derby was still being contested, though in a different arena: a courtroom. The change in scenery had occurred after the winner, Dancer's Image, had been disqualified when a postrace analysis revealed the presence of a prohibited substance, Butazolidin. Naturally attendant to the litigation was extensive media coverage, some of it sensational and inaccurate, which further inflamed a volatile situation.

With the race traumatized, its reputation and integrity questioned, its continuity disrupted, and the sport that the Kentucky Derby symbolized tarnished by the affair, few felt that the race would recover quickly. To most, it appeared that the race would never be the same again. To a degree, they were both right.

It never was the same again.

With an electrifying victory that vividly reminded everyone of what was best in the Thoroughbred sport, the Kentucky Derby, and the Thoroughbred, the aptly named Majestic Prince single-handedly rendered peace and forged a new future.

When the longest Derby ever run was legally resolved in April of 1973 with the awarding of the 1968 Kentucky Derby trophy to Calumet Farm, owners of declared winner Forward Pass, it rated little media coverage.

Behind lay the greatest Kentucky Derby ever run, ahead stood another chestnut who would become the sport's first Triple Crown winner in 25 years, his foray starting with a record time in the Kentucky Derby.

HISTORY

Presidents and Thoroughbreds have always mixed well.

According to racing historians, George Washington once served as a steward. Thomas Jefferson owned and bred Thoroughbreds, as did Andrew Jackson, an avid racing man who kept a few in the White House stables that he raced under the name of his secretary, Major A. J. Donelson. Ulysses S. Grant enjoyed both runners and trotters.

In the twentieth century, Presidents Truman, Eisenhower, and Kennedy all attended the races, though not while in office.

The 95th Kentucky Derby not only maintained a precedent, it set a precedent.

The first president ever to attend a Kentucky Derby while in office, Richard Nixon was also the first chief executive to attend the races while in office since Rutherford B. Hayes in 1879. (Actually, a present and *future* American president attended the 1969 Kentucky Derby: accompanying Nixon that day was avid horse-racing fan Ronald Reagan, then governor of California.)

RECORDS

Measured statistically, the 1969 Kentucky Derby was an unqualified success.

Total Derby Day wagering was $6,106,346, and Kentucky Derby betting was $2,625,524, at the time both pari-mutuel records for the event.

The figures were the product of the biggest crowd ever to see a horse race in America. Official records put it at 106,333, though others placed the attendance closer to 120,000 in light of the record Kentucky Derby handle figures.

For rider Bill Hartack, the 1969 Kentucky Derby triumph marked his fifth Derby score, tying Eddie Arcaro's record. It was Hartack's fourth of the decade (an outright "pop" record), and his first—ironically—aboard a favorite.

The quintet also included two Kentucky Derby time records, with Decidedly in 1962 (2:00²⁄₅) and Northern Dancer in 1964 (2:00 flat). All

The principal connections of Majestic Prince—rider Bill Hartack, trainer Johnny Longden, and owner Frank McMahon (*The Thoroughbred Times*)

of this success, remarkably, had come from just nine mounts evenly spread over a 14-year period from 1956 through 1969.

(By contrast, Arcaro had ridden in the Kentucky Derby a then-record 21 times between 1935 and 1961, the year of his retirement. Indeed, a case could easily be made for Hartack as the best rider ever in the long and storied history of the Kentucky Derby.)

To trainer Johnny Longden went the most unusual record.

The rider of 1943 Triple Crown champion Count Fleet, Longden became the first man in Kentucky Derby history ever to take the roses initially as a rider and later as a trainer.

The 1969 Kentucky Derby, unquestionably, was the richest triumph ever enjoyed up to that time by the sport's two major industries: breeding and sales. Bred by Leslie Combs II at his Spendthrift Farm outside Lexington, Kentucky, Majestic Prince was a son of undefeated champion and leading sire Raise a Native and out of Gay Hostess, an unraced but well-bred daughter of top sire Royal Charger.

A gallant and courageous Majestic Prince holds off Arts and Letters (outside) and Dike (inside) to win the 1969 Kentucky Derby. (Keeneland Library)

Sold at Keeneland in 1967 for a world record $250,000 to Canadian oilman Frank McMahon, Majestic Prince did not disappoint as so many expensive yearlings had before him.

His Kentucky Derby triumph, which ran his career earnings to nearly $260,000, made him at the time the highest-priced yearling ever to return his purchase price. Any doubts that remained about expensive yearlings, after such a payoff in the country's biggest race, were completely dispelled when McMahon the next year returned to Keeneland and bought Majestic Prince's full brother for a record $510,000. Named Crowned Prince, he was sent to England and in 1971 earned champion juvenile-colt honors.

THE FINISH

Close finishes in the Kentucky Derby are a rich part of the race's history. To date, 21 finishes have seen the winner separated from the runner-up by a margin of a neck or less. Seventeen of those were strictly two-horse affairs. One Derby became a race only after the winner went lame in the stretch after building up a big lead and just barely held on to win by a nose.

Two others saw late-closing moves just fail to get to the winner, one of them the tightest on-the-board Derby finish ever posted, the 1947 running, in which a pair of heads separated Jet Pilot, Phalanx, and Faultless.

The 1969 Kentucky Derby finish was a horse of a different color, something never seen before: a protracted duel from the top of the lane between three horses who had a chance to win it all.

The stage was set for the incredible finish when Top Knight, who had taken over from early leader Ocean Roar, stopped badly midway into the final turn. As he drifted out under Manny Ycaza, Arts and Letters slipped through on the rail, Majestic Prince went by on the outside, and Dike began his rally from the second flight.

At the top of the lane with a quarter mile to go, the all-out war began as the trio moved away from the rest of the field. Arts and Letters held a half-length advantage over Majestic Prince. Three lengths back was Dike, perfectly placed to uncork the final lick he had displayed in his six previous wins.

Lacing into Majestic Prince with his whip, Hartack pushed him to a half-length lead with a furlong to go. Arts and Letters, however, refused to yield. Making matters worse for them was Dike, who was steadily gaining ground on the outside, the earlier three-length advantage having been cut to two.

With a sixteenth of a mile to go, Arts and Letters courageously came back with another run, but it was not enough. Gamely fighting off the resurgence, Majestic Prince hit the wire in 2:01⅘, a neck in front of his shadow on the rail. A half length back was Dike, who had hung in the final strides to finish third.

Though some felt the finish would have been different had Shoemaker been aboard Arts and Letters, including the usual group of California detractors, none objectively could deny the quality of the victory.

Majestic Prince had prevailed despite losing ground on the first turn when he had been forced five-wide; the slow, early fractions, which more benefited a true off-the-pace horse like Dike; and the prolonged stretch duel, which had seen Majestic Prince challenged as never before.

The acid test was the final quarter kick of :24⅕.

Nearly matched by Arts and Letters and exceeded by Dike, the time more than met Colonel Bradley's famed formula for a Kentucky Derby victor: a horse who could take the last quarter in 25 seconds or less. That two rivals had done so and yet failed to win the roses only furthered the power of Majestic Prince's victory.

In heart and body, Majestic Prince was the best horse in the finest Kentucky Derby ever run.

Injured five weeks later in the Belmont, finishing second to Arts and Letters, who denied his bid to become the first Triple Crown winner since Citation in 1948, Majestic Prince never raced again.

Retired to stud with nine wins in 10 starts and nearly $415,000 in earnings, Majestic Prince sired a number of top stakes winners before dying prematurely on April 22, 1981, of a heart attack.

Included in his get was Coastal, who in 1979 stopped Spectacular Bid's Triple Crown bid with a victory—ironically—in the one race his sire never won: the Belmont Stakes.

Majestic Prince's impact continues today as his son, Eternal Prince, thrust himself into this year's Kentucky Derby picture with an impressive score in the Gotham Stakes. (Eternal Prince, however, was unplaced in the 1985 Kentucky Derby, won by Spend a Buck.) Besides Eternal Prince, other top get by Majestic Prince included Majestic Light and Prince Majestic.

Arts and Letters, who played second fiddle in the first two legs of the 1969 Triple Crown series, then put on a second-half show of six straight stakes wins that included the Metropolitan, Belmont, Jim Dandy, Travers, Woodward, and the Jockey Club Gold Cup.

At season's end, he had eight wins and six placings in 14 starts for earnings of over $555,000, and was an easy choice for 1969 Horse-of-the-Year. Retired in 1970, his get includes Winter's Tale and Codex.

Dike, the hard-running show horse who just missed in the 1969 Kentucky Derby, left the track with seven wins and 11 placings in 25 starts and more than $350,000 in earnings. As a sire, he proved to be good but not notable.

For Top Knight, the 1969 Kentucky Derby represented the beginning of the end.

Retired to stud because of an injury, he proved to be a true product of his St. Germans line. Though the line had produced four Kentucky Derby winners in Twenty Grand, Bold Venture, Assault, and Middleground, plus a multiple handicap-male champion in Native Diver, all were failures as sires except Bold Venture. Returned to racing in 1972, Top Knight raced on through 1975, a bare trace of his former self.

At year's end, Arts and Letters and Majestic Prince were co-highweights on the *Daily Racing Form* Free Handicap rankings, each getting 136 pounds.

Dike and Top Knight, part of a four-way tie for second, each received 126 pounds.

The Blood-Horse magazine separated all four a shade lighter, Arts and Letters getting the top assignment of 133 pounds, Majestic Prince 132, Dike third in a three-way tie at 127, Top Knight tied in fourth place with Al Hattab at 126.

The cold numbers did not reflect their parts in the 95th Kentucky Derby.

No single description, in pictures or words, exceeds that of *The Blood-Horse* Kentucky Derby issue that year. Locked in time and frozen in motion, the spectacular finish hangs like a priceless portrait over a headline describing the 1969 Kentucky Derby as the "grandest Kentucky Derby of all."

In all the time since, nothing has happened to alter that assessment.

The Record-Breaking
Season of Shane Sellers

WHEN SHANE SELLERS RODE his 182nd winner of the current season at Arlington International Racecourse on Wednesday, September 11, he broke the previous record of 181 set by Randy Romero in 1982.

Moreover, Sellers has done more in less time than Romero—and he can do even more, since the 132-day meet, which began May 12, runs through October 9.

Romero set the previous standard during a 121-day meet in 1982 that ran from May 17 through September 30, tallying 181 winners from 832 mounts for a solid 21.75 percent win rate (rounded off from 21.7548 for mathematical purists).

Sellers, by vivid contrast, in just 107 days of racing through September 11, had racked up 182 winners from only 683 mounts for a gargantuan win rate of 26.65 percent (rounded off from 26.6471).

Broken down by month, Romero took 24 scores in May, 38 in June, 45 in July, 40 in August, and 34 in September. Interestingly enough, Romero's record 181 triumphs included four wins by virtue of a disqualification, one of them a stake (the Shecky Greene Handicap, in which Straight Flow was awarded the victory upon disqualification of the original winner, Golden Derby, who was subsequently placed second).

Ladies and gentlemen—presenting the gifted Mr. Shane Jude Sellers of Erath, Louisiana, whose glistening career work includes a record 219 victories at Arlington International Racecourse in 1991 (Keeneland Association/Bill Straus)

Sellers's monthly victory total through Wednesday, September 11, read like this: May (37), June (46), July (39), August (46), and September (14). That total is known to include at least one win by virtue of a disqualification (on May 31 in the seventh race).

Romero's overall 1982 numbers were 832-181-135-128 and purse earnings of over $1.7 million.

Through his record-breaking day (Wednesday, September 11), Sellers's Arlington ledger read 683-182-115-78 and purse earnings of nearly $2.5 million.

For the record, Romero equaled Ray Sibille's old mark (137 winners, set in 1980) on August 25, 1982, aboard the aptly named Queen Tye (rhymes with tie, get it?) in that afternoon's seventh race. He broke the record aboard the prophetically named Borntorun on Friday, August 27, 1982, in that afternoon's sixth race.

That record-breaking score, incidentally, came two days before the second running of the Arlington Million, won in record time by Perrault. Romero was unplaced in that year's Million aboard Al Nasr, his first—and to date, only—mount in the world's first million-dollar Thoroughbred race.

Sellers, who was unplaced in his first Million appearance this year with 1990 turf-male champion Itsallgreektome, tied Romero's mark on Wednesday, September 11, aboard Cecconi in the fifth race and broke it the same day aboard Bustopher in the seventh race.

While Sellers's final victory total will be dramatically different than Romero's, both men began their record-breaking treks with glittering opening-day action.

Romero bagged three winners in the 1982 seasonal opener, including the very first race of the meet. Sellers was even more sensational in his seasonal opener this year, garnering five wins, one of them the featured Governor's Stakes.

Certainly, every record has personal tidbits that numbers cannot describe, and Sellers's new standard is no exception.

For example, Sellers's agent, Ronnie Ebanks, was competing at Arlington in 1982 when Randy Romero set the record that Sellers will have decimated by the end of the current season at Arlington. And Romero's agent that season was Fred Aime, who now books for Pat Day, the brother-in-law of Ray Sibille, whose record Romero broke.

Interestingly enough, three men in 1982 exceeded or equaled Sibille's standard (137 wins in 1980): Randy Romero (181), Pat Day (159), and Earlie Fires (137).

Finally, and here's some food for thought, the last three record-setting champion riders at Arlington—Sibille, Romero, and Sellers—are all natives of Louisiana, a state long renowned for its output of top-class riders. That company also includes such talents as Eddie Delahoussaye, Kent Desormeaux, and Larry Snyder, to name but a few more.

It's been said of Louisiana-born reinsmen that they'll ride anything with four legs—including the kitchen table. That's an overstatement, of course, but not by much. And Sellers's recent record work at Arlington International Racecourse is proof paramount of that fact.

Author's Note: Sellers wound up with 219 victories for the 1991 season. Through the end of 1998, his top career horses and wins included champion Skip Away (Blue Grass Stakes, Jockey Club Gold Cup, Woodbine Million, and the Suburban Handicap); champion Countess Diana (Breeders' Cup Juvenile Fillies); champion Black Tie Affair (Washington Park Handicap); Buck's Bid (Breeders' Cup Turf); Pulpit (Blue Grass Stakes); Do It With Style and Lunar Spook (both winners of the Ashland Stakes); Talkin' Man (Wood Memorial); and Explosive Red (American Derby). Sellers's career work also includes thirds with Wild Gale in the Kentucky Derby and the Belmont.

Lady Star

THIS AFTERNOON'S 46TH RENEWAL of the Alcibiades Stakes (G2) honors the champion classic-winning filly who left an indelible mark on American Thoroughbred racing as both a runner and a broodmare.

Bred and owned by Hal Price Headley—the founding father of Keeneland Racecourse—and trained by W. W. Taylor, the prosaically named Alcibiades was foaled February 10, 1927, at Headley's Beaumont Farm near Lexington, Kentucky. A glistening chestnut, Alcibiades— ironically enough—was named after a Greek general and statesman.

By any name, though, she would have been a great warrior.

Champion two-year-old filly of 1929 off a stellar campaign that saw her win four of seven starts and place second once (in the Kentucky Jockey Club Stakes), Alcibiades that season took her major triumphs in the Debutante Stakes at Churchill Downs and the Clipsetta Stakes at old Latonia (now Turfway Park).

Brought back the next year, Alcibiades turned out another banner season to earn champion three-year-old filly laurels.

Sent out 16 times in 1930, Alcibiades either won or hit the board in exactly half of her starts, her top victories coming in the Kentucky Oaks and the Arlington Oaks. Her work also included thirds in the Latonia

Alcibiades (*The Thoroughbred Times*)

Oaks, the Illinois Oaks, the Hawthorne Gold Cup, and the Arlington Matron. This interesting campaign included a tenth-place finish in the 1930 Kentucky Derby (won by eventual Triple Crown champion Gallant Fox), which was run within days of the Kentucky Oaks. For the record, Alcibiades is the last runner to have competed in both of Churchill Downs's signature races—the Kentucky Derby and the Kentucky Oaks.

And, at age three, as she had done at age two, Alcibiades showed no fear of running against males or over "off" tracks.

Her glorious racing career ended abruptly in November of that year when she suffered a torn tendon while setting the pace for the Latonia Championship. But Alcibiades and the racing sport were hardly done with each other.

At stud, Alcibiades proved to be as great as she was on the racetrack, possibly better. From eight foals, she produced seven runners—all of them winners, four of them stakes winners.

That quartet of stakes winners included Latonia Oaks victress Sparta; Menow, the 1937 juvenile-male champion off scores in the Belmont

Futurity and the Champagne who later sired 1953 Horse-of-the-Year Tom Fool (also brilliant at stud himself); Alabama and Ladies Handicap heroine Salaminia, a well-bred daughter of Man o' War; and Lithe, a blue-blooded Pharamond II daughter whose career work included scores in the Arlington Matron (twice), the Comely, and the Demoiselle.

A champion on and off the track, Alcibiades—who died at age 30 in 1957—was one of a kind, a gift of the gods.

Like Keeneland, she lives on grandly today, her name synonymous with the qualities that embody what is best in the Thoroughbred race-horse and Thoroughbred racing.

Fully in keeping with the horse that gives this race its name, the Alcibiades Stakes over the years has been home to a number of this country's top two-year-old fillies, including six (through 1997) who went on to earn juvenile-filly championship honors.

Those titlists include inaugural 1952 Alcibiades victress Sweet Patootie, as well as Doubledogdare (1955), Leallah (1956), Moccasin (1965), Eliza (1992), and Countess Diana (1997).

In addition, the list of two-year-old filly champions turned out by the Alcibiades Stakes also includes the 1987 runner-up, Epitome.

VII

THE MECHANICS
OF THE GAME

Keeneland magazine (Spring/Summer 1981)

Gone Are the Days
of the Unsure Start

The starter shall give all orders necessary for securing a fair start.
(Sec. 14, Rule 140, Paragraph A: Official Jockey Club Rules)

SLOWLY BUT SURELY OVER the past 75 years, modern technology has permeated every level of Thoroughbred racing, improving it with safety helmets, photo finishes, pari-mutuel machines, film patrols, videotape replays, and electronic timers. Chief among those improvements is the mechanical starting gate, which emerged in the early 1930s.

Gone now are the days when unsure starts began with the beating of a drum, the waving of a flag, or the dropping of a web barrier.

Yet the mechanical starting gate has not changed the temperamental and often mercurial nature of Thoroughbreds; they still act up as much at the start as their ancestors ever did.

No one knows this better than 49-year-old Tom Wagoner, the official starter at Keeneland Racecourse, who schools horses six mornings a week (Sundays excepted), then starts the afternoon card of races five days a week.

"It's a long day, no doubt about it," he says. "I generally get up around quarter to six on the days we school and come to the track, where we start schooling whenever it gets light. We run to around 9:15 in the morning.

"Then I go home, rest for a couple of hours, come back around quarter to one, pick up my programs, and start the races. By the time I'm through and get home, it's well past dinnertime."

Tom Wagoner (Keeneland Association)

Tanned, gray-haired, and built like a football player at a stocky six feet and 205 pounds, Wagoner possesses the lived-in face and track savvy that Damon Runyon and Joe Palmer immortalized in their turf characters.

More than two decades of experience at the starting gate tend to do that to you.

After graduation from Athens High School in Athens, Kentucky, Wagoner spent two years as a physical education major at the University of Kentucky before enlisting in the U.S. Marines when the Korean War broke out. After being wounded (and receiving a Purple Heart), Wagoner was discharged halfway through his four-year hitch.

Back home in 1952, he enrolled again briefly at UK before turning to training. That uneventful venture lasted just long enough for him to find out that, in his words, "I'd better find me another profession."

He found that profession in 1959 when he began working the gate first under the late Roy Dickerson, the Keeneland starter, and later Dickerson's successor, the late William Simpson.

During those years, Wagoner honed his talents, working both as an assistant and head starter at various tracks around the country. His first head-starter job came at River Downs in 1968 when he handled a meet abbreviated to only ten days due to a flood.

In the fall of 1970, Wagoner started his first Keeneland meet while Simpson was working a "conflicting" date elsewhere, and then took over at Keeneland when Simpson died in 1978.

Wagoner's circuit is now well established.

In January, he begins the year at Oaklawn before moving on to Keeneland for the last six days of the spring meet, taking over from substitute Donald Plunkett (who fills in for Wagoner now that the dates of Oaklawn and Keeneland overlap).

Then Wagoner ships west to Churchill Downs, and later up to Delaware Park, before finally returning home to finish the year in Kentucky.

Wagoner starts any number of big stakes races, including the Blue Grass, the Kentucky Derby and Kentucky Oaks, the Delaware Oaks and Delaware Handicap, and the Arkansas Derby.

His first Kentucky Derby, the centennial running in 1974, was particularly memorable.

"That was a hell of an initiation for me. I took over the last 35 days of the spring 1973 meet after James Thomson became ill. The next year was the '74 Derby, the 100th running, when they had 23 horses, the largest field ever. We had to use two 14-stall gates plus 18 men. There was a lot of pressure, and I was kind of green, but I feel it was my best start ever.

"Probably one of the things that contributed to the pressure was the fact that it was televised. Starting on time in those type of races is crucial because the requirements of television are so precise. You don't get a few minutes extra at the post then. I've started every Derby since then, so I feel I must be doing all right."

Wagoner is a firm believer that a starter is only as good as the crew he works with, particularly in the big stakes races.

"Mine are a real tough breed of people. One of my men worked up at Churchill Downs this year with a broken hand, to give you an idea of what I'm talking about. And, out of the crew of seven I regularly carry with me, four of them are ex–rodeo riders. The good ones make it easy for you. Of course, the key to good starting is schooling them properly."

So, Monday through Saturday, from approximately 7:00 A.M. until 9:15 A.M., Wagoner has a 12-stall gate out on the Keeneland track at the head of the 4½-furlong chute "standing" and "breaking" horses.

With the former, Wagoner simply allows the horse to stand in the gate without actually racing; in the latter, the horse stands, then breaks from the gate in an actual simulation of racing conditions.

Horses are schooled for a variety of reasons.

Some have made their way onto Wagoner's list, which means they must demonstrate a proficiency starting before Wagoner sends in a small starter's card certifying to the stewards that the horse can handle the gate.

Included among those are chronic slow-breakers, dwellers, refusers, and fractious horses. And it's automatic that if a horse is adding or taking off blinkers, they have to prove they can handle the equipment change from the gate before Wagoner will send his okay to the stewards.

Other horses come to be schooled, either at Wagoner's request or at the desire of the trainer, to break them of bad habits they may be starting to accrue while in the gate.

Regarding blinkers, Wagoner is outspoken.

"They're probably the most overused and overrated piece of equipment around. A trainer and rider take a horse out on the track, the horse gets scared, and they decide he needs blinkers. Well, of course, the horse gets scared. It's only natural. All those sights and sounds are new to him. If they just gave him a little time to adjust, though, he'd get along fine without the blinkers.

"Which is the smart thing to do, since a horse can see about 360 degrees. Put those blinkers on, and you artificially restrict his natural vision. I believe there's a lot of horses hurt more than they've been helped by blinkers."

The schooling is important from a numerical standpoint, too. Usually, the horses in a race outnumber the crew members, so the assistants are dispatched to handle the really bad actors. For obvious reasons, Wagoner and his crew don't need a gate filled with bad actors.

One particular morning, on the day of the 1980 Fayette Handicap, Wagoner was schooling horses to avoid just this situation, square in the face of constant bantering from Herb Stevens, the trainer of the 1979 juvenile-male champion, Rockhill Native.

With five horses loaded and ready to go, Wagoner turned the key located at the side of the gate that activated the electrical circuit. Then he stepped away about 10 feet and picked up the other end of the electrical cord, on which hung a handle and a button he would push to open the gates all at once.

However, he couldn't start yet.

A pair of riders, about 200 yards away and barely visible in the early-morning mist, just stayed there, delaying his break. Wagoner was getting impatient; the five horses and five riders in the gate were getting anxious. Finally, he barked down the chute entrance, "C'mon down there. Let's do something. We're getting ready to break, and I can't wait all day." The pair of riders responded instantly, getting out of the way. But then Wagoner got a request from one of the riders in the gate, which he just as quickly and summarily handled: "Can you have another few seconds?" he retorted in mock disbelief and anger. "Hell, you been in there for an hour!"

The exchange cracked up Herb Stevens, who waited until the quintet left quickly in standard Wagoner fashion, then told him, "I think he was trying to tell you you're not a good starter, Tom."

Before Wagoner could rebut the veteran trainer, Stevens walked off quickly—sound, secure, and satisfied that he had gotten in the last word.

"I start very fast," Wagoner explained. "That's my style. It keeps the riders and the horses relaxed. When you sit on 'em for a while, everybody starts getting edgy and nervous, and there's more of a chance of someone getting hurt.

"Of course, like I said before, it all goes back to how much you school them. Now, you take a good trainer like Herb Stevens. He schools his entire stable, if possible, probably two or three times a week. That keeps them educated, and certainly less fractious.

"I rarely have any trouble with his horses because of that schooling. He keeps them settled because they know what they're doing in there. And that's where schooling really pays off.

"Very few fractious horses make good runners. Oh, there are the exceptions, but by and large, most of them use up all their energy in the gate fighting you. They get so stirred up they can't run their race. They just leave it in the gate.

"I can't make a trainer school his horse, but if the horse acts up and the trainer won't listen to me, then I'll put the horse on the list. But most trainers are cooperative and glad to know about it.

"A lot of times, their jocks don't tell them anything, which can hurt them. 'Cause if your horse doesn't break with the field, he won't win as a rule, particularly in a short-distance race where a good start is crucial. So, you see, the schooling really is a benefit to them.

"I'm not a slip-writer, though. I'd rather ask a trainer to school than tell them to. But every once in a while, you get a hardhead who won't listen to you, and the only way to deal with them is put their horse on the list.

"And I found out one thing. Sex, class, or age doesn't have anything to do with it. You might have to school the stakes horse a little less because they're a higher-grade animal, but they all still need to be schooled."

There's another side to schooling that proves that too much of a good thing can be bad.

"If you break them constantly," Wagoner continued, "you actually defeat the purpose of schooling. Every time that horse sees the gate, or gets into it, they think they have to break and run like the wind.

"We call that 'speed-crazy.' You can make a horse a bundle of nerves that way real easy. The smart thing is to change their mind constantly. Break them one morning, then just stand them the next time you come back to the gate. It relaxes them, because they know they don't have to exert themselves every time they come near the gate."

According to Wagoner, a good starter can earn up to $50,000 annually (and more in the East or on the West Coast) if he's willing to travel nonstop year-round.

Wagoner chooses not to push that hard. The several months he gets off every year he enjoys spending with his wife of 21 years, Mildred, daughter Shirlie, sons Gary and Kenny (the latter works for him), and his five grandchildren.

And what Wagoner doesn't earn schooling horses, he more than earns starting the races five days a week at Keeneland.

Even after the schooling, Wagoner still gets bad actors, frequently necessitating a variety of persuasions to load them.

A standard piece of equipment is a 10-foot lead-up strap, which racing fans frequently see draped around crew members' necks. This is a mainstay that allows the crew to merely hook up to the halter in order to lead a slightly balky horse in the gate.

On the gate lies a five-foot buggy whip, which is snapped behind the more recalcitrant horses. The snapping sound usually is enough to make them move forward; occasionally, the buggy whip is flicked slightly against the rear legs for ones who prefer touch to sound.

Others need ear or nose tongs, a set of aluminum handles covered with thick rubber joined in the middle with a hinge. On occasion, crew members will use them to bring a horse in the gate when the simpler methods won't work, enabling them to hold the horse still with his head pointed straight ahead.

Once the race begins, the horse literally runs out of the tongs as the crew member releases the pressure. The tongs inflict no pain, but they do get many a horse's attention.

Some horses have to be blindfolded, a method Wagoner rarely uses and has always disliked because of the danger posed by a blindfolded horse getting loose on the racetrack.

Trainer Herb Stevens (Keeneland Association)

Then there's the flipping halter.

Like its relative, the flipping harness, it firmly secures a horse in the gate who really wants to move around or try to lie down. However, the latter can only be used in schooling, because a horse cannot run out of it.

The flipping halter, however, firmly secures a horse in the gate, then when the doors open, he can run out of it.

A final trick of the trade is tailing, in which a crew member simply lifts and holds the tail of a horse firmly. If the horse moves, the resultant pressure will convince the horse to act otherwise.

Sometimes, a horse will not respond to any of these methods, or schooling, posing a danger to everyone concerned. He may be a chronic refuser, a wheeler, or just a viciously fractious horse. Whatever the reason, Wagoner will bar him. It's a rare occurrence, but it does happen.

During the races, Wagoner climbs a 12-foot stand where he can look down into the gate and see everything. Below him on the steps sits a phone, a direct line to the stewards. In his hand, he holds a mike that enables him to give instructions to the crew.

As the horses are brought in, Wagoner looks at the last one loaded, then goes back to stall one and works his way out, his eye constantly looking for any trouble.

Occasionally, a rider will ask for help; other times, Wagoner will see a horse's head turned, standing wrong in the gate, or trying to lie down in the gate, and he'll order a crew member over to the trouble spot.

Right before the last horse is loaded, the crew member loading that horse will yell out, "Last one, boss!" to tell Wagoner that all the horses are

Tom Wagoner started the first grass race ever at Churchill Downs on April 29, 1987. The one-mile contest was won by Thunderdome (#6, obscured), trained by Harry Trotsek, and ridden by Steve Bass. (Churchill Downs Incorporated/Four Footed Fotos)

loaded and none will be left behind, causing distraught stewards, an irate public, and an embarrassed starter.

The last check emphasizes the historical anonymity and negative reinforcement that all starters seem to endure and toil in. Start a hundred perfect races, and no one will remember you; miss one, and your name will be on a thousand tongues.

For proof of that adage, you have to look no further than Thoroughbred racing's best-known starter, the legendary Mars Cassidy.

Today, he is still best known *not* for the countless scores of races he sent out perfectly over his lifetime, but for the one he missed literally: the 1919 Sanford Stakes, in which Man o' War lost the only race of his career, to Upset, following a poor start by substitute starter C. H. Pettingill.

Clearly, a starter's value, particularly a good one's, cannot be overstated.

"We're the last contact those horses have," Wagoner says, "before they start racing. We want to protect the public with a clean start. If they school right, they'll probably start right.

"And if they start right, they've got a fair shot in the race. It's hard to drive home a good point, but easy for them to learn a bad habit. That's why we're constantly working with them."

As with all the other races that afternoon, including the featured Fayette Handicap, Wagoner sends this 1⅛-mile affair off quickly, cleanly, and efficiently.

Old Mars would have been proud.

VIII

ESSAY

Song of the Trainer

YOU GRABBED SOMETHING WILD and free, and made it for your own, as much as you could. It is a tenuous alliance—you and that horse, though, and well you know, held together by leather, steel, iron, aluminum, cotton, wood, luck, love, skill, and all the fragilities of life.

You may change it somewhat, calm the spirit, slow down the pace occasionally, but always—always—you live with the knowledge that the really good ones only *tolerate* you and your human eccentricities.

For, indeed, the power you seek to control is the very element you must unleash in a race if you are to win—their unfailing spirit.

You stand close to this spirit and let it warm you on cold days and chill you on warm afternoons—in the paddocks, around training-center strips, on the racetrack, along the shed row, on planes, trains, and vans.

You are exultant alongside the wild spirit that entrances you beyond regard for your own safety and well-being.

Just like a moth drawn to a powerful light, you are inexorably drawn to this incandescent spirit, though it can mean your end if you are not careful.

You have been touched; you cannot live without it, although at times you swear you can barely live with it. The fire that warms can also burn . . . and vice versa.

It's being protruded on your consciousness so suddenly that before you know it, you enter into and become part of a vibrant, new world, as if no other world—or life—existed before this one.

It is a world where race, color, and religion mean little or nothing, just the ability to get a check . . . and get it consistently.

This magical world is filled with wondrous names and legends like Darley Arabian, Eclipse, Tremont, Colin, Sysonby, Exterminator, Man o' War, Equipoise, Citation, Native Dancer, Round Table, Kelso, Northern Dancer, Secretariat, Seattle Slew, Affirmed, Sunday Silence, Easy Goer, Cigar, Holy Bull, and hundreds more, including ladyloves like Miss Woodford, Imp, Pan Zareta, Regret, Gallorette, Twilight Tear, Busher, Moccasin, Susan's Girl, Genuine Risk, All Along, Winning Colors, Personal Ensign, Go For Wand, and Flanders, to name but a few from a staggering list of all-time greats.

It is a world whose pages of rich history have been written by a magnificent and mercurial blend of Arabs, Brits, the French, Moors, Spaniards, Italians, Orientals, Australians, Canadians, the Irish, Germans, Poles, and Americans.

In your world, you're voraciously well read; outside it, you're a virtual illiterate. You devour magazines, books, and newspapers by the score, but only ones that have to do with the horses.

To you, they are your lifeblood—that *Daily Racing Form*, those copies of *The Thoroughbred Times* and *The Blood-Horse*, that sales catalogue from Saratoga, those reams of stallion registers and scores of other basic reference journals.

To the average layman, far outside the realm of your sport and kingdom, they are indecipherable logs. To you—one of the privileged few on the inside of the looking glass—they speak volumes, literally and figuratively.

If you're successful enough, you'll be seen haunting the sales pavilions around the country, looking for your next big star. No doubt, somewhere along the line, you'll travel to the Mecca of it all, the bluegrass region of central Kentucky, hoping that one day you'll get your hands on one of those "heavy heads" they seem to turn out in assembly-line fashion.

It is not easy training horses for a living unless you get the perfect blend—big stock and big owners.

You travel long and hard year-round on a variety of circuits to places like New York, Maryland, Florida, Kentucky, Chicago, Louisiana,

California, and all points in between, and even mixtures thereof, armed with a "home" in name only and addresses in at least three different cities.

Like all the good ones before you, you learn the game from the ground up, with claimers. You quickly learn that game because you must if you are to survive. You learn that there are few friends at that level because those purses are the smallest—the cheapest—in racing, and they can only be split so far, and then there is no more.

In time, you learn the art of answering stupid questions from the media. With good humor, you open your world and your stable to countless visitors, including that occasional village-idiot fan who wanders in trying to get a souvenir from the mane or tail of your prized charge, who would have most certainly put that fan into another world had it not been for your timely, lifesaving intervention. With the wisdom of King Solomon and the patience of Job, you quietly instruct your stable help, the sole qualification of many of them being their naive love of the horse.

And when you get that "big" horse, spiritually, if not physically, at least once a day you get down on your knees and thank your Maker for having endowed you with one who so dramatically changes your life, simultaneously wondering why your Maker picked you above all others to train this big one, a thought that lingers just long enough to keep your mental defenses honest so you don't get too full of yourself.

The big ones, though, can exact a heavy price if you're not careful.

They can play havoc with your marriage, your physical health, your sanity. They can cause you to lose or alienate your best friends, turn your wife and children into strangers, deprive you of any form of privacy—particularly with the press—and put your stable into an uproar in ways you never imagined.

At times, they so exasperate you with their prima-donna antics that you'd like nothing better than to go up and knock the big son of a bitch on its butt.

But that big one has got you, and you know it.

You can't do that, because the owners would frown on it, and even more important, you know that there are at least a hundred trainers out there who would gladly take that "star" off your hands instantly, with no questions asked, and no reservations about enduring whatever the star might dish out to them.

So, as long as things remain in reasonable control, you deal with it. It's part of the price of greatness, they say.

And, truth be known, you're glad of it.

Admit it, now. You talk to that big horse when people are around, when people aren't around, and sometimes when absolutely no one is around, and it's just you with your dreams and a silent audience that hangs on your every word—your imagination of what might be.

Don't deny it now; we heard you, on many an empty and starry night in the stable.

And we see you, too.

We watch as you nurse them, stand by them, plead with and cajole them, pamper them, bribe them, trick them into doing something that's good for them, and spoil them worse than an only child. We see you attend to the star's every need—the best vet money can buy, the best shoes money can buy, the best training (yours) money can buy, and the best feed money can buy for the best health you can provide (that "best health" including those candy bars he has grown used to on a regular basis, without which no day will start or end).

The candy is a demand you yield to so the star will not kick down half the barn and start a stampede, or punt a groom half the length of a football field.

You put up with these incidental shenanigans because at your age what you have learned to do over the years is to follow the path of least resistance as much as possible.

You're not the first to make this compromise, and you won't be the last. Your company includes more than one Hall of Fame trainer, dating back in time more decades than you can count on the fingers of both your hands.

If you need a further barometer of your star's value, remember what Man o' War's groom—that great American of racing letters Will Harbut—said when the owner of Big Red turned down a *$1 million offer* for the epic star during the heights of the Great Depression.

"Lots of people can have a million dollars," Harbut said, "but only one man can have Man o' War."

And so it is with you and your stars.

After all, you could be in a factory punching a time clock, or in a wall-to-wall office job figuring out your coffee breaks and lunch versus quitting time.

But you're not.

You're here, tending to something alive and wonderful and great. Could it get any better?

You have heard it said that music is the universal language, but you know this is not true, because that calls for either proficiency at an instrument or an appreciation that can only be gained over a long period of time.

The runner is the universal language.

They need no interpretation, no explanation, no introduction. Their mere being precludes all that. And, when the "big one" comes along, capturing all in their tidal wave of victory, electrifying a crowd, the bulk of whom do not know a gelding from a furlong but nonetheless appreciate the big one for all they are worth, making the hearts of all present sing in a triumphant revelry of life, then those people learn—if only for a brief instant—what you have known for ages, that the horse is more than a sport or business.

It is all the great art in the world combined together with the soul of those who care for it, colored with a beauty and grace and power and history that translates the same in all languages, a music you cannot only hear and feel, but see.

The horse is the essence of being.

It is life, art, sport, everything. No other living thing on the planet can lay claim to being such a phenomenon.

And perhaps the grandest thing about the horse and the sport of Thoroughbred racing, two of the oldest entities on the planet, are their eternal rebirths, grand denials of one of the great forces in the universe—time.

For, even as the old and great stars pass from the stage, young ones arise to take their place. Though you may be eighty and change, it makes no difference. There is always the prospect of that new one around the corner, waiting to make you half that age again, alive and young with a glittering future just down the road.

It is a marvelous thing, you say.

Unlike the outside world, time is not measured on the track in years, only horses and races. Other people may grow old with no memories of their life's work to keep them warm and to give them company.

You, on the other hand, have managed to bamboozle time a bit, by spending your years in the presence of a special light that has enabled you to feel the very pulse of life itself and given you a unique kind of freedom, a home in every corner of the world where they have a racetrack. It is a grand thought, a grand life.

Three kings of the turf—the late Charlie Whittingham, rider Bill Shoemaker, and Horse-of-the-Year champion and Kentucky Derby and Breeders' Cup Classic victor Ferdinand—head for the track. (Santa Anita Park/Four Footed Fotos)

A motion at your side breaks your train of thought, instantly attracting your attention and hurling you quickly back into the present and the realm of reality and everyday business.

It is "Baby," that enormously talented and precociously bred two-year-old who never gives you a moment of peace. You suddenly realize that your idle thoughts have carried you to the door of his stall.

Well, it's your damn mistake. Now you've done it, pal.

That equine man-child, who has made your good name a curse upon the lips of the starter in a very short time, is back in your face . . . and he's hungry.

And not for the good stuff.

He wants his treat, a frozen Milky Way candy bar . . . and he wants it *now*.

You shake your head at the wonder of it all, and then give him the candy bar like the spoiled child he is, smiling tentatively as you watch him devour it.

When he's through, you will lead him out into the bright sunshine of a new morning. Another racing day—indeed, another racing season—is upon you.

Your hands are full, you know, your work cut out for you. As you head up toward the track, away from the rich aromas of coffee, leather, ointments, hay, and straw, you also know one other thing.

You would not have it any other way.

Author's Note: This chapter is dedicated to Jimmy Croll, Bob Baffert, D. Wayne Lukas, and to Charlie Whittingham, who died at age 86 on April 20, 1999.

IX

REFLECTIONS

Unpublished (1998)

At the Top of the Game

I T'S 1998 AND I'M back at Churchill Downs, where I have witnessed a host of Kentucky Derbies (from a variety of angles) and a pair
of Breeders' Cups.

My angle is a bit different now. I'm no longer in publicity or working
as a turfwriter; I'm in something magical called "racing television." As
a consequence, I'm on the roof looking down at an extraordinary world,
realizing that I'm literally and figuratively at the top of my game.

It will never get any better than this. Can I live with this? I believe so.
Why? Because like any other player at one of my favorite haunts, I have
my memories. Lots of them. And here come the apparitions.

Like Native Dancer, "the Gray Ghost," television's first racing star and
the horse who introduced me to the sport, whose lone career loss in 22
starts was the 1953 Kentucky Derby.

Like the prosaically named Tim Tam, who lost the 1958 Triple Crown
when he broke his leg in the stretch run of the Belmont, though he courageously held on for second behind Cavan, giving me my first true
testament of courage and class from a Thoroughbred.

Like 1943 Triple Crown winner Count Fleet, whom I saw in his
waning years at Stoner Creek Stud when he was swaybacked, losing hair,
dim-eyed, and had to be brought in at night because he was afraid of the

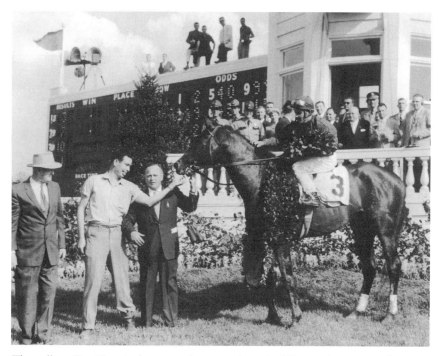

The gallant Tim Tam is shown in the winner's circle following his win in the 1958 Kentucky Derby. Milo Valenzuela is in the saddle, while trainer H. A. "Jimmy" Jones is at the immediate left of the horse. To the far left is Ben Jones, father of Jimmy Jones. (Keeneland Library/J. C. "Skeets" Meadors)

dark. I tempered that sight with the searing thought that they hadn't called him Count Fleet for nothing (in some instances, he didn't just merely win, he *crushed* his opponents).

Like my first Breeders' Cup here in 1988, because I made good on my losses at the Arlington Million that year at Woodbine in Canada (where the Arlington Million had been run while Arlington, host track of the Arlington Million, was recovering from fire damage).

I hit on the Great Communicator–Sunshine Forever exacta in the 1988 Breeders' Cup Turf, and it paid $78.80. It was particularly good because a young kid in Publicity who was down to his last two dollars (so he said later) yelled at me at the last moment to give him a winning combo on the Breeders' Cup Turf.

I gave it to him, COLD. And I gave it to him at the last minute, too. Great drama, great theater, this Thoroughbred racing game. He came back with money in his hand, a wide smile on his face, and a mesmerized

The author's first great Breeders' Cup/Churchill Downs "hit"—winner Great Communicator (right) and "Sunny Boy," as runner-up Sunshine Forever (left) was nicknamed (Breeders' Cup Photo)

look that heralded me as a genius . . . yea, a demigod. *"How did you know?"* he wanted to say. Kid, I been carrying that exacta since Canada.

A poor, destitute run-out only moments before, now he is at the top of his game. And he emphatically thanks me for his incredible wealth. Heads turn and nod. I'm somebody. This kid won't let it go until everyone knows that. I love a good agent. This could only happen on the racetrack. But it wasn't luck, no sirree bob.

In that same Breeders' Cup of 1988, I picked Is It True for the Breeders' Cup Juvenile, just to be stubborn. Remember him? You should remember him. He upset 30 cents–$1 odds-on favorite Easy Goer (later the vaunted archrival of 1989 Horse-of-the-Year Sunday Silence, another one of my personal favorites).

Is It True paid $20.40. *"How do you do this, sir?"*

What can I say? It's a gift, ladies and gentlemen, *a veritable gift from the gods.* I hardly understand it myself. *Mirabile dictu,* as they say in Latin.

Not all favorites get beat, though, and in the process, some of them redefine courage and heart for all of us.

In the minds of many, including the author, this was *the single greatest race* ever seen in the history of both Churchill Downs and the world's greatest racing extravaganza—the 1988 Breeders' Cup Distaff. Many of those people also say that "there were no losers in that race that day." Personal Ensign is on the far left, and Winning Colors is on the far right. (Breeders' Cup Photo)

Pictured here is the famed One Dreamer "score," which secured more Breeders' Cup/Churchill Downs handicapping acclaim for the author. This was based upon the sound handicapping principle that Gary Stevens is one of this generation's finest riders, a lesson we learned to an extreme in the 1990 Arlington Million when he piloted home Golden Pheasant and loaded our pockets up with across-the-board wagers and exactas. Had we not been so stubborn, we easily would have scored the trifecta, too. One Dreamer is on the far right. (Breeders' Cup Photo)

In 1998, the author proudly reached the summit of his handicapping career when he picked five out of six winners for a lucrative $335.80 return off a $16 ticket. (Some pros we know spent $1,600 for the same Pick-Six consolation ticket.)

The horse that stood between him and the Breeders' Cup Pick-Six payoff of $35,000 was Da Hoss, seen here winning the 1996 Breeders' Mile. Because of a nagging set of injuries, Da Hoss raced only once (a win, notably) over the next two years before his victory in the 1998 Breeders' Cup Mile. This astonishing win, achieved via the magical trainership of Michael Dickinson, gave Da Hoss a special and permanent niche in turf history. (Breeders' Cup Photo)

Like in 1988, when 1-to-2 odds-on choice Personal Ensign, trying to become the first major, undefeated racehorse in this country since Colin (15-for-15 in 1907 and 1908), with her left rear leg held together by screws and driven by a heart bigger than life itself, negotiated a stretch

Trainer Bob Baffert, unquestionably *the* trainer of the late 1990s (Keeneland Association/Bill Straus)

that was a sea of mud, coming from far off the pace to nip another gallant heroine—that year's Kentucky Derby victress, the fabulously named Winning Colors—by a nose at the wire in the Breeders' Cup Distaff.

No one wants to say it, but that may be the greatest race ever seen at Churchill Downs and in the Breeders' Cup . . . and it involved the "fairer sex."

A Grade 1 stakes winner every season she raced, Personal Ensign left the game unbeaten in 13 starts, and a startling reminder of what a truly great horse is. Her work manages to overshadow that of another "signature horse" of the Breeders' Cup series at Churchill Downs, the magnetic Arazi, who took the 1991 Breeders' Cup Juvenile by five lengths, just devouring his foes and immediately stamping himself as the horse to beat for the following year's Kentucky Derby (he ran eighth).

Touch Gold (left) denies Silver Charm victory in the 1997 Belmont—and a Triple Crown sweep. A year later, Baffert would lose another Triple Crown bid in the Belmont when Victory Gallop upset Real Quiet. Despite those losses, the late 1990s clearly remain the province of Baffert. (New York Racing Association/Adam Coglianese)

Now my mind and heart turn to the 1994 Breeders' Cup at Churchill Downs, where the only race I played was the Breeders' Cup Distaff. What a field: topflight New York stakes winner Heavenly Prize in at $2.10–$1, West Coast gem Hollywood Wildcat in at $1.80–$1, New York Filly Tiara winner Sky Beauty (who can't win outside New York) priced at $1.90–$1.

And then there's One Dreamer (coming out of the four hole), who's ridden by my favorite jock, Gary Stevens (whose Triple Crown work includes a Kentucky Derby win with a filly, Winning Colors), and trained by one of the cagiest handlers around, Tom Proctor, one of them good ole Texas boys who never runs anything without a good reason (that is, he thinks he can win).

I want some money, so I play her—One Dreamer—across the board, then hook her up in a superstitious 4-1 exacta ("Four-one for the poor one!").

It's like a beautiful dream. A "One Dreamer" kind of dream. Heavenly Prize (with Pat Day up), the most consistent of the top three here at Churchill Downs, runs second; Hollywood Wildcat finishes sixth; Sky Beauty runs ninth and last.

Victory Gallop (left) edges out Real Quiet in the 1998 Belmont Stakes. (New York Racing Association/Adam Coglianese)

I'm rich. I got One Dreamer (let go at $47.10–$1 odds) across the board for a $2 bet, and I got the 4-1 exacta ($340.80). I've turned $4 into megabucks. I've succeeded beyond my wildest dreams. You need only one race like this a year.

Do you notice something missing here from the résumé? It's called success in the Kentucky Derby. For the record, I've had *one* Kentucky Derby winner since I entered the game in 1970—Winning Colors in 1988. I came to her *intelligently*: I liked her color (roan), her sex and the histor-ical land-mine record attached to it (she was the third and the latest of three fillies to win the Derby), her running style (on the front), and her jock (the gifted Gary Stevens, perhaps the most underrated rider of this generation). I didn't give a damn whom she was running against. They could have resurrected Man o' War. I was betting her with both hands.

And that's it. One Kentucky Derby winner. I've also got a slew of runner-ups during that time frame. That has a rather frightening edge to it, since it means I've missed all the Triple Crown winners in the last 29 years (Secretariat, Seattle Slew, and Affirmed). Think about that.

This glorious Kentucky Derby work also includes the year that I gave the Derby exacta COLD to a friend because I couldn't make the Derby (I was recovering from several major eye surgeries).

"All right, you want a price?" I said. He bobbed his head up and down like a village idiot. "Here it is. Lil E. Tee (who went off at $16.80–$1) over Casual Lies (who went off at $29.90)."

"Why those two?" he queried.

"Please," I said, "I'm an artist. I can't be revealing secrets of my craft, my trade. Oh, what the hell. [Pat] Day [on Lil E. Tee] is overdue for a Derby win, and Whiting [Lynn Whiting, Lil E. Tee's trainer] never runs a horse in a race like this unless he thinks he's got a legitimate shot. I like the name [underdoggish in tone]. As for Casual Lies, it's trained by a woman [Shelley Riley], and you know how I feel about women in the derby. Also, Lil E. Tee's going to be ridden by Gary Stevens, who's always dangerous if he's got any type of horse under him."

My friend comes back the next day with an enormous smile on his face, having cashed a 7-3 exacta for $854.40. And, that doesn't include what he made in straight wagering (win, place, and show betting). He thanks me profusely. What can I say? To this day, he still thinks I was serious.

I don't think I'm overstating my lack of Kentucky Derby success. My number of winners equals my number of Eclipse Awards for turfwriting (one). It also equals my number of winners handicapped (selected) abroad. In 1974, thanks to my late godfather (Judge Dan Fowler), I attended the Arc de Triomphe at Longchamp in France (box seats overlooking the finish line, flowers, champagne, wine, etc.) and easily found the winner—the brilliant champion filly Allez France.

Go figure. When it comes to handicapping the Kentucky Derby, I am without honor or acclaim. I shall have to learn to live with it.

Sometimes, you can't measure your winners in dollars and cents.

Take the 1997 Kentucky Derby, for example. I'm up on the roof, working as a production assistant for ABC-TV. The door to the far right of me opens, and I can hear partying. *Great* Kentucky Derby partying.

It's all coming from the most exclusive club at Churchill Downs.

All afternoon long, I go in and out of Millionaire's Row. It's my lone source for basic necessities like the rest room, food, soda pop, and Kentucky Derby wagering. As luck would have it, I land up hobnobbing and eating with the party of (ready for this?) Rick Pitino, who are right inside the door. Pitino is on his way to the Boston Celtics from the

Trainer Elliott Walden, whose Victory Gallop denied Bob Baffert and Real Quiet a sweep of the 1998 American Triple Crown with a narrow and electrifying score in the Belmont Stakes (Keeneland Association/Bill Straus)

University of Kentucky, and this is his last Kentucky Derby party with his family and friends as the head coach of the University of Kentucky basketball team.

I consider the ramifications of all of this.

All my life I've coveted a ticket to Millionaire's Row, and now I'm going in and out of there for free. Go figure. I can't buy a ticket, but on this date in history I can go in for free.

But the Pitino party is the least of the gifts from this ABC-TV credential that hangs around my neck, shining in the sun like a bar of gold. I'm almost 50, and I shouldn't feel this way, but I do. It's Kentucky Derby fever. When they finally hung that credential on me, I was like a little boy. I felt like I was being knighted.

And there is the other gift of that credential: on a warm, sunny afternoon beneath a blue sky, I got an unobstructed rooftop seat to one of the greatest Kentucky Derbies ever, a driving finish that sees Silver Charm hold on to win by a head from a dead-game but dog-tired Captain Bodgit, who's sporting a bowed tendon.

In 1998, I find myself even closer to the action, helping to work the ABC jib camera just outside the winner's circle. Once again, the Kentucky Derby proves to be an extraordinary prelude to a fabulous Triple Crown series, which in the last two years has done for racing, thanks to trainer Bob Baffert and a host of ancillary heroes, what Mark McGwire and Sammy Sosa did for baseball in 1998—woke it up, and put one of the two greatest sports on the face of God's earth (baseball is the other) where it belongs: on the front pages.

The end of the 1998 Kentucky Derby (winner Real Quiet, Kent Desormeaux up, on the right; runner-up Victory Gallop, Alex Solis up, on the left) and the beginning of the 1998 Triple Crown Series (Churchill Downs Incorporated)

(That Triple Crown brilliance continued this year with trainer D. Wayne Lukas, rider Chris Antley, and the former claimer/blue-collar workhorse Charismatic—the 1999 Kentucky Derby/Preakness winner whose Triple Crown bid and career ended with a courageous third, on a broken leg, in the Belmont Stakes.)

My reflections also cover some hallowed ground, reminding me of two grievous losses the Thorough-bred racing sport has suffered in the last couple of years, both with major ties to Churchill Downs and the Kentucky Derby: Jim Bolus, this country's greatest Kentucky Derby writer and historian, and the peer-less Eddie Arcaro, tied with Bill Hartack as the Derby's top-ranked rider, each having five wins.

Jim Bolus (Kentucky Derby Museum, Louisville, Kentucky)

Those thoughts also include mighty Arlington (where I worked for a number of years), a part of the Midwest circuit that incorporates Kentucky.

The plug has been pulled on it for the 1998 and 1999 seasons, though there is now talk—and hope—that they'll finally reopen for the millen-nium racing season. If they do come back in 2000, that return will be long overdue (complete with the revival of their two trademark races—the mighty Arlington Million and the elegant Beverly D), since their pro-tracted absence has left a gaping hole in that circuit. All of this because a dysfunctional public sector wants more money—much more money—than it's entitled to.

I know this "revival" would thrill Bolus and Arcaro, who heartily believed in both the tradition and continuity of the sport and who worked tirelessly in that direction all their lives; one a distinguished turf-writer whose life's work was covered in gold and silver, the other a riding legend whose very name and easily recognizable face were trademarks—signatures—of the racing sport itself.

Eddie Arcaro

Signed jockey card of Eddie Arcaro (Horse Star Trading Cards; Philip Von Borries Collection)

Backside view of Hialeah Park clubhouse looking through the palms (Hialeah Park)

And I know one more thing.

I know we will carry on because we have to, since their shining example demands that we do so if we are to stay true to them, ourselves, and the sport.

Index

Racing memorabilia (Philip Von Borries Collection;
photography by Sharon Hoogstraten)

Racing memorabilia (Philip Von Borries Collection; photography by Sharon Hoogstraten)

Horses making their way to the track from the barn at beautiful and historic Hialeah
Park via picturesque Fitzsimmons Lane (Hialeah Park)

Horses leaving the paddock for the racetrack at Hialeah Park (Hialeah Park)

	WIN	PLACE	SHOW

START◆
6 FURLONGS
◆FINISH

MAIDEN
PURSE $25,000

5

HAPPY BIRTHDAY EDDIE ARCARO

FOR MAIDEN FILLIES THREE YEARS OLD. Weight 120 lbs.
Track Record: 1:07.4, MR. PROSPECTOR (3) 119 lbs.; March 31, 1973

MAKE SELECTION BY PROGRAM NUMBER		PROBABLE ODDS
OWNER ⬇ TRAINER		JOCKEY

Red **1**	WINTERHAWK FARM — KIMBERLY DEPASQUALE Gray, Blue Circled "WF", Blue Hawk, Blue Bars on Sleeves, Blue Cap **LEAVEME LONESOME** Ⓕ 120 Ch. f.'93, Risen Star-Dancing Sal,by -Northern Jove (FL)		10 GARY BOULANGER
White **2**	LA ISLA STABLE — R. MILLS Royal Blue, Black Polka Dots, Royal Blue Cap **GO GIPSY GO** Ⓕ (L) 120 Dk.b/br. f.'93, Regal Search-Gipsy Princess,by -The Prince's Pants (FL)		8 RUBEN HERNANDEZ
Blue **3**	J. D. MURPHY — W. W. PERRY Green, Pink Diamond Belt, Pink Sleeves, Pink Cap **STAR DE LADY ANN** 120 Dk.b/br. f.'93, Star De Naskra- Lady Vixen,by -Sir Ivor (KY)		3 SHANE SELLERS
Yellow **4**	G. W. HUMPHREY JR. & PAMELA FIRMAN — G. R. ARNOLD, II Forest Green, White Diamonds, White Stripes on Sleeves, White Cap **DREAM SCHEME** 120 B. f.'93, Danzig-Dream Deal,by -Sharpen Up (GB) (KY)		4 PAT DAY
Green **5**	NANCY A. VANIER — H. L. VANIER Maroon, White Diamond Belt, White Sleeves, White Cap **BARN SWALLOW** 120 B. f.'93, Iron Courage-Bird House,by -Yukon Eagle (IL)		12 ROBERT LANDRY
Black **6**	MARIE M. MONTOTO — H. MONTOTO Blue & White Halves on Front, White "MM" on Red Back, White Sleeves, Blue Cap **NOEL'S HALO** Ⓕ 120 B. f.'93, Prospector's Halo-Hellenis,by -Greek Answer (FL)		30 RAPHAEL VERDEROSA
Orange **7**	J. MACK ROBINSON — F. GOMEZ Coral, Coral "R" on White Ball, White Bars on Sleeves, White Cap **GALA EVENT** 120 Ch. f.'93, Academy Award-Ravel,by -Secretariat (KY)		10 SEBASTIAN MADRID
Pink **8**	T. CROLEY — T. A. HILLS Orange, Black Polka Dots, Orange Cap **JUST JEB** Ⓕ 120 B. f.'93 Jeblar-Kiss The Wind,by -Smile (FL)		12 AARON GRYDER
Turquoise **9**	BARBARA HUNTER — STEVEN M. RIESER Scarlet, Black Belt & "B", Black Sleeves, Scarlet & Black Cap **RAMPALLION** 120 B. f.'93, Farma Way-Biddy,by -Greenough (KY)		15 DAVE PENNA
Purple **10**	CAROLYN HINE — H. HINE Red, Gold Stripes, Gold Chevrons on Sleeves, Red Cap **CHIP** 120 Dk.b/br. f.'93, Norquestor-Big Pride,by -Bet Big (MD)		6 RICK WILSON
Grey **11**	J. BRODY — J. C. KIMMEL Yellow, Red Sash & "G", Black Bars on White Sleeves, Yellow Cap **INCOMPARABLE** 120 B. f.'93, Alleged-Rose Helen,by -Lyphard (NY)		8 MIKE SMITH
Lime **12**	J. AMEGLIO — H. HERRERA White, Green Diagonal Sashes, Green Cap **HARD ROCK FEMME** 120 Dk.b/br. f.'93, Rock Point-Siwolki,by -Chieftain (FL)		15 GARY BAIN

Ⓕ Registered Florida Bred - (L) Treated with Lasix
Equipment Change: (BLINKERS OFF) **CHIP**
Scratched: **MARK TO MARKET**

Probable Favorites 3 - 4 - 10 - 11

This race was part of a 1996 birthday party that Gulfstream Park threw for Eddie Arcaro. Autographs are those of Arcaro and Hall of Fame trainer H. A. "Jimmy" Jones. (Gulfstream Park; Philip Von Borries Collection)

G. Edward Arcaro
Rode 31 years (1931-61), 24,092 mounts, 4,779 victories (19.8%)

Six times America's leading money-winning rider, Eddie Arcaro never led the list in winners, although upon his retirement, his career total of winners ranked second only to Longden's, and his total purse earnings of $30,039,543 placed him millions ahead of any jockey then or before his time. Born in Cincinnati in 1916, Arcaro began riding in the 1930s, before the film patrol, and he gave more than he received, until September 1942, when stewards noticed his attempt to unseat another rider and suspended him for a full year. Thereafter matured, Arcaro became the very best, The Master to his peers and the public. He had great hands and seat, was unexcelled in switching the whip, possesed a sure sense of pace, and for two decades won the important races with casual excellence. He won five Kentucky Derbys, six Preaknesses, six Belmonts, the Triple Crown twice, the Suburban eight times, the Jockey Club Gold Cup 10 times. His superb talent was sought for all the good ones, Kelso, Nashua, Native Dancer, Bold Ruler, Assault, High Gun, Hill Prince, Sword Dancer, Jaipur, One Count, Whirlway, First Landing, Pavot, Battlefield, Dedicate, Real Delight, First Flight and Nellie Flag. He could make a $5,000 claimer win for $10,000. Of all the good horses he rode or saw, the greatest, Arcaro declared, was Citation.

Eddie Arcaro's Hall of Fame plaque (Gulfstream Park; Philip Von Borries Collection)

Up on the rooftop with the talented Mark Hall of the United States Trotting Association for the start of the 1998 Hambletonian, the first leg in trotting's Triple Crown (also held at DuQuoin, Illinois); Muscles Yankee (#5) the winner (United States Trotting Association/Mark Hall)

Ron Pierce (left) drives Shady Character to win in 1998 Little Brown Jug (first leg of the pacing Triple Crown) at DuQuoin, Illinois. (United States Trotting Association/Mark Hall)

A thing of rare beauty: the highly popular Patchen Beauty, a rare white Thoroughbred, is shown racing at Turfway Park in December of 1998 (Turfway Park/Pat Lang Photos)

The late William H. King, the promotional genius who made a substantial contribution to Kentucky—and American—harness racing via two great dreams that came true—Louisville Downs and the Kentucky Pacing Derby (United States Trotting Association)

Old Louisville Downs, once the home of the nationally prestigious Kentucky Pacing Derby and, to the end, one of the "funnest" half-milers in the country (United States Trotting Association)

(Photo by Bill Straus)

About the Author

KENTUCKY NATIVE Philip Von Borries is a national award-winning sportswriter and screenwriter who has written extensively about horse racing and baseball.

His numerous Thoroughbred and Standardbred racing credits include *The Thoroughbred Times, The Thoroughbred Record*, the *Daily Racing Form, The Blood-Horse, The European Racehorse, Racing Times, Racing Action, The Kentucky Derby Magazine* (1986–88), *Turf & Sport Digest, The Horse-player, Keeneland, The Horsemen's Journal, The Jockey News, The International Festival of Racing/Arlington Million Magazine, The Florida Horse, The Arizona Thoroughbred, The Chronicle of the Horse, Illinois Racing News, Spur, Hoofbeats, Hub Rail, Trot!, The Standardbred, The Illinois Standard-bred and Sulky News, The Red Mile Magazine*, and *Harness Horseman International*.

The author of *The Official Kentucky Derby Quiz Book* (1986), Von Borries—whose first public racetrack appearance coincided with Nashua's last public racetrack appearance (in 1956)—has earned four awards for his turfwriting.

Those awards include a 1990 Eclipse Award (Thoroughbred racing's highest accolade) for "Black Gold," a local television feature on the winning black riders and trainers of the Kentucky Derby; a 1980 John Hervey Award (Standardbred racing's highest honor) for best harness-racing magazine article of that year, "The Twilight Zone Pacer"; and a 1984 Iris Award for another local-television Kentucky Derby feature, "The Roses of May."

In addition, he was runner-up in the magazine division of the John Hervey Awards in 1985 for another harness racing article, "Requiem for a Pacer."

His racetrack publicity experience includes stints at such major American Thoroughbred and Standardbred ovals as Arlington International Racecourse, Gulfstream Park, Calder Race Course, Woodbine, Hialeah Park, Churchill Downs, Louisville Downs, the Red Mile, and Maywood Park. As a publicist, he has covered such major racehorses as Holy Bull, John Henry, Manila, Niatross, Rambling Willie, and Whamo, and has worked such top races and racing extravaganzas as the Arlington Million International Festival of Racing, the Kentucky Derby, the Kentucky Pacing Derby, the Florida Derby, the Flamingo, and the Festival of the Sun.

Von Borries is the son of the late Frank B. Borries Jr. (1914–68), who found the long-lost grave of the legendary black rider Isaac Murphy (America's first great black athlete) after a three-year search. Other major turf credits by the senior Borries included radio and newspaper coverage of the November 1947 funeral of Man o' War (which took place just days before his son was born).

Philip Von Borries's mother, Betty Borries, is a writer of note as well, she being the author of *Isaac Murphy: Kentucky's Record Jockey,* a definitive biography of the legendary nineteenth-century jockey.

Philip Von Borries is the author of two baseball books as well: *Legends of Louisville* (1993) and the groundbreaking *Louisville Diamonds.* The latter, published in 1997, was the first complete major- and minor-league history ever on the "lost city of historical baseball"—Louisville, Kentucky.

A cousin of old-time St. Louis Browns pitcher Frank "Dixie" Davis (and All-American Navy running back Fred "Buzz" Borries as well), Philip Von Borries has contributed baseball articles to such publications as *The Oakland Athletics Magazine* (1989), *The Chicago Cubs Program Magazine* (1983), *Sports Collectors Digest, The Washington Times, Oldtyme Baseball News, Baseball Bulletin, Grandstand Baseball Annual* (1997), *The*

Minneapolis Review of Baseball, Louisville, Chicago Sport Scene, and *Baseball Research Journal.*

His historical baseball work also notably includes the co-designing of a new four-and-a-half-foot-tall marker for the grave of fabled nineteenth-century batting champion Pete Browning, the man for whom the first Louisville Slugger bat was made in 1884 by John A. "Bud" Hillerich.

Unveiled at Louisville's historic Cave Hill Cemetery in 1984 (the 100th anniversary of Hillerich & Bradsby, maker of the world-famous Louisville Slugger bat), the new marker—Von Borries's idea—was erected through the joint efforts of Von Borries, the Hillerich & Bradsby Company, and then–Louisville Mayor Harvey I. Sloane.

The new marker, whose inscription was also written by Von Borries, replaced a weathered stone that misspelled Browning's name and failed to carry any of the pertinent career statistics of this legitimate Hall of Fame candidate.

Other bylines by Von Borries include *Virginia Today, Kentucky Sports World, Lexington, Louisville Today, Kentucky Monthly, Kentucky Images,* and *The Lexington Weekly.*

His fiction includes one published short story ("Smokeout") and one unpublished novella (*Seizure*).